Inside Teaching

The Teacher Development Series

Inside Teaching

*Options for English
language teachers*

Tim Bowen
Jonathan Marks

Heinemann English Language Teaching
A division of Heinemann Publishers (Oxford) Ltd
Halley Court, Jordan Hill, Oxford OX2 8EJ

OXFORD MADRID ATHENS PARIS FLORENCE
PRAGUE SÃO PAULO CHICAGO MELBOURNE
AUCKLAND SINGAPORE TOKYO IBADAN GABORONE
JOHANNESBURG PORTSMOUTH (NH)

ISBN 0 435 24088 9

First published 1994

Series design by Mike Brain
Illustrated by John Gilkes

The authors would like to thank all the teachers and learners from
many countries who were directly or indirectly involved in the writing
of this book. Their views and feelings have formed the basis on which
the book was written, and we are greatly indebted to them.

Cover photo by Paul Brierly

Printed and bound in Great Britain by The Bath Press

95 96 97 98 99 10 9 8 7 6 5 4 3 2

Contents

The Teacher Development Series

TEACHER DEVELOPMENT is the process of becoming the best teacher you can be. It means becoming a student of learning, your own as well as that of others. It represents a widening of the focus of teaching to include not only the subject matter and the teaching methods, but also the people who are working with the subject and using the methods. It means taking a step back to see the larger picture of what goes on in learning, and how the relationship between students and teachers influences learning. It also means attending to small details which can in turn change the bigger picture. Teacher development is a continuous process of transforming human potential into human performance, a process that is never finished.

The Teacher Development Series offers perspectives on learning that embrace topic, method and person as parts of one larger interacting whole. We aim to help you, the teacher, trainer or academic manager to stretch your awareness not only of what you do and how you do it, but also of how you affect your learners and colleagues. This will enable you to extract more from your own experience, both as it happens and in retrospect, and to become more actively involved in your own continuous learning. The books themselves will focus on new treatments of familiar subjects as well as areas that are just emerging as subjects of the future.

The series represents work that is in progress rather than finished or closed. The authors are themselves exploring, and invite you to bring your own experience to the study of these books while at the same time learning from the experiences of others. We encourage you to observe, value and understand your own experience, and to evaluate and integrate relevant external practice and knowledge into your own internal evolving model of effective teaching and learning.

Adrian Underhill

About the authors

Tim Bowen

I am a teacher and teacher trainer at International House Hastings (ILC Group). I have worked with students and teachers in a number of different countries and in the UK with multi-national groups. I particularly enjoy this international, multi-cultural aspect of my job and, as a committed linguist and language learner, I am always very fortunate to be in contact with people from such diverse linguistic backgrounds.

My particular interests in language teaching are phonology, vocabulary and contrastive linguistics. The little free time I have from my work permits me to indulge my twin passions of translation and long-distance running.

Jonathan Marks

I have been running courses and workshops for teachers for about ten years, based in the UK (at ILC Hastings), in Germany and now in Poland. I have always been attracted to education in general, and the field of English language teaching enables me to combine this with my interest in languages and language learning. I am more and more interested in how language acquisition studies on the one hand, and the rich and varied classroom experience of teachers and learners on the other, can illuminate each other, and how teachers can really facilitate learning.

Introduction to *Inside Teaching*

THIS BOOK takes you, the individual reader/teacher, as its starting point. It is not intended as a methodology training course or as a menu of recipes for classroom techniques and procedures, although you will find suggestions to try out and evaluate. Our main intention is to help you become more self-aware as a teacher, and to enable you to take a constructively and compassionately critical view of your own teaching, of the teaching of others, and of methodological recommendations you come across. The book will encourage you to reflect on your own experience and build on it. It will help you to identify your own strengths and build on them. It will also attempt to help you to come to terms with areas of language teaching and learning with which you may not feel entirely comfortable. It will, in certain cases, challenge you to take action in these areas. But it will also attempt to reassure you by placing your teaching in a wider context. By including the views of other teachers, it will show you that you are not alone in what you do, and that any perceived 'bad habits' are not unique to you. It will help you to identify areas for possible change and development, where you may feel discontent or even inadequacy. *Inside Teaching* will provide guidelines for self-directed action to be taken in these areas, and encourage change, risk-taking, experimentation and movement forwards.

An important feature of the book is its use of the views of teachers and learners. This element is included for a number of reasons. We want to give readers the opportunity to 'listen' to the views of their colleagues and peers and to be able in a sense to enter into dialogue with them. You may identify with and empathize with these views and, in some cases, draw comfort or derive confidence from them. On the other hand, you may disagree with some of the opinions expressed and this may have the effect of encouraging you to identify or reconsider your own views on a particular topic and, once again, to question and analyze your own classroom practice in the area concerned.

The book will also provide you with an opportunity to develop and sharpen your awareness of aspects of the English language, such as grammar, phonology and lexis. It also deals, as approachably as possible, with other areas perceived by many teachers as 'difficult' or even to be avoided, such as language-teaching theory, methods and approaches, and certain aspects of pure and applied linguistics. We hope that you may discover something new about language and the other issues that impinge on language teaching, and perhaps adopt a more positive attitude towards them.

In dealing with these 'difficult' areas, we will try to put into perspective some of the incomprehensible jargon that confuses relatively simple concepts and leads teach--ers to avoid them. We will encourage you to confront difficult areas at a level appropriate to you, by asking questions like *What on earth does X mean? Do I really have to read X? or Why am I afraid of X?*

In our lengthy experience of working with both native English speakers and foreign teachers on in-service courses we have observed a pervasive guilt among practising teachers – a feeling that they are doing something wrong, that they should be doing something they aren't doing, that there's something new that they don't know about and should be incorporating into their teaching, that they need to be up to date, whatever that means – and, underlying this, the feeling that their own experience somehow falls short of the mark. We aim to raise these issues directly and help teachers to see their own performance and practice in a more positive light, channelling negative perceptions in a more positive direction and leaving teachers feeling better about themselves, their job, their learners and their future.

Inside Teaching is aimed at language teachers – not exclusively teachers of English, although we use English for the majority of our examples and contexts – either with some pre-service qualification, or perhaps with no formal pre-service training but with some kind of induction, perhaps on-the-job training or support, and with one, two or more years' experience. We regard experience as the key requirement for making the most of the book, as the reflective classroom-based approach will be of most benefit to teachers who can relate it to their own classroom practice. It can be used by teachers who speak English as a first, second or foreign language, and could be used on in-service courses as well as teacher development groups and for private study.

Inside Teaching is not an introductory handbook to the teaching of English as a foreign language. It assumes that readers are already familiar with basic notions of the systems of language and current methodological principles. As such, it will be of limited use to people who are considering language teaching as a career, or who are looking for a set of immediately usable practical techniques. It relies on the principle of weighing up alternatives and evaluating experiments, and in this respect some classroom experience is a pre-requisite.

We hope that *Inside Teaching* will supplement your own valuable experience and enable you to evaluate your experiences and beliefs from a number of different perspectives, and broaden your range of options for your further development as a teacher.

This book has grown out of our many years' experience of work together on numerous kinds of courses, workshops and seminars for teachers. These encounters have been the catalyst for our development of our own ideas and beliefs.

Chapters 1, 4, 6, 9, 11 and 12 were written mainly by Jonathan, and Chapters 2, 3, 5, 7, 8 and 10 by Tim, but the book has also, of course, developed through our collaboration during the writing process.

Tim Bowen
Jonathan Marks
Gdańsk, Poland
October 1993

Chapter 1 Faith, guilt and doing the right thing:
Theory applied and theory discovered

1 Introduction

Teaching is obviously an intensely practical undertaking. We think many teachers believe, or assume, that the practice of teaching is, or should be, based on the application of theories elaborated in parent or feeder disciplines, especially linguistics and psychology. This type of top-down approach to professional education, whereby knowledge is handed down to practitioners by experts remote from the everyday realities of the workplace, is common in many fields apart from teaching. In this 'applied science model' (see Schön 1983 and 1987, and Wallace 1991) professional competence develops through practice informed by the results derived from scientific knowledge and experimentation. Since scientific knowledge is in a continuous state of flux and development, professional competence needs to undergo periodic in-service updating. And committed teachers who are keen to optimize and develop their professional competence tend to look to the purveyors of seminars and training courses, and the authors of teaching materials and books for teachers, as the immediate source of the latest knowledge.

In this chapter, and indeed throughout this book, we would like to suggest that although teachers can certainly benefit from such initial training and subsequent updating, over-dependence on this model can lead to neglect of teachers' own expertise, resources and potential for self-development, to an impoverishment of their work, and to unnecessary feelings of guilt and embarrassment. After all, who is in a better position to be an expert on teaching – the doer or the theorizer?

But in order to do justice to this role as experts, teachers need to bring to conscious awareness as much as possible of the knowledge they have of what they do, and how and why they do it, so that they can properly evaluate it, experiment with it and develop it. In this chapter, and throughout the rest of the book, we want to offer some frameworks for conducting this investigation.

2 Bad habits

Here are some typical remarks which we have heard from experienced teachers at the beginning of in-service training courses and seminars. Perhaps you yourself have said, or at least thought, things like this:

I've been teaching for a few years now and I'm sure I've got into all sorts of bad habits.

I'd like to get some feedback on all my mistakes.

You can't teach well in the school where I'm working 'cos they haven't got any decent materials.

My methodology needs updating.

I think I need to give my classes more comprehensible input, but I don't really understand what it is.

Here in Hammerfest we're so out of touch with current developments.

I bet you'll have a fit when you see how I teach.

Statements like these bear witness to the guilt teachers sometimes feel at not doing things the right way, and the faith they often place in experts to tell them what that right way is. Some of the assumptions that underlie these heartfelt cries include:

- There is a straight and narrow Way of Teaching, from which we sometimes stray like lost sheep.

- I don't mind exposing my teaching to my learners, but the prospect of an expert observing one of my lessons is fraught with fear, guilt and embarrassment.

- If I make mistakes in my teaching, you will be able to identify them better than me.

- Today's methodological recommendations are better than yesterday's.

- The world of EFL has a centre and a periphery, and if I have the misfortune to be on the periphery, I have to look to the centre for guidance and inspiration.

- I can't function fully as a teacher without the support of certain tools.

- I have to understand current key ideas in linguistics and applied linguistics so that I can put them into practice in my teaching.

Task 1
Which assumption could go with each of the above statements?

Commentary ■ ■ ■

I've been teaching for a few years now and I'm sure I've got into all sorts of bad habits.
- There is a straight and narrow Way of Teaching, from which we sometimes stray like lost sheep. The Right Way may be conceived of as eternal or, more commonly, subject to historical development. It is perhaps recorded in the pages of teachers' methodology books or the notes in the files of tutors on training courses, but often seems ethereal, and housed, if anywhere, in the collective consciousness of other, anonymous but better, teachers.

I'd like to get some feedback on all my mistakes.
- If I make mistakes in my teaching, you will be able to identify them better than me. Because of your position and your experience, and because you are more in touch with current trends and recommendations, you are equipped to measure me against certain standards, and to note and report the nature and extent of my shortcomings.

You can't teach well in the school where I'm working 'cos they haven't got any decent materials.
- I can't function fully as a teacher without the support of certain tools. Perhaps the coursebooks are out of date, perhaps there is a limited selection of supplementary materials.

My methodology needs updating.
- Today's methodological recommendations are better than yesterday's. Faith in science and belief in progress are deeply established in us, despite doubts thrown up almost daily in the news. Whether from a general feeling that we could do better, or from specific instances of obvious failure, we are eager to at least consider any new ideas in the hope that they will enable us to take a small step, or maybe even a great leap forward in the effectiveness of our teaching.

I think I need to give my classes more comprehensible input, but I don't really understand what it is.

- I have to understand current key ideas in linguistics and applied linguistics so that I can put them into practice in my teaching. And this is made difficult by the fact that these ideas are often expressed and discussed in a language which is impenetrable for those not regularly involved in such discourse.

Here in Hammerfest we're so out of touch with current developments.

- The world of EFL has a centre and a periphery, and if I have the misfortune to be on the periphery, I have to look to the centre for guidance and inspiration. This is partly, but not only, a question of geography. The 'centre' may be identified with the 'developed' countries, the 'west', the national capital, a particular university department, a particular group of schools, a team of authors, and so on.

I bet you'll have a fit when you see how I teach.

- I don't mind exposing my teaching to my learners, but the prospect of an expert observing one of my lessons is fraught with fear, guilt and embarrassment. So I feel ambivalent about the prospect of you coming to see my lessons: on the one hand I want the benefit of your expert eye to note where improvements need to be made, but at the same time I'd feel more comfortable if you stayed away. ■

3   Enquire within: being your own expert

In this section, we'll look at the relative roles of outside sources and internal personal resources in contributing to teachers' professional development.

Task 2

What outside sources do you use in order to continue developing as a teacher? Can you think of examples which have been particularly beneficial or enriching, or any which have disappointed you, and not given you what you had expected?

Commentary ■ ■ ■

Teachers can benefit greatly from:

- being observed and receiving feedback;
- observing other teachers and finding out how at least a few members of their huge invisible peer-group go about the task of teaching;
- taking an active interest in current ideas in the fields of language pedagogy and applied linguistics, not least those emanating from innovative and productive sources (people, places, institutions, publishers);
- taking part in courses, workshops, seminars and conferences where they are introduced to new ideas and activities for classroom use;
- enjoying access to a range of teaching materials and technologies.

However, we and many other teachers we have talked to have often been disappointed because, for example:

- observing other teachers can result in the feeling 'That was really good, but *I* could never teach like that';

- what observers say to us after our lessons reveals more about them than about us;
- presentations at conferences sometimes don't quite seem to give us anything that's exactly applicable to our teaching situation;
- when we try to read about current issues in applied linguistics we find them obscured by jargon and difficult to relate to the classroom;
- the sheer range of published materials available can appear bewildering. ∎

What's more, if the *only* channels of enquiry into professional development which teachers use lead *away* from them, towards outside authorities of various kinds, the result can be an unnecessary and debilitating degree of disempowerment. And this can degenerate into an abdication of responsibility for personal development, a feeling that it isn't worth trying to do things better, perhaps combined with a sense of guilt about not doing things right, and a retreat into secrecy at the prospect that anyone might find out how we teach. Learners, of course, see every day how we teach, but very often they aren't credited with possessing the faculty of critical observation.

There probably isn't much point in expecting 'experts' to give an ultimate, unequivocal answer to the question 'How should we teach?', since there has been a succession of so many different – often mutually contradictory – recommendations over the last century or so, to say nothing of the less well-known earlier history of the field (see Howatt 1984). And there is no definitive evidence that English language teaching as a whole is any more effective than it was ten, or twenty, or fifty years ago. Indeed, it's hard to imagine how this question could ever be researched, or whether it would be reasonable to expect any clear answer, given the diversity of circumstances, reasons for learning and possible ways of assessing effectiveness.

In his *Introducing Applied Linguistics* (1973, p 11), S. Pit Corder writes:

> ... applied linguistics deals with that part of the language teaching operation which is potentially susceptible of some sort of rigorous systematization. We are still a long way from achieving such a systematization ... For this reason linguistics can, as yet, scarcely claim to give firm answers to any but a few problems in language teaching.

The *as yet* indicates a faith that linguistic science *will* deliver the goods in the future, but it is also implied here that there are other parts of teaching which are not amenable to 'rigorous systematization'. We think it may well be the case that these other elements constitute *most* of the language teaching operation, that they depend on numerous variables which make every class – and every teacher – different from every other, and that the individual teacher is not just the best but actually the *only* person in a position to observe and respond fully to these variables.

From a different point of view, Anthony Howatt, in his introduction to *A History of English Language Teaching* (p xiv), suggests that the idea of putting theory into practice accounts only partially for whatever development there has been in this field.

> ... if there is a latent point of view beneath the surface [of this book] it is a belief that progress in the teaching of languages, as in many practical arts, is neither a function solely of the application of theoretical principle, however persuasive, nor of an unthinking reaction to the demands of the immediate market, but of the alchemy which, whether by accident or by design, unites them to a common purpose.

Although we will emphasize educational factors rather than strictly market ones, we hope that a similar underlying attitude to the role of theory will emerge from *this* book.

Donald Freeman, in a 1986 paper on Training, Development and Teaching Teaching (pp 4-5), writes:

> While knowledge which reflects various facets of teaching – applied linguistics, language acquisition, methodology and so on – increases, the understanding of teaching itself, and how it is learned, does not.
> (...)
> Let me make three assertions about the state of language teacher education: First, while we recognize the results of successful language learning, we have an uneven, often hypothetical, understanding of how language is learned. Second, because we lack that understanding of the learning process, we have only a hazy sense of the actual teaching performance which brings about successful language learning; language teaching remains a highly idiosyncratic, often hit-and-miss, operation. Third, because we don't have a clear, integrated understanding of language learning and the teaching performance which fosters it, we cannot define the teaching competence on which such teaching performance ought to be based.

We would add to this that the answers to these three challenges will be to some extent, and perhaps to a large extent, different for different teachers, and that teachers, with their intimate knowledge of their own classes and lessons, hopes and fears, successes and failures, are uniquely well placed to be their own 'experts', and to *discover* their own personal theories, rather than only attempting to *apply* theories which have been elaborated by other people in other contexts. Carl Rogers' idea that 'learning is persons' implies the inadequacy of assuming that teachers can be taught everything about what to do when they teach, and that this knowledge of what to do will stand them in good stead in their work, regardless of the particular realities of who they are and who their learners are. In contrast to 'teaching as behaviour' and even 'teaching as thought linked to behaviour', Freeman, this time in the IATEFL *Teacher Development* newsletter no. 18, 1992, proposes a third view of teaching as 'knowing what to do'. In this view,

> ... the classroom context and the people in it become central and crucial. They are not just settings for implementation; they provide frameworks for knowing.
> (...)
> This third view of teaching as knowing what to do introduces some points which should be of interest and concern to anyone in education. First, it suggests that teachers themselves, and not others like administrators, curriculum or materials writers, or researchers are in the best position to examine and define the knowledge-base from which they operate. Second, it suggests that the prescriptivism in much of teacher education and professional credentialing is largely pointless if the aim is to guarantee qualified practitioners. Such efforts are bound to be ineffective because they do not account for, because they cannot within their static and a contextual frameworks account for, these highly context-dependent ways in which teachers know what to do.

We hope this book will help you to account for what you do and how you know what to do.

4   Opening your classroom door

Task 3

Take a sheet of paper and jot down in a few sentences or phrases how you would describe your teaching to someone who wanted to get a feeling of what it's like to be in your classroom. If possible, tell or show these notes to a colleague; they may wish to ask questions or comment.

You could also use these notes as the basis for identifying things you are happy with, things you would like to change or improve, or things which simply interest you about your own teaching and which you would like to investigate and get to know better. In any case, file your notes away in a safe place with a view to coming back to them in the future and re-assessing their validity.

If you feel the relationship between you is right, you could also ask your learners to report on what it's like to be taught by you, perhaps in the form of a writing exercise.

Commentary ■ ■ ■

Classrooms have often been characterized as 'black boxes' because once the door is shut and the lesson starts, no one outside has any idea what goes on inside. But it may be that even we ourselves as teachers don't really know what goes on, and the task of articulating what kinds of places our classrooms are may help to force our awareness of how we see our classrooms and perhaps where our blind spots are. This awareness may be thrown into sharper relief by being reflected off another person. It may also be a way in to literally opening the classroom door and inviting someone else to report their impressions of what they see. We believe that being observed *can* be one of the most fruitful experiences for a teacher engaged in professional development, and we will explore this possibility in Chapter 3. ■

5   Articles of faith

Here is an exercise to help throw some more specific light on what kind of a teacher you are.

Task 4

Decide whether each of the following statements applies to you wholly (1), partly (2) or not at all (3):

- ☐ I always correct learners' errors.
- ☐ I talk as little as possible in lessons, so that the learners have as much opportunity to talk as possible.
- ☐ I always ask my learners to speak in complete sentences.
- ☐ I think it's a waste of time for learners to do lengthy writing exercises in the classroom.
- ☐ I gave up drilling years ago.
- ☐ I use authentic materials as much as possible.
- ☐ I don't explain meaning; I illustrate it.

☐ I don't show learners how to spell a word until they've heard it and practised pronouncing it.

☐ I don't like to allow silences of more than a few seconds during lessons.

☐ I always try to elicit from learners first, rather than giving them language myself.

☐ I use a lot of songs and games to lighten the atmosphere on Friday afternoons.

☐ I don't use translation, and I don't allow my learners to use their mother tongue during lessons.

☐ I make sure everyone in the class can say the word or sentence being practised before I move on to the next point.

☐ I always stand and never sit when I'm teaching.

If possible, discuss your responses with colleagues, and exchange and discuss other similar statements of personal principle. Are your beliefs and principles really as absolute as you think? How long have they been true? How did you learn them or become convinced of their value? Have you ever tried to go against them? If so, what happened?

You could also consider this: Are there any statements in the list which you would *like* to apply to you? Why do they appeal to you? Why don't they apply to you, in fact, and what would you need to do in order to make them apply?

If you have the benefit of being able to discuss teaching regularly with colleagues, listen to what you say, perhaps particularly when you and your colleagues disagree. You may well find other statements of principle to note and examine.

6 A dispassionate view

Now take a dispassionate view of the statements in Task 4.

Task 5

Reformulate each statement into a recommendation for any teacher (eg *Always correct learners' errors*, *Talk as little as possible in lessons*, etc) and brain-storm three arguments in favour of, and three arguments against each recommendation. If at all possible, do either the initial brainstorming or a reporting and discussing phase together with other teachers. Setting your own convictions aside for a moment, see how many arguments for and against you can muster.

Commentary ■ ■ ■

Example: I talk as little as possible in lessons, so that the learners can talk as much as possible.

This is a recommendation quite firmly established and influential in some ELT circles, either officially or in the form of folklore, and failure to follow it is a frequent source of teacher guilt. Perhaps it has its origin in the fact that, whereas teaching is often assumed to consist of telling and explaining, the teaching of a living language calls for a different approach: it seems obvious that people learning a language for productive use – and in most cases this means primarily for oral production – should practise speaking it in the classroom. Talking on the part of the teacher perhaps needs more justification, particularly if it is seen as taking away speaking opportunities from the learners. Teachers sometimes feel that they talk unnecessarily much because they are inefficient in classroom management, and they waste time which could be used more productively. And if it turns out that a substantial proportion of teacher talk is unnecessary, this does indeed suggest that some reorientation is desirable. But simply taking a quantitative approach and minimizing teacher talk is probably too crude a solution.

The *so that* in the statement under discussion implies a causal connection. Whether there actually is such a connection is an empirical question, and it is likely that the answer will vary according to numerous factors. Nor can it be taken for granted that the best use of learners' classroom time is necessarily talking. It may be that they will benefit equally, or more, if some of this time is set aside for reflection, writing or listening. A reduction in the *quantity* of learner talking may allow for a higher *quality*, however this is defined. Minimizing the quantity of teacher talk may deprive the learners of access to valuable listening practice, opportunities for incidental learning and for communicative interaction with a more fluent speaker of the language they are learning.

What is important, then, is to investigate not only the quantity but also the type and function of talking done by the participants in the classroom, and then experiment to see whether the quality of learning can be improved by making any adjustments. In addition, those teachers who tend to talk uncontrollably and fill as much air space as is available, might usefully work on the discipline of not talking at all during activities or phases where it is not strictly necessary; it is only by adding no-talking options to their repertoire that they will subsequently be able to *choose* whether or not to talk according to the demands of the situation, instead of automatically falling into the habitual option of talking.

You may find in doing this task that you discover new arguments that support your view, or persuasive arguments in the other direction. These may suggest experiments with unfamiliar – or rediscovered – techniques. Most importantly, we would like them to suggest that any technique or style is likely to have a reasonable rationale – and to be effective – in certain circumstances, but can, if not kept in awareness and questioned, become an unthinking habit or empty ritual divorced from its original justification. So, for instance, it may be that, especially in some teaching situations, learners can benefit enormously from opportunities to listen at length to the teacher's voice, and the conclusion might be that there is a need to balance this with the wish to give the learners as much high-quality speaking time as possible. ■

7 Glimpses through classroom keyholes

In the following short extracts, we see glimpses of different teachers at work, and imagine a possible rationale – no doubt only one of many – behind what happens.

1 The class are practising saying a word which is difficult to pronounce. As each learner has a go, the teacher says: 'Good!' 'Well done!' 'Very good!' 'Not bad ... try again, like this ... listen ... good! Much better!' and so on. Everyone is smiling, attentive, trying hard, laughing good-humouredly at the difficulty of the task and the mistakes being made.

Comment: We can speculate that this teacher has discovered from experience that this class, at least, works very well in an atmosphere where she is constantly challenging the learners, rewarding them, emphasizing their successes and encouraging them when they can't quite manage the task of the moment.

2 This class is engaged in a similar task to the first one. But the atmosphere and the interaction are very different. In their own time, and in no set order, the learners try to pronounce the word. Some of them make several attempts, until they seem satisfied, or tire temporarily of the effort. The learners listen to each other very carefully, and often there is a consensus of nodding and 'Yes, it's good' when they recognize a successful version of the word. The teacher also listens intently, but says little, except that when one of the learners says the word to her in a questioning manner, she says 'Yes,' or 'Say it like this,' and taps the rhythm of the word on the table, or mouths the sequence of vowel sounds in the word.

Comment: We can speculate that this teacher believes in allowing learners to pay careful attention to their own pronunciation and develop their own criteria of what is correct, or what is acceptable and the best possible at the moment. She lets them work primarily with their own collective resources, but is ready to intervene when these resources fall short of what is needed.

Task 6

How would you describe the rationale for the glimpses that follow?

3 The teacher is introducing some vocabulary which the learners are going to meet in a reading passage. The teacher writes the words on the board one by one, and asks the class if anyone can provide an explanation. Sometimes the learners give explanations in English, sometimes translations into their L1. If no one knows a word, or a wrong explanation is offered, the teacher explains; in these cases, the learners often check by suggesting a translation, which the teacher confirms if correct. There are supplementary questions about some of the words; the teacher answers these briefly.

4 A similar activity to 3 above. But in this class the teacher explains or exemplifies each word without saying the word itself. The learners are invited to say the word if they recognize it from the information given; if not, the teacher says it and gets the learners to repeat it before she writes it on the board.

5 This teacher is also going to use the same reading text as in 3 and 4 above, with a class of the same level, but does no preparatory work on vocabulary at all.

6 The learners are reporting back on a decision-making task. One says 'We have choose this one.' The teacher replies 'chosen'.

7 The same situation as in 6 above. But this teacher replies 'You've chosen this one, have you? Why?'

Commentary ■ ■ ■

In considering alternative approaches to a certain type of teaching task, you may find yourself clearly favouring one rather than another. The above exercise may be helpful in looking beyond personal preference and thinking your way into alternatives. ■

8 The archaeology of methodology

The next task will help you investigate where such preferences come from.

Task 7

Now reflect on how your practice has developed since you started teaching, and why you teach the way you do now. The answer to this will probably be quite complex, and it may be that you can only sketch it out at the moment, but it may well include reference to:

- theories you hold about teaching and learning;
- what you were taught on training courses (for English language teaching or other subjects);
- what you've read in books and magazines for teachers;
- exchange of ideas with colleagues;
- observing other teachers;
- ideas you've developed yourself through experience.

But dig deeper into the past, too, for example into the way your teachers taught you when you were a child.

Commentary ▨ ▪ ▪

Here is part of one response to this task:

The whole impression I got from the initial ELT training course I did – which I should say was great, and the best educational thing I'd ever done – was that lessons should be busy, with lots of 'pace', lots of oral practice, which often meant drilling, and correcting, relentlessly but nicely, and then giving the learners gradually a bit more scope and a bit more, until in the end they were using a new item 'freely'. It was certainly great fun and very different from what I'd considered teaching to be like previously, and I went along with it quite happily for a while. But then it gradually began to seem less and less like me, I wanted to slow things down, give more time for working things out, trying things out. And as I needed to spend less energy on thinking about what I was doing and see the lesson more from the learners' point of view I began to realize that for some of them it was really a bit of a game, that they could apparently reach the point where they were getting it right, as long as the focus of the lesson was clear and they were channelled towards saying certain things, but it didn't help them much when they came back the next week and they'd forgotten it all, or when we met outside the school and chatted in English.

And I started reading a bit about how people need to be actively involved mentally with a language and not just perform tricks with it, and how they go through different stages of hypotheses and make different types of errors. And that made sense because I noticed that I could 'correct' the same error again and again and when it did eventually start coming right it was often a long time later and it didn't seem to have anything to do with me directly, it just sort of corrected itself. So I tend not to take such a rigid view of correction, and emphasize more giving opportunities for use and experimentation, and encouraging people to develop their own criteria of what's right and wrong, although even in this I've come to realize the importance of pointing out errors and helping people to work on them if they're really concerned about it. And if I think it helps, I'll deal analytically with grammar. That didn't use to be the done thing, as far as I could see, but some people really expect it and I think it can help them if it's made approachable. And if you don't allow for that they'll probably do it anyway on their own, and get it wrong, more than likely.

In retrospect it seems there was a sort of conspiracy that there were certain things that were OK to do and others that weren't. Maybe a lot of it was just a fashion for a while, and maybe just in a small sector of the English teaching world, although I learned a lot through it and I think it was an excellent starting point for me. And maybe people like me even contributed to that conspiracy, or fashion, 'cos we allowed ourselves to be led by it. I feel much more relaxed now – I mean relaxed in lessons, 'cos I'm not trying to keep things moving fast all the time, but also relaxed about being able to choose how to do things, depending on what suits my style and what I think will work in that particular class, without worrying that the Teaching Police are going to come knocking on the classroom door to make sure I'm doing the right thing. (JONATHAN) ■

A principled and professional approach to teaching needs to be based on something more than keeping up with fashion. The relationship between principle and practice is complex. On the one hand, ideas filter through from education, applied linguistics, psychology, neurology and so on, and seem to suggest more or less direct applications to teaching. But we should be wary of embracing any of these ideas wholesale and assuming that by implementing them we absolve ourselves of responsibility for further critical thought and decision-making. Above all, we should be careful not to assume that one set of recipes will work for all learners, all teachers, all contexts.

On the other hand, we may through intuition, deliberate experiment or chance arrive at discoveries of Things That Work. Out of a sense of responsibility to our own development and the collective development of EFL teaching, we might then want to find out if these discoveries are generalizable and capable of yielding some new guiding principle for our practice, and, ideally, *why* they are valid, if they seem to be so. In other words, as well as subjecting recommendations from outside to critical examination, we can also begin with observational data concerning our own practices, prejudices and habits, and derive principles, theories, models, or rationales from these. Theory and practice are linked by a two-way street.

And even if a discovery resists any attempt to assign a rationale to it, we shouldn't dismiss it. If I discover that a certain class of mine learn better with their seats facing east than west, I would be well advised to make use of that fact, although I would be equally well advised not to be too hasty in recommending it as a universal panacea for effective language learning.

9 Beyond methods

Clearly, people *do* learn languages (and have learned them through the ages) by all sorts of methods, some involving classrooms and teachers and others not. Perhaps what matters is not so much what methodology we use, but other more basic underlying factors to do with how people feel about the place they are in and the people they are with.

Task 8

Think about classrooms you have been in, as a learner, a teacher or in any other capacity. Which of these metaphors express something of your feelings towards those classrooms?

The classroom is:

- a workshop;
- a playground;
- a courtroom;
- a factory;
- a greenhouse;
- a parade ground;
- a prison;
- a minefield;
- a church.

Are there any other metaphors that suggest themselves to you? Compare your answers with colleagues.

Commentary ■ ■ ■

For example, a classroom is a courtroom where the learners have to plead their knowledge of the subject to the teacher facing them behind the desk, and the teacher judges whether or not their performance is convincing. If it is, they can be acquitted, at least for the time being; if not, they are punished, by harsh words, by low marks, by being given extra homework and so on. A classroom is a greenhouse where special fertile conditions for learning are set up in an atmosphere deliberately different from the one outside, and learners are tended by teachers who monitor their progress and give them any additional mental nourishment necessary, but where it can get uncomfortably hot and stuffy sometimes. And so on. ■

Task 9

Now think about your ideal classroom. What metaphors would describe it? What can you start doing now towards achieving it?

Commentary ■ ■ ■

Metaphors can be dangerously seductive and lead us away from accurate perception of reality. But they can also act as spectacles to enable us to see things from a different perspective and therefore perhaps more clearly, or to have new insights – to see into things which were previously hidden. ■

As another way of looking at and thinking about classrooms from a viewpoint innocent of methods, theories and techniques, here is a summary called *What I hope for in a classroom* by Earl Stevick (1976, p 159) which is divided into observations about the students and observations about the teacher.

Task 10

You might like to jot down your thoughts under that title, *What I hope for in a classroom*, before you read. Otherwise, read what Stevick says and decide whether you would subscribe to the same views, or if there are things you would want to change, add or take away.

As the years go by, I find myself less concerned with which method has been chosen for a particular class, and more interested in how it is being used. I am particularly aware of what I see when I look at students and teacher.

Students

1 I hope to find the students involved in whatever they are doing, contributing to it and getting satisfaction from it on many levels of personality.

That is to say, I hope *not* to find them concentrating on merely coming up with correct responses (even in a structure drill), or on grinding out correct sentences or free conversations just for the sake of grinding out correct sentences or free conversations.

2 I hope to find the students comfortable and relaxed, even in the midst of intense intellectual activity or vigorous argument.

This does not mean that they are loafing on the job. In fact, students who are really comfortable with what they are doing are less likely to loaf.

This also means that the students are not apprehensive that they will be punished if they fail to live up to the teacher's expectations.

3 I hope to find that the students are listening to one another, and not just to the teacher. I also hope that they will be getting help and correction from one another, and not just from the teacher.

This means that the students are not like separate lamps plugged into a single power supply, in such a way that the power used by one diminishes the voltage available to the rest.

Teacher

4 The teacher is in general control of what is going on.

This does not mean that everything the students do comes as a direct response to a specific cue from the teacher.

5 The teacher allows/encourages/requires originality from students, whether in individual sentences, or in larger units of activity, or in choice among a range of techniques.

This does not mean anarchy or chaos.

6 One of the first things I notice is whether the teacher seems relaxed and matter-of-fact in voice and manner, giving information about the appropriateness or correctness of what the students do, rather than criticizing or praising them.

The teacher does not, either by word or by unspoken message, say to students, 'Now always remember ...,' 'You shouldn't have forgotten ...,' 'You are a good/poor student,' or 'Now try to do this so that I may judge you on it.'

Commentary ■ ■ ■

Here, the focus on the *how* rather than the *which*, and on looking at the *people* in the classroom, is an expression of an interest in the *process* which goes on within and between the participants in a lesson. Probably Stevick's hypothetical observations of teachers and learners are compatible with the use of any method at all, or with instances of teaching which are not recognizable as any particular method; rather, they would suggest that the teacher is working in accordance with some personal knowledge of 'what to do' in a particular context. There may be various routes to this knowledge, leading through intuition, introspection, attending courses, participating in formal and informal peer networks, and so on, but depending crucially on the teacher's awareness of that context, not as a 'setting for implementation', but as a 'framework for knowing'. ∎

The model of professional education appropriate as a description for this kind of development would seem to be the one conceived of by Douglas Schön and Michael Wallace as the *reflective model*. In this model, practice is initially informed by *received knowledge* from authoritative sources and by the practitioner's own already-exisiting knowledge derived from experience. But competence then develops through a repeated *reflective cycle* of practice and reflection. Top-down transmission of authoritative knowledge is not discounted, but is allotted only a limited role, and one which is likely to diminish with time in the development of an individual. Theory can be discovered and developed through practice.

Task 11

How do you rate yourself on your achievement of those criteria from the above extract which are important for you, together with your own additions? If you're not sure, how can you find out? What steps can you take to improve your rating?

10 Recommended reading

Training Foreign Language Teachers by Michael Wallace applies the concept of reflective professional training to the context of language teaching.

Anthony Howatt's *A History of English Language Teaching* illustrates in a thoroughly readable way that the work we do is part of a long-established tradition of interaction between theory and practice, and that what appear to be new ideas are often old ones recycled, refurbished or reinvented. In this way the book emphasizes the importance and value of the historical perspective which is so often lacking in discussion and writing about English language teaching.

11 References and bibliography

Corder, S.P. 1973 *Introducing Applied Linguistics* (Penguin)
Freeman, D. 1986 *Training, Development and Teaching Teaching: A descriptive paradigm of teaching an examination of related strategies for language teacher education* (School for International Training, Brattleboro, Vermont)
Freeman, D. 1992 Three Views of Teachers' Knowledge. In *Teacher Development* (newsletter of the IATEFL Teacher Development Special Interest Group) no. 18
Howatt, A.P. R. 1984 *A History of English Language Teaching* (OUP)
Schön, D.A. 1983 *The Reflective Practitioner: How Professionals Think in Action* (Temple Smith)
Schön, D.A. 1987 *Educating the Reflective Practitioner: Toward a New Design for Teaching and Learning in the Professions* (Jossey Bass)
Stevick, Earl W. 1976 *Memory, Meaning and Method* (Newbury House)
Wallace, M. 1991 *Training Foreign Language Teachers: A Reflective Approach* (CUP)

Chapter 2 **Into the inner sanctum:**
Teachers and terminology

1 Introduction

For many teachers, language teaching, and particularly linguistics, seems to be riddled with complex terminology, much of it seemingly incomprehensible to those not versed in its inner secrets. The more unkind critics of over-complex terminology have suggested that it owes its existence to the fact that it represents a quasi-science, that linguistics is not a true science and that it has therefore invented for itself a blanket of obscure terms to disguise the fact that 'the emperor has no clothes'. Indeed, it is hard not to be swayed by this argument when one comes across *lexical item* used to mean *word*, or *semantic function* used to represent *meaning*.

To some, the use of such terminology may even be intimidating. There may appear to be a highly complex, secret language that demands a high level of intellect if it is to be understood, let alone used. To many it may appear to be the preserve of a select group of linguisticians who communicate in their obscure argot to the exclusion of the real world. This view has led to an active resistance to terminology (and through it to linguistics itself) in the minds of many teachers. Terminology, it appears, has uncomfortable associations for many of us with 'theory' and is thus 'difficult'. It is fair to say that there is even a 'counter culture', teachers who actively resist the use of such terminology and who regard it as unnecessary, over-intellectual and out of touch with the realities of the classroom. At the heart of this lies the often discussed question of the relevance of linguistic science to practical language teaching. This chapter will not attempt to address that question directly (for the simple reason that it has been discussed many times before), but it will attempt to put the use of terminology into a practical context and to show that it can be both useful and, at a certain level, even entertaining.

2 What terminology do teachers use?

Critics of terminology generally argue that it is over-complex and simply a way of avoiding 'calling a spade a spade'. This criticism can, of course, be levelled at other fields of professional practice far removed from the world of foreign language teaching. Most fields of human activity from football to astrophysics have their own peculiar jargon, often incomprehensible to outsiders. Even the everyday language of the language school staffroom would seem strange, even impenetrable, to someone unfamiliar with its jargon. What would the lay person make of these snippets of 'teacherese'?

I think I'll do a jigsaw listening with my elementary class this afternoon.
Juan's still having trouble with the 3rd conditional.
Why is it that I can never make a substitution drill work?
Where's that infinitive vs gerund exercise you used yesterday?
My students really seem to enjoy jumbled readings.
Have you got a good exercise for practising tags?

Probably not very much. Yet how many teachers would regard some of the expressions in the above utterances as examples of terminology? The *Shorter Oxford English Dictionary* defines *terminology*, inter alia, as 'the system of terms belonging to any science or subject'. The above examples are surely just that. Where else other than in the context of language teaching could one use the expressions *jigsaw listening* or *substitution drill*? The language-teaching profession, just as any other, has generated, and is still generating, its own set of terms to identify, define and differentiate both its subject matter and the ways in which this subject matter is presented. There is nothing strange about this. What is noticeable, however, is the frequently encountered reaction by some teachers that terminology is something unnecessary, superfluous to their practical classroom needs. It is perceived as the creation of the 'mother discipline' of linguistics, the 'theory' that supposedly lies behind all language teaching. In rejecting terminology, some teachers are implicitly rejecting the claim of linguistic science to form the theoretical basis of language teaching. The practical classroom practitioner will say that just as he or she has no time for linguistics, applied or otherwise, in his or her construct, then he or she will also have no truck with the terminology that this science has created for itself. The above examples show, however, that things are not quite that simple. Methodology, of course, has created its own branch of terminology (*jigsaw listening, jumbled reading*), but can we really get by without the basic terminology of linguistic description? Is it possible to teach effectively without reference to grammatical terms, technical terms relating to phonology, vocabulary and discourse? We asked a number of teachers to give us their reaction to terminology in language teaching (it was not specified whether the terminology referred to methodology exclusively, to linguistics exclusively or to both).

Question: What is your reaction to terminology in language teaching?

Teacher responses:

a *I can get by perfectly well in the classroom without any of this terminology.*
(PHIL, USA)

b *I get frustrated when I come across terms I don't understand. It affects my confidence and makes me feel I should know them.* (HELEN, UK)

*c I enjoy using complex terminology, but only with my colleagues. Some words are
really funny. I wouldn't dream of using these terms with my students though!*
(SEAN, UK)

d Some terminology is very useful. It helps learners to categorize words, for example.
(PETER, GERMANY)

*e A lot of it seems to be terminology for terminology's sake. Some of the terms seem to be
completely unnecessary.*
(JOANNA, UK)

*f What's more important – talking about the language using terminology, or using the
language itself? I think the answer is obvious.*
(MIKE, UK)

*g We have to learn all this terminology at university. It's difficult at first, but now we
know it, although I must say I rarely use it in class, with the exception of
grammatical terms.*
(ÉVA, HUNGARY)

*h I haven't got the patience to learn these terms. If I come across one I don't know in a
book, I just ignore it.*
(ANTHONY, UK)

*i Sometimes I find a word I really like the sound of and then I take the trouble to find
out what it means.*
(LIZ, UK)

*j Students only need a very limited amount of terminology – noun, verb and so on.
The central question is how much terminology teachers need. I think that if it helps
them to understand the nature of language, then they need as much as possible.*
(DIETMAR, GERMANY)

Commentary ■ ■ ■

Four main strands emerge from the above comments. The first is that some
teachers simply reject the idea of using terminology at all. They will probably, of
course, as indicated in the examples of teacher language earlier in this chapter,
use terminology at a certain level without realizing it, although for them terminology per se has strong negative associations. It is associated with 'talking about
language' rather than actually using language and thus it has theoretical overtones. The second strand is that some teachers find terminology intimidating.
Their own perceived lack of understanding and knowledge of terminology makes
them feel inadequate. Our discussions with teachers suggest that this feeling is
fairly widespread and, as with the first group, may lie in the first place with the
fact that they have simply not thought about the amount of terminology they
already use in the classroom and outside it as part of their everyday teaching.

A second factor, particularly as regards the feeling of inadequacy expressed by
one of the teachers quoted above, is that for some teachers it is difficult to identify
which terms are necessary and which are simply 'luxury items' that they do not
need anyway. Such teachers may also assume that terminology is endless and that
there are simply hundreds of complex terms that they feel they *should* know. For

teachers who feel this way, a certain amount of demystification of terminology will usually be of considerable benefit – once again, deciding which items are necessary and which are simply terms used in various forms of linguistic description and which may be of less immediate practical value.

A third strand emerging from the teachers' comments quoted above is that many teachers think a certain amount of terminology is necessary for their learners. These terms are regarded as being part of everyday classroom metalanguage and, as such, necessary in terms of explaining grammatical concepts, categorizing items of language and clarifying meaning. Clearly, if these terms are useful for learners, then they are essential for teachers. The final strand is that, although it might seem curious, some teachers actually like terminology. New or strange terms might be seen as an intellectual challenge, a means of entering a new area of language teaching theory, or simply as just fun. Certain terms sound or look interesting or amusing and are thus worthy of investigation. As with strange-sounding items of vocabulary, these are the ones that are memorable for whatever reason, and these tend to be the ones that some of us retain, irrespective of their practical usefulness. Amongst some of the more intriguing terms the authors of this book have found memorable for a number of reasons are:

- *lathophobic aphasia* – unwillingness to speak for fear of making a mistake (a condition we have suffered from ourselves);
- *felicity conditions* – the conditions which must be fulfilled for a speech act to be satisfactorily performed (please check that the felicity conditions are in order before you open your mouth).

Even those who are firmly in the 'anti-jargon' camp appear to accept that some terminology at least is necessary for classroom metalanguage purposes and for clarifying concepts and grammatical categories. To the relief of those who find themselves overawed by terminology, there may not be an excessive number of terms in the list of those judged to be essential. What do teachers regard as essential terminology for classroom use? Which terms are best reserved for background reading on language teaching theory? In focusing on the kind of terminology learners may need, the following task may help teachers to reflect on the jargon they actually use and whether it is essential or not. ■

3   What terminology do learners need?

Some terms form the basis of classroom metalanguage, which teachers use to set up tasks and clarify concepts to learners. Without such basic terminology, teachers inevitably must have recourse to the mother tongue of the learners to explain these fundamental terms. Arguably, however, there is a limit to the number of terms that can be usefully employed in the classroom and there are those which are best avoided as their main purpose is to talk about language rather than to enable learners to understand and use it. In some cases there is a simple 'non-terminological' alternative which we would, in any case, normally use in everyday speech (*word* or *phrase* to replace *lexical item* is just one example). In other cases, however, it is difficult to find a simple equivalent term and an explanation or illustration of what we mean may be necessary. An example of this is the word *syllable*, which is variously defined as 'a unit of pronunciation' (too general), 'a minimum rhythmic unit of spoken language, consisting of a vowel or sustained consonant, often preceded or followed by unsustained consonants' (too complex) and 'a vocal sound or set of sounds uttered with a single effort of articulation and forming a word or an element of a word' (potentially confusing). In this case, an illustration of what a syllable actually is (via sounds, diagrams, Cuisenaire rods) and reinforcement of the concept could be followed by subsequent use of the term whenever it is necessary and useful to do so.

Task 1

1 In the broad categories of grammar, phonology, discourse, vocabulary and classroom practice, write down words that you commonly use with your learners.
2 Read through the following terms related to these five areas of language and language teaching and decide which you feel would be helpful to learners as a reference point in lessons. (Please note that this list is not intended to be either exhaustive or essential in any way. The items chosen were selected at random and are intended to be a mixture of common and more obscure terms used in linguistic description and in describing language teaching methodology.)

> ### A: Some terms connected with grammar
> *noun verb adjective adverb pronoun gerund tense passive subjunctive progressive perfect past future auxiliary conjunction modal clause modifier formula infinitive article stative phrasal verb aspect negative question particle dynamic preposition interrogative*

> ### B: Some terms connected with phonology
> *sound phoneme syllable rising tone prominence vowel diphthong consonant voiceless open vowel stress voiced alveolar elision glottal stop schwa spread aspiration rounded primary stress plosive pitch assimilation weak form*

> ### C: Some terms connected with discourse
> *function exponent notion concept appropriacy formal informal register style discourse status context*

> ### D: Some terms connected with vocabulary
> *affix prefix suffix root collocation synonym hyponym homonym antonym homophone lexical set morpheme*

> ### E: Some terms connected with classroom practice
> *inductive deductive accuracy fluency*

3 Now decide which of the terms you have selected you regard as essential for classroom use at an elementary level.
4 Add to the list any words related to the categories of grammar, phonology, discourse, vocabulary and classroom practice which are not included in the four general categories and which you regard as essential for classroom use.

- How many in your list of useful terms are from Section A? And from Section B?
- How many of the words you regard as essential are from Section A?

We asked a group of twenty practising native-speaker teachers to choose the terms from the above list that they regarded as essential for classroom meta-language purposes at an elementary level. We also asked them to say why they regarded these terms as essential.

Results and commentary ■ ■ ■

The immediate and simple result of this brief survey was that not many terms are regarded as essential, at least as far as this group of teachers was concerned. Almost all the terms selected by the group came from section A, ie the section that can be loosely described as the 'grammar section'. The words chosen in almost every case were *noun, verb, adjective, adverb, tense, past, future, question, negative* and *progressive* (or *continuous*). Some members of the group said they preferred using the very accessible term *-ing form* to either of the former. The only other terms selected (and not by any means by all of the twenty in the sample) were *sound, stress, formal* and *informal*. These results suggest that the terminology most frequently used by teachers in the classroom relates to grammatical categories and concepts.

The teachers in this survey tended to regard the terms they chose as essential because they are of great help to learners in making sense of language, storing language items and relating language items to concepts in their own language. The other terms chosen were regarded as very useful for phonology-teaching metalanguage (*Where's the stress? What's this sound?*) and teaching the functional exponents of a particular functional area (*Is this formal or informal?*).

Broadly speaking, the teachers in the survey felt they could 'get by' in class with the basic terminology they selected and that it would be difficult to function without it. The other terms in the task were generally felt to be of little use to learners and more related to theory and linguistic description. Interestingly, a large number of the terms were unfamiliar to many of the teachers questioned. Some said that they had 'come across' some of these terms but were unable to remember what they meant. Some of the examples generally regarded as unclear or unfamiliar were:

Group A: *aspect, stative, dynamic, particle*
Group B: *prominence, alveolar, elision, aspiration, assimilation*
Group C: *notion*
Group D: *affix, hyponym, homonym, homophone, collocation, morpheme, antonym*
Group E: *inductive, deductive*

On further questioning, it became clear that a number of these terms were unknown or, if they were known, the concepts underlying them were not. In particular many in the group were unsure about the distinction between tense and aspect, the difference between stative and dynamic verbs, the exact meaning of various phonological terms, the distinction between a function and a notion, and what the different vocabulary terms signified. As these issues were explored, two interesting angles emerged. The first was that many of the teachers felt that, yes, the distinction between tense and aspect was interesting and even rather important in understanding the concepts underlying verb forms in English. Likewise, the distinction between stative and dynamic verbs could go some way towards understanding why certain verbs did not have progressive forms, for example. Such realizations were, arguably, important and potentially very rewarding for teachers, but were they of much use to learners? This point produced a significant level of disagreement within the group, with some arguing that an understanding of such distinctions would be of great benefit to a certain type of learner and that even reader-friendly reference books such as *Practical English Usage* (Swan, 1980) referred to these concepts. The second angle that emerged was that of the potentially confusing nature of some terms. Some teachers argued very forcibly that distinctions between pairs of concepts were often unhelpful, particularly if the terms used to express these distinctions were themselves unclear. *Inductive* and *deductive* were cited as specific examples of this.

We then widened the discussion to examine how teachers avoided using terms that expressed concepts that were important for classroom use. One example of this was the word *collocation*, which several teachers were unsure about. A few suggested that they would actually use this word with their learners, even at an elementary level, having previously established its meaning, but most avoided it by using phrases such as *words which usually go together* or *two-word expressions* or *words that we usually find next to each other*. It was interesting to note that all of these 'avoidance techniques' used a lot of words to replace a single term, but also that it was generally felt preferable to paraphrase rather than to give learners jargon, especially when the teachers themselves were unsure of the term in question. Several teachers in the group declared themselves to be terrified of students who knew and used terminology – *collocation* was one example given. One teacher recalled with horror the student question 'Is *interested in* a collocation?' There was, however, a strong feeling amongst the group that it was necessary to 'call a spade a spade'. What is wrong with the word *opposite* to replace the jargon word *antonym*? Indeed, many felt that here was a simple term that was almost essential for classroom use, given the usefulness of the idea of an opposite concept in learning and remembering items of vocabulary.

The general impression gained from this investigation was that most teachers used a restricted but essential, high-value range of terms, mostly connected with grammar and grammatical explanations, but also in the area of functional language and phonology teaching. In many cases, they used paraphrasing to avoid complex jargon or terms they were either uncertain about themselves or felt were unhelpful, unnecessary or confusing for their learners. A few said they were interested in terminology per se but did not find this interest particularly useful in practical classroom terms. ■

Task 2

Arrange for one of your own lessons to be video (or audio) recorded. On the playback note down which terms you use in the lesson. Do you use any of the terms in Task 1? Which section or sections do the majority of the terms you use belong to?

Note: If you are unable to arrange a recording of one of your lessons, try to observe colleagues teaching and note down the terminology they use, or arrange for a colleague to watch one of your lessons and note down the terminology you use.

4 Helpful and unhelpful terminology

Although many terms can perform a useful function by clarifying or simplifying concepts (helpful terms), there are some which may actually have the opposite effect and create confusion (unhelpful terms). Unhelpful terms often lurk in pairs, and have a strange propensity to be very similar in spelling and sound, as if invented with the avowed intention of causing confusion. One such pair is to be found in Task 1, namely *inductive* and *deductive*, words derived from the verbs *induce* and *deduce* respectively. The *Longman Dictionary of English Language and Culture* (Longman 1992) defines *induce* as 'to lead someone to do something, often by persuading', whereas *deduce* is defined as 'to reach a decision or judgement about a fact or situation by using one's own knowledge or reason'. *Inductive* is defined as 'reasoning from known facts to produce general principles' and *deductive* as 'reasoning from a general idea or set of facts to a particular idea or fact'. If we apply the meanings of the verbs directly to language teaching, then we might expect *inductive* to mean persuading learners that something is correct and that *deductive* means to work it out on your own. From the definitions of the adjectives we might assume that inductive teaching means working out general principles from particular known facts about the language, while deductive language teaching means working out particular facts from a general idea about the language. When these terms are applied to methodology, however, their meaning changes, as can be seen from these definitions given in *The Longman Dictionary of Language Teaching and Applied Linguistics* (Longman 1992):

> **inductive learning:** An approach to language teaching in which learners are not taught grammatical or other rules directly but are left to discover or induce rules from their experience of using the language.

> **deductive learning:** An approach to language teaching in which learners are taught rules and given specific information about a language.

Thus, the approach which involved working out or *deducing* rules is *inductive*, while the approach in which rules are given (perhaps even persuasively!) is *deductive*. It is fair to say that these terms have become confusing to say the least, while the concepts they convey are fundamental, yet relatively simple, principles of language teaching methodology. Surely there must be an easier way of conveying such important principles? The expressions 'meaning to form' and 'form to meaning' have been used to replace inductive and deductive, the first implying that the meaning underlying a particular structure or item of vocabulary is clarified to learners first before the form of the structure or item of vocabulary is given, while the second implies that the form is provided and then the meaning is arrived at somehow or other. This might appear to be a simpler solution but it hardly constitutes a whole approach and would seem to be confined to techniques for presenting language to learners. Martin Parrott (*Tasks for Language Teachers*, 1993) refers to *guiding* and *giving*, which seem to be much more appealing and helpful terms for several reasons. Firstly, they are simple non-jargon terms. Secondly, they are clearly distinguishable in meaning. Thirdly, they can be applied equally to a whole approach or to a single technique or even to a single moment in a lesson. Fourthly, they could also serve as a useful basis for classroom analysis, with teachers analyzing their own teaching style (or the teaching style of others) and observing times when they 'guide' and times when they 'give'. In the latter case, it is quite difficult to imagine a teacher saying *Aha. Now I'm being inductive.*

The terms *accuracy* and *fluency* can also be regarded as unhelpful, but for different reasons. They may not be confusing in themselves. Many teachers probably have an image of a learner who speaks accurately, ie with very few errors. Many teachers would also imagine a fluent speaker as speaking the target language with a certain amount of ease and 'flow'. Dictionary definitions of fluency are quite interesting, however. The *Dictionary of English Language and Culture* (Longman 1992) defines fluent as '... expressed readily and without pause', while *The Collins Cobuild English Language Dictionary* (Collins 1987) describes a fluent person as someone who can speak or write '... easily and correctly, with no hesitation or *inaccuracy*' (our italics). Is it possible, then, to be accurate and not to be fluent or to be fluent and not to be accurate? If English is our mother tongue, we are accurate in English, but, arguably, we are not always fluent. We sometimes stumble and hesitate through nerves, unfamiliarity with the topic of conversation or as a result of other affective factors that inhibit our sense of well-being, but surely we can nonetheless regard ourselves as fluent in our mother tongue. *Fluency* is a notoriously difficult concept to define.

We asked a group of twenty secondary and tertiary level English teachers in Luxembourg to say what they understood by the term *fluency*. There were numerous opinions, including such diverse concepts as 'without pausing', 'fast and accurate', 'good vocabulary', 'well expressed ideas', 'good content'. We then played a recording of two learners tackling the section of the ARELS Higher examination in which candidates are required to talk for two minutes about a contemporary topic. The first learner spoke rapidly, with no hesitation what-soever for the full two minutes. He also spoke extremely repetitively and made several basic grammatical errors. The second learner spoke carefully with some hesitation and finished after one minute. She spoke very accurately with very good pronunciation and used sophisticated vocabulary. The teachers were asked to grade their fluency on a scale of 0 to 12 (as the examiners do). In the first case the marks varied from 2 to 12, the latter awarded by several people because the learner spoke without any hesitation whatsoever, so, by that definition of fluency, he was fluent. The second learner was generally awarded around half marks for fluency because she hesitated and appeared to be searching for what to say at times. In terms of the examination as a whole (ie including the other five sections of the examination), the 'fluent' speaker actually failed, while the 'accurate' speaker passed easily.

We have often heard teachers saying they intend to give their learners some 'fluency practice'. What do they mean by this? Do they intend to get them to speak quickly without hesitation and to hell with accuracy? Probably not. What most people seem to mean when they talk about 'fluency practice' is giving their learners the opportunity to speak freely and in an unpressurized way within a pair or small group, or even within the class as a whole. What they say will be more or less accurate depending on their language level. It will not necessarily be the error-strewn free-for-all that the presentation of accuracy and fluency as opposing extremes suggests.

What we regard as helpful terminology falls into two distinct areas: either those areas where a term can be clearly applied to a concept useful for classroom practice (*noun*, *verb*, etc), or those areas where a term refers to something concrete and describes it in a way that avoids overlong paraphrasing. In other words, the term acts as a convenient short-cut. Terms in the former category have been discussed earlier in this chapter, but the second category merits some brief attention. One area where there are a number of helpful terms of this type is in the field of phonology. The terms used in phonetic description present a quick and accurate reference point for the items they describe and would appear to be preferable to, eg, 'that soft bit that hangs down at the back of the mouth'. With few exceptions, the terms used to describe methods and place of articulation are unambiguous and relatively accessible, eg *nasal*, *dental* and *voiceless*. Even those terms which are less obvious in meaning can be easily linked to words which help to reinforce their meaning, eg *plosive* to *explosion* as in 'an explosion of air' and *fricative* to *friction*.

5   Staying informed

In the wider sense, an investigation into terminology can also open up for the teacher a whole range of new areas of language and language learning. Simple curiosity about the meaning of terms can, via dictionaries of linguistic terms, bibliographies, articles and so on, lead to a greater awareness of the different facets of language itself. For example, an investigation into the meaning of *assimilation* in phonetics might lead to an increased awareness of where this takes place in English and, indeed, in other languages known by the teacher. Terminology itself can be a 'way in' to this awareness. This, in turn, can lead to a more confident teacher, no longer feeling disadvantaged by the weight of all the unknown terminology 'out there', but empowered by a realization that what is required in classroom terms is limited and achievable and that what goes beyond that is not essential but is potentially rewarding. In this sense, terminology is part of 'finding out', part of moving rather than standing still, a potential key to the door of finding out more about how language itself operates.

Some terms are attractive in themselves, even if the concepts they refer to are possibly less than central in the list of language teaching priorities. Here are some terms drawn at random from *The Longman Dictionary of Language Teaching and Applied Linguistics* that we particularly like the sound of: *pragmatics*; *heuristics*; *semiotics*; *phatic communion*.

These are not terms that we use in everyday conversation! We should stress that in many years of language teaching and teacher training we have never felt the need to use any of them. Nor have we felt disadvantaged by any lack of fluency in their use. We just like them.

Task 3

If you are curious about the meanings of *pragmatics*, *heuristics*, *semiotics* or *phatic communion* or you would like to incorporate them into your personal vocabulary, the following short task might help.

Here are the meanings of the four terms but in jumbled order. Unscramble them and see if your answers match those given on p 27.

1 A term used to refer to the language used for establishing or maintaining social contact rather than seeking or conveying information. Examples would be comments on the weather or enquiries about health, eg *Nice day, isn't it?* and *How are you today?*

2 The study of the use of language in communication, and in particular the relationships between sentences and the situations and contexts in which they are used and the influence on the structure of sentences and the relationship between speaker and listener.

3 From the teacher's point of view, procedures which allow learners to learn through personal discovery and experience. From the learner's point of view, conscious or unconscious inquiry and discovery.

4 The analysis of systems using signs or signals, both natural and artificial, for the purposes of communication.

In terms of a framework for analyzing our own use of terminology and for possibly extending it in the future, we have found it useful to follow this framework:

a basic terms
  What terms do I use regularly in the classroom and which of these
  do I regard as utterly essential?

b avoiding unhelpful terms
  What complex terms could I replace with user-friendly expressions?

c moving on
  What areas of language teaching and linguistics would I like to
  investigate further?

We can survive quite happily with the first stage. The second stage can be extremely satisfying. The third can prove to be interesting, stimulating and even fun!

6   Recommended reading

The Longman Dictionary of Language Teaching and Applied Linguistics is a useful reference work, containing as it does clear definitions of terms related to both language and classroom practice.

Teaching Language as Communication by Henry Widdowson is a good example of a work which introduces new terminology and redefines commonly used terms in a way that may at first appear confusing but which guides the reader to think more critically about key issues in language teaching and which provides several new insights into these issues.

7   References and bibliography

Crystal, D. 1971 *Linguistics* (Penguin)
Crystal, D. 1980 *A First Dictionary of Linguistics and Phonetics* (Andre Deutsch)
Leech, G. and Svartvik, J. 1975 *A Communicative Grammar of English* (Longman)
O'Connor, J. 1973 *Phonetics* (Penguin)
Palmer, F. 1965 *A Linguistic Study of the English Verb* (Longman)
Parrott, M. 1993 *Tasks for Language Teachers* (CUP)
Pit Corder, S. 1973 *Introducing Applied Linguistics* (Penguin)
Quirk, R., Greenbaum, S., Leech, G. and Svartvik, J. 1972 *A Grammar of Contemporary English* (Longman)
Richards, J., Platt, J. and Weber, H. 1992 (new edition) *The Longman Dictionary of Language Teaching and Applied Linguistics* (Longman)
Seaton, B. 1982 *A Handbook of English Language Teaching Terms and Practice* (Macmillan)
Swan, M. 1980 *Practical English Usage* (OUP)
Widdowson, H. 1978 *Teaching Language as Communication* (OUP)

Answer key (Task 3)

4 semiotics
3 heuristics
2 pragmatics
1 phatic communion

Chapter 3 **On the inside looking in:**
Collaborative classroom research

1 Introduction

Let's begin here by defining what we mean by research. This is not the kind of research that involves reading numerous books in order to become better informed about one's subject, although that is not excluded. The idea of becoming better informed and more aware is central to this idea of research. What we are primarily concerned with here is teachers researching their own teaching (and the teaching of others) and thereby becoming better informed about the strengths and weaknesses of their teaching performance. Research of this kind encompasses the teachers themselves, what they teach, how they teach and how they interact with their students. It also encompasses their learners and what it is like to be taught by these particular teachers. In short, this is an invitation to exploit fully the rich vein of research material that can be found, without much difficulty, in any language classroom, and on the basis of this material to learn a great deal about one's own teaching and the learning of one's students.

2 Self-evaluation – finding a starting point

A starting point for any investigation into your own teaching must be a willingness to examine critically what you are doing. This might stem from a sense of personal dissatisfaction with what you are doing at a particular time, a feeling that things could be better. It may also be precipitated by the comments or reactions of your learners (see Section 5 of this chapter for a discussion of this). It may even be a case of feeling that, in fact, everything is fine and you are simply 'coasting' through your work, doing it reasonably successfully, with reasonably happy learners, but that you are in a rut of some kind. One approach that we have found fruitful in focusing ourselves on areas of our teaching that we can affect in a positive sense is to write (and then answer) a brief personal questionnaire. The following is an example of this kind of personal questionnaire:

1   Am I satisfied with the way that I am teaching at the moment?
     If not, what aspects of my teaching cause this dissatisfaction?

2   Am I happy with the materials I use with my learners?
     If not, what is it about these materials that causes this feeling?

3   Are my learners happy with what I do and the way I teach?
     If not, what are the possible reasons for this dissatisfaction?

4   Which of the above problems can I affect directly myself?

5   Which of the above problems could an observer help me with?

Here is an example of the answers one teacher gave to these questions:

1 Not really. I suppose there's always room for improvement of some sort, even if things are going quite well at the moment. I think I could introduce more variety into what I do. I seem to rely on groupwork and problem-solving a lot. I am happiest when my learners are working in groups and I tend to avoid addressing the whole class. I think I'm a bit of a time-watcher too. I often see my classes as something to be got through and I'm always happy when I find something that will last a long time, irrespective of whether it's useful for my learners or not.

2 No, a lot of the time I think my learners might be bored by the materials I use, especially texts. I also rely a bit too much on homework tasks based on grammar or vocabulary exercises, which I then go through in class time. The materials are rather unimaginative, even the coursebook materials I use. I'm also very disorganized. I find a good piece of material and use it once, then I lose it and I can never remember where I've put it.

3 They always seem fairly happy. I try and remember to ask them from time to time, but that's precisely the kind of thing I often forget to do. Sometimes there are problems with individual learners, particularly ones who are self-opinionated and tend to dominate proceedings. I know that this often makes other members of the group unhappy.

4 I could affect all of them in some way. For example, I could adopt a more balanced approach to whole class and groupwork. I could start by asking my learners what they think about the balance and variety in my lessons. I could also try and avoid time-watching in the negative sense. I could be more imaginative in my choice of materials. I could spend some time actually looking for stimulating reading materials, for example. It wouldn't take too long to devise some motivating tasks for them and I could always use the materials again. I really must start filing material in places where I can find it easily when I need it again. That wouldn't take long and would probably save a lot of time and effort in the long run. I could also do much more to find out if my learners are really happy. I could make much more time for feedback and I could also do something about group dynamics by talking about problems such as dominant students with the group as a whole.

5 I would welcome some help with the question of balance and variety in my classes. It's difficult to evaluate this easily when you're at the centre of things all the time. I would also benefit from some comments on timing, about how long I spend on different activities and whether it's appropriate. An observer might also be able to give me an objective opinion about the class dynamics in my classes.
(TIM, UK)

We use this framework ourselves and we have found that, simple though it is, it can be very productive in highlighting areas that may need attention. We have also noticed that the process of completing the 'questionnaire' in itself usually produces a positive effect and a determination to take action, and the act of writing can in itself be a catalyst for the discovery of hidden issues. Whether that action is actually taken and those issues confronted (as in the case of resolving to be more systematic about filing materials!) is another matter, of course.

3   Being observed – the roles of teacher and observer

As mentioned earlier, the starting point for this type of research is openness and willingness. An openness, first and foremost, to the idea of action, to the idea of change and a willingness to take both of these on board. Also involved in this kind of research is an openness to the views and opinions and help of others. Teachers are by nature vulnerable creatures. They may argue, with some justification, that they put their head on the block in every lesson, just as actors do in every perform-ance. They may prefer that performance to be witnessed only by its participants, ie the students and not by an audience of would-be critics. Indeed, to many teachers their classroom is a private domain. What goes on when they close the classroom door is their responsibility and hence their preserve. Outsiders can only interfere and affect the special relationship they have with their learners.

It is difficult not to sympathize with this view and it is probably fair to say that most teachers have experienced this feeling at times, even when they know the observer has the best intentions. Resentment of whatever kind residual in the teacher as a result of some part of their job is directed against the unfortunate 'guest'. Yet the choice is clear. Do you prefer to continue within your private domain, untroubled by feedback and outside comment and only occasionally opening your door to the dreaded observer (and then when required to do so rather than requesting the visit), or do you see the benefit of inviting an objective 'second opinion', of seeking the help of a colleague? Openness is central to classroom research.

Task 1

Make a list of the words you would normally associate with the idea of one of your lessons being observed (by a colleague, a director or an outsider).

We asked a cross-section of teachers (twenty in all) to do the same task. Some were fairly new to the profession and had the recent experience of being observed regularly on their pre-service teacher training course, while others were teachers with several years' experience and presumably used to the presence of observers in their classrooms.

Here are some of the words the group produced:

nervous	worried	irritated	resentful	unconcerned
put upon	annoyed	scared	uncomfortable	disconcerted
negative	reluctant	oblivious	intrusion	indifferent
harassed	neutral	concern	uptight	overburdened
pleased	flattered	fed up	not bothered	extra pressure

Commentary ■ ■ ■

The reactions seem to fall into four main categories. There are some, albeit very few in the case of this particular group, who are worried about the prospect of an observer sitting in on one of their lessons. One person was actually frightened of being observed. The second category, and a much more widespread one, consists of those who resent the presence of a 'foreign body'. The third group, roughly equal in size to the second group, professed to be indifferent about observation, while the fourth group, which was relatively small in number, actually seemed to welcome observation.

The teachers were then asked to explain their reactions to observation. This produced a number of revealing comments. Those who had said they were nervous about being observed, or even frightened of it, talked about the possibility of the observer criticizing what they did or undermining their confidence. The resentful members of the group attributed their negative feelings to two main factors. The first was the alleged negative effect on classroom dynamics and rapport of an outsider sitting in the back of the classroom, often unsmiling and scribbling furiously. The second factor was put down to heavy-handed management, imposing observation on teachers on a regular basis for administrative purposes without the teachers getting much in return. Those who felt indifferent or neutral towards observation tended to feel this way because they were working in institutions which had an 'open door' policy to observation and, consequently, they were completely used to it. The small number who appeared to welcome observation were positive towards it because they had personally derived great benefit both from observing and being observed. In the latter case, they had all received a great deal of constructive feedback on their teaching and this had helped them to develop and become more confident.

Reactions to being observed depend almost entirely on the perception of the purpose of the observation in the mind of the teacher being observed. If the observer is seen as a critic, an intruder, an institutional assessor or simply an unwanted distraction, and if the teacher can perceive no personal benefit in having this person in the classroom, then feelings of anxiety, indifference or resentment build up. The idea of being criticized is an uncomfortable one for most individuals, whether they be policemen, gardeners or nuclear physicists. Teachers are no exception to this general rule. Negative criticism, and particularly destructive criticism aimed at the individual rather than what he or she does, can be especially damaging in teaching, where confidence in the classroom is such a key factor in rapport and motivation. Similarly, the prospect of being assessed for an institutional purpose (a kind of 'quality control') can induce feelings of panic or animosity. Most teachers rightly understand that it is possible to criticize any lesson subjectively, depending entirely on the criteria and the motives of the observer, and unless teacher assessment is handled carefully, bad feeling can easily build up. ■

In the light of the above, we feel that contact between the observer and the teacher prior to the observation is crucial. If the teacher understands the purpose of the observation and if the observer too is clear about his or her motives in observing the lesson, there is a much greater possibility that the observation will be seen in a better light by both sides, provided the observer's intent is benign. In this sense, a 'pact' between the teacher and the observer prior to the lesson is essential. This pact might encompass the following basic elements:

1 The teacher and the observer agree on the purpose of the observation. Examples might be:

For the teacher
● to get general feedback on his or her teaching style.
● to get specific feedback on a particular aspect of his or her teaching.
● to get feedback on the effectiveness of a particular lesson.
● to get feedback on a particular technique.
● to get feedback on the effectiveness of the materials used.
● and the observer to explore alternative ways of doing what was done in the lesson.

For the observer
● to watch the performance of the class as a whole or that of individual students.
● to get ideas from watching the lesson.
● to evaluate the strengths and weaknesses of the lesson.
● to grade the lesson formally according to criteria previously made known to the teacher.

2 The teacher and the observer agree on the role(s) and activities of the observer. A starting point could be how the observer will be introduced to the class. There are several possibilities here: colleague, visitor, guest, another teacher, assessor, examiner, assistant, trainee teacher. This might seem relatively trivial, but the role of the observer as perceived by the students can have an effect on the classroom atmosphere and make the teacher's task easier or more difficult as a consequence. Similarly, the question of where the observer will sit needs to be addressed. Should the observer sit at the back of the class? Inside or outside the semi-circle of students? At the front with the teacher? To one side? Clearly, the wishes of the teacher in this respect are the main consideration and he or she is best placed to know which position will have the most positive effect on the class and the lesson.

The question of whether the observer will participate in the lesson or not also needs to be agreed in advance. Unexpected interruptions and interventions (to the extent in some cases of 'taking over' the lesson) can be both undermining for the teacher and disturbing for the learners. Will the teacher invite the observer to contribute? Will the observer be asked to express an opinion? Will the teacher turn to the observer for advice? If the observer is there explicitly to learn from the teacher, will the observer be able to ask questions during the observation? Will the teacher give the observer the freedom to intervene whenever he or she feels it necessary to do so? Will the observer talk to the learners, participate in group-work with them or monitor what they do by walking around the room and looking at their work? Finally, will the observer write? If so, what? Notes? A blow-by-blow account? Formal feedback? Informal feedback? A list of alternatives? Again, it is up to the teacher and the observer to organize all of this in advance so that the observer's role and activities during the observation are clear to all concerned.

3 The teacher and the observer agree on the nature and purpose of the feedback. A number of variables are possible, including:

- The observer will give no feedback at all to the teacher.
- The observer and the teacher will discuss the lesson in the light of the original purpose (eg they will explore alternatives, look at the strengths and weaknesses of the lesson, etc).
- The observer will give the teacher a written report focusing on the area(s) agreed in the pact.
- The observer will give, without comment, a list of apparent facts expressed without using *not* in the introducing clause, eg *You said ...*, *You wrote ...*, *You stood ...* .
- The teacher will evaluate what he or she has done and the observer will listen and/or question.
- The teacher will discuss what he or she has done in the lesson with the aim of clarifying it for the benefit of an observer who is observing in order to take ideas from the lesson.
- The teacher and the observer will discuss the lesson with the students.
- Any combination of the above

Clearly, there would normally be insufficient time for the teacher and the observer to work through a list like this in advance of the observation, but if the principle of establishing clearly the purpose and the outcome of the observation in the minds of both sides is adhered to, then the whole process can become less confrontational and less of an ordeal for the teacher, in particular. Openness about the nature of the operation can enable both sides to focus much more clearly on the mutual benefits of the observation and the whole process can be seen in a much more positive light.

The purpose of the pact between teacher and observer is to encourage a positive attitude towards the concept of observing and being observed with the aim of promoting the idea of classroom research as a means of improving one's own teaching and, of course, the teaching of one's colleagues. In the sense of encouraging a positive attitude towards observation, Adrian Underhill, founder of the IATEFL Teacher Development Special Interest Group, talks about the 'privilege of being observed', pointing out that someone has given up an hour or two hours of their time to watch *you* teach. This presents an intriguing image; that of teachers the world over welcoming observers into their classrooms and thanking them for the privilege. It may seem idealistic, but there is a great deal of merit in projecting the positive side of an activity often seen as negative. Observation is very much a two-way process: teachers can learn so much from observers and observers can learn an enormous amount from observing teachers. Seen in this light, observation is, indeed, a privilege, and not only for the teacher. If classroom research is to work for the benefit of all concerned, then an open policy of colleague-to-colleague observation is one way of setting this in motion. How many bank managers, estate agents, university professors, dentists, etc regularly get a chance to see a colleague at work and/or to get feedback from a (respected) colleague? Regular, open, two-sided observation and feedback is fundamental if the idea of classroom research as the basis for improving one's teaching is to succeed.

4 The teacher as researcher

Traditionally, observation focuses on two general areas – the teacher and the lesson. In the case of the teacher, there are generally various sub-divisions from voice and mannerisms to classroom management and rapport. In the case of the lesson, the focus is generally on the effectiveness of the techniques employed to present or practise items in the different language and skills categories and on more general categories such as pace, variety and balance. This type of observation focus tends to be based on a checklist drawn up by the observer or by an official body represented by the observer. Although teachers are usually (but not always!) aware of the contents of such checklists, they themselves will tend not to play any part in actually drawing them up. If the type of open observation outlined in the previous section is to succeed, thereby making a significant contribution to classroom research, then arguably the approach that places a checklist in the hands of the observer is not the most effective means of achieving this goal, as it removes any responsibility for the process from the hands of the teacher, the central figure in the classroom research. Perhaps a mutually discussed checklist might form the basis for an initial diagnostic observation, but, as most checklists tend to be exhaustive, the sheer number of items on the list can often obscure the key areas that really need attention. If developing awareness and more effective teaching are the aims of classroom research, then the teacher needs far more involvement in what the observer does and the kind of things the observer looks for. Teachers will often know, although they may not like to admit it, which areas they are least confident in or least effective in. Even in those areas where they are particularly effective at present, they may seek alternatives to give them a wider perspective. So the suggestion is that the teacher presents the observer with a specific observation task in an area where the teacher feels there is a need for some change, some movement or some improvement. If this task can be drawn up as part of the 'pact' between teacher and observer, then so much the better.

Task 2

Read through the three case studies below and decide what specific observation task is suggested by each one. Then compare your answers with the tasks that emerged in each of the situations.

Case study 1

I have a lot of problems with this class. I have trouble getting their attention and getting them to understand exactly what I want them to do. They're quite rowdy and boisterous, not in a malicious way, but it's beginning to get to me. I find I have to raise my voice a lot, and this sometimes just makes matters worse. Two students in the group particularly get me down. Sometimes things go reasonably well, but I find the class really difficult and by the end of the hour I'm absolutely exhausted.

Case study 2

I think I'm doing more or less the right kind of things in my teaching. My classes go quite well and the students don't complain about anything. The lessons aren't very lively, though, and I find a lot of my classes are fairly quiet. I can't seem to get much out of some of the students no matter how many questions I ask.

Case study 3

There are a lot of texts in the coursebook we use and I find the way they're presented pretty boring. The tasks that follow them are not very interesting either. We've got to use the book and I get the feeling that my students are bored with the reading lessons. I use all the usual pre-reading activities and so on, but it doesn't seem to make much difference. The lessons are not exactly what you could call lively.

These are the specific observation tasks reached by agreement between the teacher and the observing colleague:

Observation task 1

Focus on the following:

a Teacher 'presence', body language, facial expression, voice.
b Classroom management, especially instructions.
c Use of different interactions and groupings within the class.
d Use of different activities, including reflective activities such as reading and writing stages.

Observation task 2

Focus on the following:

a Type of teacher questioning, variety of questioning.
b Opportunities for learner initiative within the class.
c Amount and nature of pair- and groupwork activities.
d Interest level of material used.

Observation task 3

Focus on the following:

a The effectiveness of the pre-reading activities.
b Options for the ways the texts are presented.
c How the learners react to the reading tasks.
d Opportunities for interactive stages.

Commentary ■ ■ ■

The problems outlined in the case studies are fairly typical ones. They are the kind of problems that teachers often experience and usually have to deal with alone. When such questions are raised in the staffroom, colleagues, usually for lack of time, tend to respond with *Have you tried a roleplay with them?* or *What about using that exercise on page 112?* Such 'solutions' are fine in the short term, of course. They may well solve the problem of what the teacher in question is going to do during the next hour. But they do not actually get to the root of the problem. Talking through the problem in advance of the observation can help to focus both the teacher and the observer on what the likely causes might be and then, both during and after the observation, they can begin to work towards solutions. You will see that the observation tasks are fairly short and also that possible solutions have already been generated by the pre-lesson discussion between teacher and observer.

Observation can provide a wealth of data to help teachers in classroom research. We have found that collaborative research of the kind described above can be particularly productive because it can be directly focused on areas perceived to require attention. Clearly, it will demand a considerable amount of good will on the part of institutions to introduce and operate on a regular basis this kind of observation, but the experience of the authors is that when such a system is in operation, the repayment in terms of happier and more open teaching staff far exceeds the initial outlay. ■

5 Evaluating methods, materials and the teacher – the role of learners

If teachers are generally interested in obtaining data from their classes that they can use in order to become more aware of the strengths and weaknesses of their teaching, observation by peers is only one means of acquiring this data. Perhaps a more direct method is to get this information from the direct recipients of the teaching, ie the learners. It does, however, require a certain amount of courage to ask learners directly for feedback. And indeed, in response to questions such as *Well, what did you think of that?* learners may well, for reasons of politeness, give a fairly bland response, which, ultimately, is of no real use to anyone. The result of 'faint praise feedback' can often be that the teacher becomes even more comfortable in his or her particular rut and sees no reason to question or change what he or she is doing. The principle of getting feedback from learners is fine, but what is important is how it is done, the effectiveness and relevance of the feedback given, and what action is taken as a result of it.

Given that *What did you think of that?* can produce an ineffective response that is of little practical use to the teacher, it is worth considering the kind of learner feedback that can provide useful data for classroom research. A useful starting point is to divorce the teacher from the teaching. Learners may often be reluctant to criticize lessons because they do not wish to offend the teacher. They may feel that any criticism of a particular exercise, technique or activity is simultaneously a direct criticism of the teacher. It is perfectly possible for students to dislike lessons intensely but at the same time to like their teacher very much as a person. If you begin by separating the two, you can often get a much more objective response from learners. That is not to say that teachers should not invite feedback on themselves as teachers and as people and on how they come across to their students, as we shall see later, but as a starting point, particularly with learners who are not used to being asked their opinion of lessons, focusing on the lesson and the activities and materials in it can be extremely productive.

Task 3

Consider the following options for obtaining feedback from learners on activities, techniques and materials and decide which you think would be most productive in terms of providing data.

a   *What did you think of that text? Was it interesting?*

b   *Evaluate this exercise for usefulness on a scale of 1 to 10 and for enjoyment on a scale of 1 to 10.*

c   *We do a lot of speaking in groups in this class. Can you tell me what you think of this?*

d   *For homework over the weekend, write me a letter about what we've done this week. Try and divide the activities into things you liked, things you didn't like and things you felt were just OK.*

e   *Here's a list of the things we've done this week. Work in groups of 4 and rank them in order of preference from 1 to 15. Make a note of why you liked the things you ranked from 1 to 5 and why you didn't like the ones you ranked from 10 to 15.*

f   *Think about the things we've done so far and the way we've done them. Then, in small groups, say which things you would like to change and which things you would like to do more of.*

(See also Chapter 8 on reading for a further example of a learner questionnaire on the merits or otherwise of what and how they have been taught.)

Commentary ■ ■ ■

Technique **a**, with the word *text* substituted by a range of other terms from exercise to lesson, is probably the most common and can often produce some very interesting responses. The problem with the question as it is phrased here, however, is that it is followed by a much more restrictive *yes/no* question which limits what learners can say. In this case they are often likely to say *yes* simply to be let off the hook. A profitable discussion along the lines of *What did you think of ...* depends heavily on there being a good deal of trust between learners and teacher and a considerable degree of openness existing in the classroom.

Technique **b** gives learners the chance to consider their response more carefully. It also gives them the opportunity, should they so desire, to remain anonymous, as this particular type of feedback can easily be done in written form. It can either be done in rough form, simply supplying a number, or in a more systematic way, eg 10 = extremely useful and very interesting.

Technique **c** invites the class to debate the issue. As with technique **a**, it will depend heavily on whether learners feel confident enough to express forthright opinions in open class, but it is certainly open-ended and it tackles a particular issue head on.

Technique **d**, like technique **b**, gives learners time to reflect and think about their response in a more considered way. It is not completely open, as it calls for learners to categorize the week's activities into good, all right and not so good. Variations are clearly possible – perhaps a combination of **b** and **d**.

Technique **e** is more systematic in one way in that it reminds the learners clearly what has been done and asks them to respond to each activity. Giving reasons for decisions is also likely to provide more research data.

Finally, technique **f** focuses learners on the possibility of actually changing what is done and the way it is done, as well as giving the teacher further information about what has been successful and what has not.

We do not include the above examples as prescriptive models, and they are not intended to be ideal in any way. They are simply verbatim examples of some of the ways we (and teachers we have worked with and/or observed teaching) attempt to elicit feedback on materials and activities from our learners. Clearly, much depends on the good will and trust within the group and a willingness on the part of all concerned to work towards improving both teaching and learning. Asking questions like the ones above may seem awkward, even uncomfortable, to both sides at first, but once established it can be a relatively simple and quick way of getting feedback that goes beyond the simple 'It's going well', 'It's all right' or 'It isn't going well' that teachers can normally gauge from observing the responses of their learners.

The idea of separating the teacher from the lesson is intended to obtain more objective and direct feedback on the latter. Inviting feedback on oneself as a teacher is an altogether more sensitive matter, both for the teacher and the students. *Do you like me as a teacher (or even as a person)?* is a much more difficult question to ask, however carefully it is framed, than *Do you like what I do?* However, if a problem is allowed to deteriorate for too long, feedback of this kind will often come in an unsolicited form. Here are some typical examples:

Why don't you ever correct my mistakes?

I don't like your lessons. You speak too quickly and I can't understand you.

The lessons are boring. I think it's because you don't make us work hard enough.

You never ask me a question. You always ask the other students.

A lot of students speak Spanish all the time and you don't stop them. It really makes me angry.

Feedback of this kind is extremely valuable because it goes directly to the heart of the problem. What the teacher needs to do, however, is to take action before this state of affairs arises, because by the time students feel compelled to intervene with the teacher in this way, it may already be too late to 'rescue' this particular class. The problem is how to get this feedback in a direct and open way, without causing unnecessary embarrassment to either side. ■

Task 4

Consider the following options for obtaining feedback from learners on what they think of the way in which the teacher conducts the class. Decide which you think would be most productive in terms of providing data:

a *Are there any problems with this class and the way I teach it?*

b *I don't feel comfortable with this group and I feel there's a problem. Shall we talk about it?*

c *Is there anything you think I should do differently?*

d *Work in small groups and make a list of the things you like about the way I teach this class and the things you don't like so much.*

e *Work in groups and make a list of what you believe are the qualities of a good teacher.*

Commentary ■ ■ ■

The first technique might have the effect of producing a muted response or no response at all. Politeness and convention often obstruct constructive comment. The second approach, by stating at the beginning that there is a problem, is more likely to elicit a response, although again, embarrassment might prevent a fruitful discussion. The third technique suffers from the same potential problems as the first one, although the invitation to ask for changes and differences might prove more profitable. The fourth approach is very direct, but by enabling the students to collaborate away from the direct presence of the teacher, it may elicit the required information. It will probably also produce comments about materials and activities, but asking questions about the *class* can often have the effect of eliciting a lot of information about learners' perceptions of their teacher. The final technique has the effect of distancing the teacher from the discussion and allowing the learners to direct their comments at an abstract, 'ideal' teacher, rather than the class teacher in person. It does, however, need to be followed up with a question along the lines of *Which of these qualities do you think I need to work on?* or similar, which, again, may not be such an easy question to ask or answer.

The kind of classroom research data on materials, activities and teachers provided by learner feedback may often be uncomfortable for the teachers, but it is of immense value if teachers intend to change what they do and how they do it in any way at all. It is valuable because it is directly targeted at where the problems lie. ■

6 Classroom research and self-assessment

Leaving aside the valuable data that can be obtained from observers and learners, there is another source of material for classroom research and that is, of course, teachers themselves. The demands of the classroom and the amount of time needed for preparation, marking and administration often mean that teachers are not in a position to devote much time to feedback from observers (colleagues, directors of studies and so on) or from learners. Teachers labouring under a full timetable are equally unlikely to be willing to devote precious 'recovery' time to reflection and analysis of what they have just done. Perhaps they would like to do so, but the reality of the average teacher's workload is often such that any such analysis is destined to remain little more than wishful thinking. The idea of answering questions on a questionnaire or ticking boxes on a checklist may seem extremely unappealing under such circumstances, and may be seen by teachers as relatively unimportant in their list of priorities. In a sense, it is the very formalization of self-assessment that can make it unappealing, particularly if it is 'imposed' from above. Some teachers may be more at ease with the idea of informal self-assessment, analyzing their teaching at those times when it seems appropriate to do so, without following any formalized procedure. But what exactly is 'self-assessment'? We asked a group of teachers to tell us what they did to assess their performance. Here are their answers:

a *If a lesson goes well, I always try and note down the particular things I did that helped make it go well – using particular materials, classroom management, atmosphere, etc. If I have a bad lesson, I try and analyze the lesson to put my finger on the things I might have done that caused this and how I could have avoided that.*
(ULI, GERMANY)

b *I try to grade each lesson on two scales from 1 to 10. The first is how useful it was for the students, and the second is how much I enjoyed the lesson myself.*
(HELEN, UK)

c *I keep a record in tabular form that's a bit like a timetable. I fill it in every evening and say how I felt each lesson went. I also observe my own reactions: pleased, bored, frustrated, and so on. It's interesting at the end of the month to compare the reactions for different times of the week and for different classes. Sometimes there are very clear patterns and I think I can influence and change these.*
(MARTIN, GERMANY)

d *I regularly record my lessons on audio tape. Sometimes I actually cringe when I play them back. Sometimes I simply can't believe how much I talk and how fast I talk. It's painful, but it's really, really useful.*
(PHIL, USA)

e *In terms of assessing how I teach, I think that being videoed is a really salutary experience. It has helped me identify so many weaknesses in my teaching. I'm sure I've become a better teacher through watching myself on video.*
(ANDREW, FRANCE)

f *It's a combination of things really. I ask my students how they felt about the lesson and then I reflect on my contribution to it. I keep a teaching diary and note the ups and downs.*
(LOUISE, UK)

All of these individual methods clearly have their benefits for the teachers involved. They may all be worth trying. The idea of identifying things that went well in a lesson and things that you were not so happy about can be supplemented by noting down when you felt comfortable in the lesson and when you felt uncomfortable. This can also be linked to the types of activities and interactions that these feelings accompanied. One teacher reported that she frequently felt uncomfortable when eliciting from the whole class and when handling group feedback, but very comfortable when students were working in groups. In this way she was able to identify an area of her teaching that needed attention. Similarly, another teacher said that he often reflected on each lesson and decided which of its stages he would use again and which he would change were he to teach the same lesson again. Grading lessons and keeping a record of those grades over a period can provide teachers with useful information about trends and patterns in their teaching in much the same way that athletes are able, by logging eating habits and training performances, to see which habits produce the best performances. One teacher reported that her most effective lessons were always on Monday mornings and her least effective on Thursday afternoons.

As far as recording lessons is concerned, both audio and video recording of lessons have their merits. Audio recording focuses fairly and squarely on issues such as the teacher's voice, clarity of instructions, proportion of talking time taken up by the teacher and the effectiveness and appropriacy of error correction, while video recording can reveal a number of aspects about the teacher's teaching 'persona'. Many teachers find both forms uncomfortable and many are resistant to using them, but the benefits are considerable and it only requires a certain amount of will-power to start audio-recording lessons, for example. The idea of a teaching diary is not, of course, a new one. Learner diaries are recommended in most fields of learning and teaching is no exception. The reflective nature of a diary can be a powerful tool for teachers in identifying reactions to and feelings about particular classes, individuals, types of lessons and activities.

In our experience, all of the above can, in their own way, function as aids to self-assessment, in the sense of teachers becoming more aware of patterns in their behaviour in the classroom and the effect on others of that behaviour. If nothing is ever done, and teaching simply becomes time-serving, then we will be left with a whole group of 'stuck' teachers, doing the same things effectively and efficiently but never changing, never moving, never addressing the question of how they might improve the quality of what they do both for themselves and for their learners. For this reason alone, self-assessment is arguably the most important of all the types of informal research outlined in this section

At the heart of self-assessment and evaluation of their performance in the classroom lie teachers' perceptions of what their classroom actually is and what their role in it is. It has been suggested that the perception of the classroom (positive, negative, indifferent) is a direct reflection of teachers' perception of themselves and their worth both as teachers and as human beings (see the classroom metaphor task in Chapter 1). Without penetrating too deeply into this area of psychology, the following, related task may be revealing.

Task 5

Look at the following list of metaphors for the teacher and see which ones you most closely identify with. Complete the sentences.

a *I see myself as an actor, because ...*
b *I see myself as a guide, because ...*
c *I see myself as a diplomat, because ...*
d *I see myself as a waiter, because ...*
e *I see myself as a chat-show host, because ...*
f *I see myself as a coach, because ...*

Now write some more metaphors of your own for your role in the classroom and reflect on what they suggest about your attitudes to your learners, your tasks in the classroom and your work as a teacher in general.

7   Recommended reading

Classroom Interaction by Ann Malamah-Thomas involves the reader in a variety of tasks which explore many of the issues discussed in this chapter.

Peter Maingay's chapter in *Explorations in Teacher Training* is a thoroughly readable account of a number of variables involved in observing lessons and being observed.

8   References and bibliography

Acker, G. 1990 Watching yourself, watching others. In *The Teacher Trainer*, vol. 4, no. 1

Allwright, D. 1988 *Observation in the Language Classroom* (Longman)

Allwright, D. and Bailey, K. 1991 *Focus on the Language Classroom* (CUP)

Deller, S. 1987 Observing and Being Observed. In *The Teacher Trainer*, vol. 1, no. 1

Freeman, D. 1982 Observing teachers: three approaches to in-service training and development. In *TESOL Quarterly*, vol. 16, no. 1 pp 21-8

Gebhard, J. 1984 Models of supervision: choices. In *TESOL Quarterly*, vol. 18, no. 3 pp 501-14

Gower, R. , Walters, S. and Phillips D.1994 *Teaching Practice Handbook* new edition (Heinemann Educational)

Hopkins, D.1985 *A Teacher's Guide to Classroom Research* (Open University Press)

Maingay, P. 1989 Observation for training, development or assessment. In *Explorations in Teacher Training*, Duff, T. (ed.) (Longman)

Malamah-Thomas, A. 1987 *Classroom Interaction* (OUP)

Wajnryb, R. 1992 *Classroom Observation Tasks* (CUP)

Woodward, T. 1991 *Models and Metaphors in Teacher Training* (CUP)

Woodward, T. 1990/91 Observation Tasks. In *IATEFL Teacher Training Special Interest Group Newsletter*, no. 3

Woodward, T. 1992 *Ways of Training* (Longman)

Wragg, E. (ed.) 1984 *Classroom Teaching Skills* (Croom Helm)

Chapter 4 **Learning to speak or speaking to learn?**

The role of mistakes in spoken English

1 Introduction

In this chapter we look at mistakes in spoken English – what they are, where they come from, how teachers and learners view them, and what we can and should do about them.

Task 1

To begin with, have a look at the following statements and see in each case whether you agree, disagree, or have no particular opinion. Make a note of your answers, as we'll be asking you to come back to them later on.

I regard all mistakes in language learning as a bad thing.

My main task is to ensure that my learners speak correctly.

I regard myself as lenient in my treatment of mistakes.

I distinguish between different degrees of seriousness among mistakes.

I'd prefer my learners not to make any mistakes.

I feel disappointed or annoyed when learners make mistakes with language I have taught them.

I feel surprised when learners get something right for a while and then start getting it wrong.

As a teacher, part of my job is to correct all my learners' mistakes.

I believe in peer correction (ie learners correcting each other).

I feel at least partly to blame for my learners' mistakes.

I believe that mistakes should never be repeated by me, or written on the board.

I recognize a distinction between 'errors' and 'slips', and find it helpful in my teaching.

I recognize various different causes of mistakes, and find this helpful in my teaching.

I believe mistakes are caused primarily by interference from the learners' first language.

I judge how good my learners are according to how many mistakes they make.

Add other statements which seem important to you in this connection.

2 Attitudes and terminology

Various different words have been used to describe the kind of phenomena which form the topic of this chapter: *errors, mistakes, slips, lapses, goofs* ... Perhaps you know others. The five we have quoted here are all words used more or less commonly outside the context of teaching.

Task 2

What thoughts, words, images, connotations or feelings do these words conjure up if you consider them divorced from teaching?

Commentary ■ ■ ■

Error is connected with *err*, meaning wander or stray, which might seem quite innocuous unless it also calls up moral or religious connotations of straying from the straight and narrow, erring like lost sheep, *the error of our ways* ... My computer and CD player sometimes give me 'error' messages which cause impatience and the fear that something serious and expensive and beyond my control is wrong. On the other hand, *trial and error* has quite positive associations, as a reasonable procedure to use where guidance or certainty is lacking.

Mistake is more common in everyday use and therefore perhaps lacks some of the gravity of *error*. The usage *You must be mistaken* emphasizes the meaning of misunderstanding or misapprehension, rather than something which is actively 'committed'.

Slip suggests something fleeting, perhaps due to lack of attention, probably without serious consequences and with little suggestion of intention or blame or responsibility.

These are the personal reflections of one of us (Jonathan), with some speculations about what other people's interpretations might be. Most teachers probably aren't conscious of these associations when they deal with, talk about, or think about mistakes in language learning, but the associations they have may nevertheless influence, or even determine, their attitude. And, of course, learners also have their associations, which affect their attitudes. ■

Task 3

Try out your associations with a few other words: *fault, failure, transgression, crime, sin* ...

Commentary ■ ■ ■

Perhaps these words seem less relevant to teaching and learning. But they may represent concepts underlying the attitude of learners who apologize to their teacher for making mistakes, or who say *I'm no good at languages*, or who feel that a mistake is an affront against the English language and the people who speak it. ■

It would be useful to have some superordinate term free of such connotations. Terminology does vary somewhat between writers. Items which the learner could correct and therefore 'knows' are often called *slips*. Items which the learner has had some experience of but cannot correct, and which represent a different norm from the target or native one, are often called *errors*. In his book *Mistakes and Correction*, Julian Edge uses *attempts* for items which result from the efforts of learners to express something they haven't yet come into contact with. The same writer suggests substituting *learning steps* for *mistakes* as a general term. This is attractive, since it casts a much more positive light on matters. But on the other hand, not all learning steps result in mistake-like or deviant utterances. In this chapter, we will use *mistake* as a term which covers all the others, except in quotations and in passages where we want to draw distinctions between types of mistakes.

Many teachers don't make these distinctions in their everyday work, even if they are aware of them, perhaps because they don't find them useful in practice, or because they find there isn't time in the classroom to be sure of categorizations.

In the classroom, when I'm talking to students, I only use 'mistake'. I think when I have more time to spend on correcting, for example when I'm correcting written work, then I may be interested in finding out whether it was just a slip of the pen, or perhaps an ingrained mistake, what some people call an error. But on the spur of the moment, when I'm teaching, I don't think I spend any time trying to judge whether what's happened is just a slip of the tongue or an ingrained mistake. (JOHN, HUNGARY)

Task 4

Interview learners to find out what associations they have with *mistake* and related words, in English and/or in their own language, and how they feel about making mistakes in English, in the classroom and outside.

Task 5

Let's see what a few other sources have to say. How, if at all, do these quotations help your understanding of the issue?

1 'An error is something you have done which is considered to be incorrect or wrong, or which should not have been done.' *Collins COBUILD Dictionary*

2 'A mistake is an action or opinion that is incorrect or foolish, or that is not what you intended to do, or whose result is undesirable.' *Collins COBUILD Dictionary*

3 'Errors like straws upon the surface show,
He who would search for pearls must dive below.' Dryden

From the field of language teaching:

4 The learner should not be given 'opportunities for inaccurate work until he has arrived at the stage at which accurate work is to be reasonably expected.' Harold Palmer[1]

5 'Like sin, error is to be avoided and its influence overcome, but its presence is to be expected.' Nelson Brooks[2]

6 'Getting it wrong is part of getting it right.' Adrian Underhill

7 'You can't learn without goofing.' Dulay and Burt[3]

8 'A mistake is a gift to the class.' Caleb Gattegno

And from a different field, that of improvisation in musical performance:

9 'You hear people trying out things, they make a mistake and they perhaps even develop that mistake and work out something nice from that which happened without them meaning it to.' Paco Peña[4]

10 'An error may be only an unintentional rightness.' T.C. Whitmer[5]

11 'Do not be afraid of being wrong; just be afraid of being uninteresting.' T.C. Whitmer[5]

---

1 Harold Palmer 1964 *The Principles of Language Study*, p 64 (OUP)
2 Quoted by J. Hendrickson in Error Analysis and Error Correction in Language Teaching. *Occasional Papers*, no. 10 (RELC, Singapore), 1981
3 H.C. Dulay and M.K. Burt 1974 You Can't Learn Without Goofing. In J.C. Richards (ed.) *Error Analysis: Perspectives on Second Language Acquisition* (Longman)
4 Bailey, D. 1992 *Improvisation – its nature and practice in music*, p 66 (The British Library)
5 Whitmer, T.C. 1934 *The Art of Improvisation*

Commentary ■ ■ ■

1 ... *considered to be* ... suggests an important role for opinion as opposed to an absolute value system. Different people will react differently to instances of language usage, depending on their personal taste and other features of context.

2 This introduces the idea that by committing mistakes you make yourself appear foolish, and perhaps expose yourself to ridicule. In foreign language learning, one way to avoid this is to play safe and only use what you are absolutely sure of – or even not to speak at all.

3 Mistakes are superficial phenomena which can detract attention from less obvious but more interesting or valuable phenomena. By focusing too much on learners' mistakes we may miss out on their underlying progress, or the messages they are trying to convey.

4 Language learning entails a progression from inaccuracy to accuracy. (The author – writing in 1922 – considers that mistakes reflect the shortcomings of the learner and of the teacher and materials. He looks forward to a golden future in which such failings will be overcome.)

5 We should avoid giving learners opportunities for making mistakes but nevertheless expect them to make them, and correct them when they do. This attitude is associated with a behaviourist approach to language acquisition, current during the 1960s, in which it was believed that people acquire languages through a process of habit formation. The teacher has an important role in reinforcing correct responses and correcting incorrect ones. There were attempts to programme learning so strictly that learners were not given opportunities to make mistakes. It is doubtful whether this is possible at all, and even if it was it would presumably result in a very impoverished kind of language competence. But habits of thought die hard, too, and this attitude, or some form of it, is probably still current in the beliefs of many teachers and learners.

6 and 7 Mistakes are not evidence of failure to learn; they are rather evidence of learning taking place. This is now the generally accepted view and applies to both first and second language learning. We learn through trial and error, by actively constructing and testing hypotheses, and revising these in the light of direct feedback and new data. We learn a language through using it, rather than learning it first before being able to use it: not so much learning to speak as speaking to learn. Mistakes are visible evidence of the invisible process of learning. The implications include:

- Opportunities for making mistakes should not be closed off.
- Mistakes are not evidence of incompetence or lack of ability.
- The exact nature of a mistake is more interesting than the fact that a mistake has been made, because it can give a clue to the stage of learning the learner has got to in a particular area and therefore how they can best be helped to move on to the next stage.
- Knowing what's right in a language also entails knowing what's wrong.

8 Mistakes are an interesting study in their own right, rather than something to be dealt with and got rid of as soon as possible. They can provide the most valuable material for a class to work on. Starting from mistakes means starting from where the learners are and giving help where they are ready to receive it.

9 There is a connection between mistakes on the one hand and creativity and discovery on the other. The 'something nice' could either be recognizably 'correct', or perhaps something idiosyncratic but successfully expressive. Language learning and language use also entail improvisation.

10 Correct forms may be generated unintentionally, by accident, 'by mistake'.

11 Correctness can exercise a tyranny which inhibits learners from experimenting, risk-taking, attempting to express what they would like to say. ■

3 Correctness

It's easy to think that there is a clear and absolute distinction between what's correct and what's incorrect in language, and perhaps learning and teaching would be simpler if it was true. At least then there would be an absolute standard against which we could evaluate our learners' performance, and always a straight answer to *Can I say ...?*

Task 6

How do you react to these instances of spoken English? Are they correct or not ? Would it make any difference if you knew whether they were spoken by native or non-native speakers?

1 *Why you wearing a tie?*
2 *We've been to Canterbury on Saturday.*
3 *I'm here for two weeks.*
4 (Talking about some T-shirts) *They died out when I washed them.*
5 *It's illicit to buy cigarettes if you're under 16.*
6 (Talking about an expected phone call) *I didn't get any coal.*
7 *xxxxxxxxxxxxxxxxxxxxxx* (An entirely incomprehensible utterance.)
8 *She live in a village.*
9 *The lake was iced.*
10 *It took me two planes to get to London.*
11 *I don't want to simply wait and see what happens.*
12 *Which shop did you go to?*
13 *Would you like to come with my friends and I?*
14 *Let me remind you that Radio 1 and Radio 2 stays on the air all night.*
15 *Can I have some table to work on?*
16 *What trouble was I then to you!*
17 *No one doesn't know Hamlet.*
18 *It's a really amazing film.*
19 *If you meet an English newspaper, buy it.*
20 *No matter how much grit the authorities have, there are miles of roads and only a limited amount of lorries.*

Commentary ■ ■ ■

Asterisks indicate that the utterance in question was by a native speaker of English.

1 You might assume, if this is said by a learner, that there's a word missing. But *are* is often (usually?) inaudible in native-speaker versions of utterances like this. We hear the *are* if we expect it to be there, even if it isn't really there!

2★ Contrary to what is usually taught, this kind of thing does happen – perhaps because people change their minds about what they're going to say after they've started speaking?

3 It's certainly correct as an instance of English grammar. But does it mean what the speaker wants it to mean? Does it mean *I'm here for two weeks* or *I've been here for two weeks*? Or something else?

4 Or should it be transcribed as *dyed*? To some listeners, this is probably very creative and evokes a complex meaning involving both *dye* coming out and *die out*. On the other hand, is this what the speaker intended?

5 *Illicit* just could be a deliberately unusual choice by a speaker fully aware of the range of possibilities; in that case, would it be 'wrong'?

6 This would probably be interpreted unproblematically in context. (The interpretation *coal* might not even cross the listener's mind.) So does it matter?

7 But the utterance could be perfectly correct, and the incomprehensibility could be attributable to the listener, who is inattentive, or distracted, or not predisposed to understand. Perhaps a lot of mistakes are in some sense co-operative, created through negotiation between speaker and listener?

8 Learners of English will probably always do this. Teachers castigate it as a 'basic' mistake because the grammatical point comes up near the beginning of beginners' courses. As long as the learner is using *she* as a singular form (and this needs to be ascertained) does it matter?

9 This is at least communicatively effective, at best commendably creative.

10 This makes use of the resources of the language beyond what is conventional. What more effective and economical way of expressing this idea could there be?

11★ The so-called 'split infinitive' is still considered by some people to be wrong. A recent report reveals that most 'grammar checker' programs for word processors pick out this structure as wrong, or at least question it. And yet most native speakers are unaware that any stigma attaches to it. Are they *all* wrong?

12★ A preposition is supposedly not a good thing to end a sentence with. Learners would be ill advised, though, to say *To which shop did you go?* for fear of unwelcome affective reactions from listeners.

13★ This is perhaps slightly different in that more native speakers would regard *I* as wrong here, but it is certainly widespread.

14★ Would many people even notice the mismatch between singular and plural here?

15 Unusual, perhaps, but another example of exploiting the resources of the language.

16★ (Shakespeare) Inversion although it isn't a question. Language changes.

17★ Unusual, but how else could you say this more concisely?

18★ The use of *really* as a basic intensifier and *amazing* as a basic adjective of approval are no doubt considered wrong by many, but they are really common in the speech of many young and no-longer-quite-so-young speakers of English.

19 A speaker aware of the more usual choices might nevertheless pick *meet* to achieve a certain effect.

20★ *Amount* is supposed to be used only with uncountable nouns, but this state of affairs is highly unstable at the moment. ■

When we conceive of correctness in language we need to bear the following in mind:

- Language, even in one place, changes with time, and now, as at any other time, changes are in progress. Although it may be prudent to err on the side of conservatism in teaching, there is no reason to teach an archaic form of the language.
- Language varies geographically, and changes can happen quickly as conventions are exported from one speech community to another. 'It's American' is probably an oversimplification and certainly not a reason for outlawing it, even if the learner does want to speak 'British English', whatever that is.
- Even within small geographical areas, groups of people use their own norms (which are also, of course, subject to change).
- Groups and individuals innovate constantly. Some innovations are taken up and become part of the shared norm. Other innovations are one-offs which fulfil a particular need and are then dumped. There's absolutely no reason why learners shouldn't be innovators, too.
- Any individual observes different norms in different contexts, depending on factors such as the degree of acquaintance with the interlocutor, the perceived level of formality of the situation, the time available, and so on. Learners must also come to terms with this variability.
- The conventions of written language are not necessarily observed by spoken language. Most classroom material used as the basis for oral practice corresponds closely to the norms of written language, and therefore represents an unrealistic target for learners. In expecting these standards of accuracy, teachers are expecting something more from learners than they do from native speakers. Evaluated against such standards, learners will always be found wanting, will always fall short.
- Anywhere outside a classroom, formal mistakes will often go unnoticed if the message is clear.
- Much more damage can be done by language which is correct but doesn't express the speaker's intention.
- Damage can also be done by language which is correct but perceived as impolite, or which is delivered in an accent which the listener finds irritating, etc.
- Some damage can be offset by tone of voice, facial expression and gesture.

All these factors will play an increasing role as English becomes more and more internationalized, and understandings have to be negotiated by speakers who use an increasing variety of different norms.

If examinations require adherence to certain well-defined norms, learners should be clear about what these are, and practise them in appropriate contexts. At the same time they should realize that there may be differences between exam English and other Englishes they encounter or are taught.

4   Types of mistakes

The areas of language affected by mistakes may be:

- pronunciation (sounds, sequences of sounds, stress, linking, rhythm, intonation);
- grammar (word form, word order, right elements but wrong construction);
- vocabulary;
- appropriacy;
- discourse organization.

As well as mistakes which are actually 'made', there may be mistakes of:

- distribution, eg using short answers with subject and auxiliary repetition much more frequently than is the native norm;
- avoidance, eg never using conditional structures with 'remote' verb forms, but expressing the same ideas in different ways;
- fluency, eg simply stopping to think of what comes next rather than using hesitation devices, approaching the topic indirectly, etc.

These are all mistakes in learners' production. There are also mistakes of comprehension – possibly more than we are aware of.

Task 7

Perhaps using recordings of learners' speech as well as on-the-spot observation, try to ascertain what mistakes of distribution, avoidance, fluency and comprehension particular learners are making.

5   Causes of mistakes

Mistakes are generally ascribed to:

- 'interference' from the L1 (or another language the learner knows);
- overgeneralization or overapplication of a rule to cases where it no longer holds good;
- poor teaching or shortcomings in teaching materials.

Task 8

Where do you think *your* learners' mistakes come from? Collect examples and try to account for them.

Commentary ■ ■ ■

Probably a lot of mistakes are caused by a conspiracy of factors. A learner may be misled into overapplying a rule by the way an item is presented in a book, or may assume that a structure can *always* be used as it is in the L1, on the basis of evidence that it *sometimes* is. Other factors can play a contributory role, too; learners may be more likely to make mistakes with a certain item, for instance, if they are concentrating on another one, or to make more mistakes altogether if they are tired. The same mistake might arise from different sources on different occasions.

According to contrastive analysis, which was pursued most enthusiastically during the 1950s, L1 would have a facilitative influence on L2 if the languages were similar, but a detrimental influence if the languages were dissimilar. Items that were similar in the two languages would be easy to learn, while items that were very different would be difficult (there would be interference) and therefore need lots of practice. It fitted well with a behaviouristic model of learning: mistakes represented the persistence of old habits and the failure to learn new ones. As advocated in its strongest form, contrastive analysis claimed to be able to predict all likely mistakes and areas of difficulty. In its weaker form it claimed a merely diagnostic role for some mistakes. The role of contrastive analysis in predicting and explaining mistakes has since been downgraded, for a number of reasons. What's different is not necessarily difficult; the formation of regular noun plurals in English, for instance, is certainly *different* from noun plural formation in many highly inflected languages, but this clearly doesn't make it difficult for speakers of those languages. It also became apparent that speakers of very different languages seemed to go through surprisingly similar stages of mistake-making in their learning of the same L2. It proved difficult, too, to conduct contrastive analyses of pairs of languages so as really to do justice to the degrees of similarity and difference between them.

The emphasis shifted to explaining mistakes in terms of the developmental stages learners go through, regardless of their L1, in actively constructing their L2 competence, and some very strong claims were made for the predominance of 'developmental' over 'interference' mistakes, and for the existence of a 'natural order' for the acquisition of grammatical elements. It was claimed that learners from a great variety of linguistic backgrounds tend to acquire certain key items of English grammar – to reach the stage of using them correctly – in a certain order, regardless of the order in which these items were introduced in the teaching programme. As in so many aspects of applied linguistics and language teaching, this particular pendulum has more recently swung at least part way back in the other direction, and it is more commonly recognized that contrastive analysis does have a certain useful role to play. ■

6   **What to do**

The first step towards deciding how to respond to mistakes is identifying them. Even for the most attentive listener, this is not always as easy as it sounds, sometimes because of the lack of a clear criterion of correctness, but sometimes also because a correct form may be incorrect in context. A learner might say, for instance, *See you on Tuesday,* but mean *Thursday.* Some such mistakes may only come to light after the damage has been done – if at all.

It can also happen that something which initially sounds wrong becomes validated by what the learner goes on to say. One implication of this is the danger of jumping on 'mistakes' as soon as they appear; they may subsequently turn out not to be mistakes at all. For example, a learner says about a book, *I bought it at the library,* and the teacher, thinking 'library/bookshop – typical interference mistake', responds *You mean you bought it at the bookshop,* but it turns out that there was sale of old books at the local library.

Options for responding to mistakes include:

- do nothing;
- store it away for later;
- correct it now.

Task 9

Monitor how you respond to mistakes in your classes, preferably using recordings of lessons, or inviting a colleague to observe and make notes about this. Also monitor the effect of your responses on the learners. Have you got any general response preference? How do you decide on which type of response to make in particular cases?

Commentary ■ ■ ■

Factors which influence teachers' decisions about dealing with mistakes may include:

● What's the purpose of the lesson or activity?

Many teachers make a distinction between activities to practise accuracy and activities to practise fluency. Many feel that immediate correction is inappropriate in fluency activities because learners need opportunities to express themselves at length, drawing on the resources at their disposal, to negotiate with what they've got without being able to rely on the teacher to see them through. This is reasonable if we assume that they are learning English in order to be able to express themselves in it and communicate with it. Fluency practice is also valuable in giving the teacher an insight into what learners can and can't do when left to their own devices. Many teachers like to note down mistakes during fluency activities for future treatment or even as the basis for future lessons.

I find that mistakes are generally very interesting, and it's perhaps a very easy way for the teacher to find out where the students stand, so they are pointers for you to know what you can work on, so that your timetable or your syllabus can be oriented towards what students need remedial work in.
(JOHN, HUNGARY)

Some learners will be attentive to their own and their peers' mistakes in fluency activities and draw attention to them on the spot or afterwards. If you think the class will respond favourably to the suggestion, you can appoint certain individuals to observe and note mistakes in a particular activity. In doing correction work later in the same lesson, or even in a subsequent one, you may find that learners have no recollection of what they said. So perhaps it's best to regard the activity as further practice or re-teaching rather than correction. In any case, some learners may be very keen to see evidence that their mistakes are being dealt with in some way and at some stage.

Even in an accuracy-oriented lesson, a teacher's policy on correction may vary according to the stage of the lesson.

My policy for correcting depends more on the stage of the lesson than on the nature of the mistake. If it's a language input lesson, I think I correct all the problems that the students have with the target language with great attention, sometimes it may be just a slip of the tongue or it may be that perhaps the language hasn't been presented properly, but at that stage of controlled practice I do correct a lot. But except when drilling a model sentence I would not at that stage correct other things which are not directly related to the target language.

(How do learners react if a mistake is corrected on one occasion but not on another?)

If I know it's going to be a course of at least four weeks, one mini-lesson is devoted to negotiating a policy for correction. When you ask students 'In these lessons, when would you like to be corrected?', most of the time they say 'Always, that's what we're here for, and we don't want to make mistakes.' And so you've got to go deeper into that and say 'Well, what would happen if you were corrected all the time? Or what do you do when you speak to people who speak the same language as you and you hear mistakes? So why should we do something different here?'

(And do you find that generally they are amenable to persuasion, given time?)

Given time, yes – if you have time to build enough confidence between students and also between the class as a whole and the teacher. Sometimes I notice when I do a discussion, if it's a whole class discussion, some students notice mistakes that I also notice, probably, but for some reason I don't want to correct, and I can see a couple of students just looking at me, as if to say 'Are you doing your job, teacher?' Well, it could mean that, or 'Did you hear that?' And I think if you haven't really negotiated something with your students or at least told them about your policy for correcting mistakes, then I think if they keep on spotting mistakes that the teacher doesn't correct, I don't really know what happens in their minds. Perhaps there's always a danger of the teacher losing some credibility.
(JOHN, HUNGARY)

- Does the mistake involve something 'known' or 'unknown'?

   If it's unknown (if the learner is making an 'attempt') and if it seems useful, the best thing might be *tell* the learner the correct form, which is actually different from correcting as such.

- Is it 'serious' in the sense of obscuring meaning or obstructing communication? Has it got a high damage potential?
- Can it be dealt with quickly/easily here and now? Is correction likely to be intrusive or inhibiting?
- Do you consider it a priority at the level of the learner concerned?
- Is it an issue for one individual or the whole class?

If you have, say, two Spaniards in a mixed-nationality class who have problems with /tʃ/, /dʒ/ and /ʒ/, if there's only two of them and the others have no problems with those sounds, you can't afford to spend too long on them, so what I've sometimes done is to give them some pointers and say there's such and such a cassette in the language lab that you could do in your self-access hour.
(JOHN, HUNGARY)

- Does the speaker 'ask' for correction, verbally (eg *Is that right?*) or non-verbally (eg by a questioning look)? Are they aware that something may be wrong, and does it matter to them?
- Is it a slip of the tongue, a momentary lapse or the result of a more serious underlying misapprehension?

In the beginning, as far as I remember, I didn't differentiate between slip and error. A mistake was just something which should be prohibited, something which should be corrected immediately. I think that's typical of young teachers. But now I'm aware of the difference and how to implement it – to correct pupils or not, depending on whether they make a slip or an error. If it's an error, I try to direct them to the correctness, but if it's a slip I don't mind.
(WOJTEK, POLAND)

If you do decide that it *is* appropriate to do something about a mistake, you might then find yourself involved in some or all of these steps:

- Not interrupting but waiting for the end of what the speaker is saying if it's something short, or a suitable pause if it's longer.
- Interpreting the intention and the nature of the incorrectness. For example, does *My friend live in England* mean *My friend lives in England* or *My friends live in England*? (or something else?) If you hear *I must to go* is it because the learner has included the word *to* or said *I must go* with a strongly released 't' sound which leaves a short vowel sound in its wake? If you hear *Shipbuilding is a very impotent industry*, is the intended meaning *important* with incorrect stress, or *weak* with an unusual choice of word? Asking for clarification may be the only way of finding out in some cases; in other cases the intention will become clear from the broader context.
- Indicating that there's a mistake. Teachers often have non-verbal signals for this. Sometimes it's important to acknowledge the general correctness, or factual validity, of what the learner has said before focusing on the mistake, so as to avoid giving the message that everything the speaker said was wrong.
- Indicating where the mistake is, if it can be localized. Some teachers count off the words of an utterance on their fingers, and stop at the one where the mistake is. Others repeat the utterance up to the mistake, perhaps including the mistake in a questioning tone of voice.
- Giving a model of the correct version.
- Telling the learner what to do, eg *Change the tense, Make it less formal.*
- Asking questions to check understanding of a structure or lead the speaker to use the correct one.
- Appealing to another learner, or to the whole class, for a correction. Sometimes it happens anyway.

I've seen students make good healthy fun of each other and correct each other in a very funny way. But if there hadn't been any confidence between them it could have been impolite or offensive.
(JOHN, HUNGARY)

- Giving an explanation of what's wrong and why.

Any of these steps may or may not be sufficient. Generally, it's probably a good idea if the learner who made the mistake is as involved as possible in the correction procedure, rather than simply being told what's right; this makes it more likely that the correction will be remembered. The learners will have been helped to develop their own criteria of correctness, and therefore the time spent correcting will have been well spent. And it's probably important to allow a learner sufficient time to self-correct and understand the reason for the correct form if there is one; otherwise the result may simply be fleeting confusion and no lasting effect.

Correction implies that in the end the speaker should be clear about what the wrong version was and what the right version is – and why, and should have had sufficient opportunity to say the correct version and, if relevant, opportunity for some further practice. If the correct version is unfamiliar, the learner may, understandably, say it hesitantly. So it's worth spending a short time getting them to practise saying it at speed, rhythmically, in as English a way as possible. On the other hand, don't expect, or demand, perfection. This may be just the beginning of a long process of familiarization. ■

7 A conclusion

Those teachers who tend to correct all the time, no matter in what situation, make it very stressful for their learners, and they close up and they don't express themselves. (WOJTEK, POLAND)

> If the teacher wants accuracy above all things and never mind what ideas the students express, then that teacher will get attempts at accuracy: no mistakes and no learning steps. (Edge 1989 p 16)

Over-cautious learners can develop for themselves a version of English which is correct but meagre, and not sufficiently robust to stand up to the demands placed on it outside the classroom. So it's important that they should be given opportunities to make mistakes and come to regard this as a normal part of learning. The teacher's attitude is vital here. Correction should not be a kind of criticism or reprimand. In order to learn a language, people need to experiment, to try things out, and they need helpful, supportive feedback on their experiments, plus information with which to conduct further experiments.

Perhaps it's helpful to bear this in mind when considering the role of mistakes and correction in the learning process.

8 On reflection

Task 10

Look back at the statements in Section 1 (p 44). Have your feelings about any of the statements changed as a result of reading and reflecting on this chapter?

Commentary ■ ■ ■

I regard all mistakes in language learning as a bad thing.

Be careful about applying moral judgements to phenomena which are an intrinsic part of the learning process. Saying this is close to saying that you regard language learning as a bad thing!

My main task is to ensure that my learners speak correctly.

Are you still sure about 'main'? What about helping them to extend the range of their competence, helping them to use what they already know more effectively, even when it appears to be inadequate to a particular demand? What's the use of being correct for the sake of correctness if you can't do anything with it? And in any case, what's your basis for deciding what's correct and what isn't, when there's so much variation in language – historical, geographical, stylistic, contextual ...?

I regard myself as lenient in my treatment of mistakes.

Using vocabulary like *lenient, liberal, allowing, accepting,* and *tolerating* still casts you in the role of a judge, the guardian of the laws, the seeker-out of profanity, limiting the damage which learners inflict on the English language. The real choice is not between being 'strict' and being 'lenient'; it's between subjecting people to a test they will always fail, and helping them to learn.

I distinguish between different degrees of seriousness among mistakes.

Consider the basis for these distinctions. There are probably very few mistakes which are serious or not serious in an absolute sense; context is all-important, and the only real criteria for judging seriousness are whether the message gets across at all, whether the listener has to make an inordinate amount of effort to understand, whether the mistake is isolated or part of a whole string of speech which is hard to interpret, whether the mistake causes irritation or offence. And it is hard to predict the potential seriousness of mistakes. Some teachers tend to accord a high priority to any grammatical mistakes as a matter of principle, but there is nothing to prove that grammatical mistakes are always, or even on average, the most serious in their effects.

I'd prefer my learners not to make any mistakes.

The reason behind this may be simply wanting the best for them, but the perfect is the enemy of the good. Trying to avoid mistakes means closing off learning opportunities. And don't forget that you need feedback on what learners still can't do, as well as what they can do. No mistakes means no evidence of misunderstandings and misconceptions.

I feel disappointed or annoyed when learners make mistakes with language I have taught them.

Perhaps it would help to put these affective reactions into perspective if you remember that learning isn't usually instant or easy, and mistakes aren't a kind of failure. Learners need to experience language extensively and process it in different ways before they can really 'own' it.

I feel surprised when learners get something right for a while and then start getting it wrong.

Learners' interlanguage (ie the version of the L2 they use while learning) is unstable and subject to variation in any direction. Perhaps they have moved their attention to a new issue and are neglecting the last one as a result. Or perhaps they have formed a new hypothesis which includes an adjustment of the rule which they previously used to form the correct something.

As a teacher, part of my job is to correct all my learners' mistakes.

Do you correct a mistake because it's wrong and offends against your aesthetic criteria, or because you think your correction will help the learner to acquire English?

I believe in peer correction. (ie learners correcting each other)

Why do you believe in it? Because it's fashionable, or because you have noticed some benefits from it? Have you also noticed any disadvantages?

I feel at least partly to blame for my learners' mistakes.

If you aren't careful you may help to mislead them, but the mistakes are still theirs, and no blame attaches to anyone.

I believe that mistakes should never be repeated by me, or written on the board.

Why not? Do you believe learners will learn them? Have you got any evidence that this happens? Do they learn everything else which is repeated or written on the board?

I recognize a distinction between 'errors' and 'slips', and find it helpful in my teaching.

If so, what practical conclusions do you draw? You could correct just errors, on the basis that slips don't betoken any underlying misconception and are random phenomena. On the other hand, you could take the view that errors will be ironed out through further exposure and practice, and are not likely to be affected by correction whenever they occur. In any case, are you always sure what's a slip and what's an error?

I recognize various different causes of mistakes, and find this helpful in my teaching.

It may help you to deal more effectively with a mistake – for example to refer a learner to a feature of the L1 which they have transferred inappropriately to English. But will it help the learner to stop making that mistake? In any case, how can you be sure that you can identify causes accurately?

I believe mistakes are caused primarily by interference from the learners' first language.

Teachers who meet learners of an unfamiliar linguistic background sometimes exclaim: *They make the same mistakes as my students!*

I judge how good my learners are according to how many mistakes they make.

One learner might say very little, very simply but perfectly correctly; another might take part successfully in much lengthier and more complicated interactions but make mistakes in the process. How are these two to be evaluated? ■

9 Recommended reading

Learner English, edited by Michael Swan and Bernard Smith, is a very useful reference source for typical mistakes made by speakers of a number of major world languages. It also highlights important differences between English and these languages in areas such as grammar, vocabulary and phonology.

The collection *Error Analysis*, edited by Jack Richards, explores the role of errors in language acquisition and takes a predominantly non-contrastive approach to error analysis.

10 References and bibliography

Aitchison, J. 1981 *Language Change: Progress or Decay?* (Fontana)
Bartram, M. and Walton, R. 1991 *Correction* (Language Teaching Publications)
Collins COBUILD English Language Dictionary (Collins 1987)
Edge, J. 1989 *Mistakes and Correction* (Longman)
Littlewood, W. 1984 *Foreign and Second Language Learning* (CUP)
Norrish, J. 1983 *Language Learners and their Errors* (Macmillan)
Pit Corder, S. 1981 *Error Analysis and Interlanguage* (OUP)
Richards, J. (ed.) 1974 *Error Analysis: Perspectives on Second Language Acquisition* (Longman)
Swan, M. and Smith, B. (eds.) 1978 *Learner English* (CUP)

Chapter 5   **Breaking the sound barrier:**
Aspects of pronunciation teaching

1   Introduction

Pronunciation is often seen by both teachers and learners as an extremely complex area of language teaching. While it is generally recognized by all concerned that a comprehensible pronunciation is both desirable and, indeed, necessary, there is also much debate about what 'comprehensible pronunciation' is and to what extent, if at all, teachers can influence this. There is also a grey area between the question of comprehensible pronunciation and that of comprehens-ible accent, with, for example, a learner pronouncing a particular sound or sequence of sounds in a way that is demonstrably not a normal native-speaker variant of those sounds but is nonetheless still comprehensible to the receiver of the message, and a learn-er pronouncing the same sound or sequence of sounds in a way that is demonstr-ably French or German. The latter case is often more acceptable to the native ear, largely because the native listener expects a French or German speaker to have a French or German accent (and may often be alarmed if this is not the case!), and it is also into this category of pronunciation that strong regional accents fall. A native-speaker with a strong Cornish accent might well find a Glaswegian less intelligible than an intermediate level French learner of English, but would be extremely unlikely to correct the former's pronunciation, while probably feeling no such inhibitions with the latter.

In terms of what is 'acceptable' pronunciation, regional and dialectical variations are regarded as 'acceptable', whereas 'foreign' pronunciation often may not be sub-titled. For better or worse, the native-speaker is perceived as correct, simply by virtue of being a native-speaker, even if much of his or her speech is unintelligible. The foreign learner is not accorded such privileges, and the listener may often lose patience with stumbling attempts to enunciate an utterance with intelligible pronunciation. Thus, while it is entirely possible that in this age of cable television and information technology in the not-too-distant future Bordeaux English, Bremen English and Bologna English may be regarded simply as regional accents in much the same way as Bolton English or Bristol English, this enlightened moment is not yet with us and foreign pronunciation is often regarded as a non-standard variety that could and perhaps should be improved. The following task may illustrate the different treatment afforded to native and non-native pronunciation:

Task 1

Do you regard the following as acceptable or not?

a We rally car about the unemployed.
b I haven't been to the Tar of London in years.
c The police need more far par.
d Wild life abinds rind here.
e Hyah, hyah.

Commentary ■ ■ ■

Semantically, almost certainly not, but what about phonologically? If you are now informed that **a**, **c** and **e** are transcripts of utterances in the House of Commons and that **b** and **d** are utterances attributable to members of the Royal Family, does this make them any more or less acceptable? Clearly, they are examples of non-standard varieties of British English (not RP – Received Pronunciation), but once one has cracked its code, this particular variety of English is no different from any other variety. It has its own allophonic variations on particular phonemes, and, indeed, its own idiosyncratic set of phonemes (fewer than the forty-four of RP). In that respect it is just another accent. It might seem odd when represented on paper in this way, but the average native speaker would not take issue with a person speaking in this particular variety, nor would he or she normally attempt to correct or modify the pronunciation.

Now imagine that these same utterances are being produced by a learner with a moderate French or German accent, for example. How do they sound now? It is likely that such a learner would be either misunderstood or corrected if he or she spoke about *the Tar of London*, with a native-speaker interlocutor pointing out (although not necessarily in these words) that the word *tower* is pronounced either as two syllables or as a triphthong.

This is just one reason why learners may often find themselves in a difficult position where the pronunciation of English is concerned. In addition, their pronunciation is heavily influenced by their own native language and thus they have an accent. They may also find native-speaker listeners lacking in patience when listening to them. They may also have been told that their particular accent is regarded positively or negatively by native-speaker listeners and this may affect their confidence when using English. Finally, they may have been told that their own particular pronunciation is adequate, but at the same time they know it is not 'perfect' but they do not know what to do in order to improve it. To the learner, pronunciation may seem to be a huge, vague, non-finite area of language. *I know it isn't right, but I don't know where to start*, was a rather plaintive comment we heard recently.

Despite the factors outlined above, it is often argued that pronunciation is of little importance when placed alongside, for example, grammar and vocabulary. Errors of pronunciation are hardly worth correcting, particularly if the utterance is broadly comprehensible. Interestingly, the same criterion is not usually applied by teachers to grammatical or lexical errors – if a word, for example, is 'broadly comprehensible' but is patently not correct, then teachers are likely to correct it. Similarly, if the use of a grammatical structure by a learner can be understood but contains syntactic or other errors, then, once again, it is likely to be corrected. Pronunciation errors are more likely to remain uncorrected. But let us consider for a moment what the impact of such errors could be. In this case we are dealing with a pronunciation error that is based on inappropriate tonic prominence and the use of a non-native intonation pattern inappropriate to the situation. ◼

Task 2

Imagine a visitor from a foreign country staying with a family in an English-speaking country. Consider which of the following errors is likely to be received most negatively by the listener:

a A lexical error: *At what hour will dinner be ready?*
b A grammatical error: *When has dinner ready?*
c A syntactic error: *When will be dinner ready?*
d An error of stress/intonation rendering the question querulous or complaining: *When **will** dinner be ready?*

Commentary ◼ ◼ ◼

It is highly likely that the other errors will be tolerated, even not noticed, but the pronunciation error might well lead to a misinterpretation of the message with a subsequent negative effect on the relationship between the guest and his or her hosts. The guest will be puzzled by the reaction and assume he has committed some dreadful *faux pas* or other without knowing what it is. An international incident caused by a pronunciation error. ◼

2 What kind of pronunciation teacher are you?

As in other areas of language teaching, attitudes to the teaching of pronunciation vary widely. There does, however, appear to be a fairly common perception that pronunciation is 'hard' and involves a lot of difficult theory that has to be absorbed before any teaching can be done. This is perfectly understandable as theoretical phonetics can, indeed, be extremely analytical and, at a certain level, is arguably of little practical value in the foreign language classroom. Similarly, many teachers are intimidated by the sight of phonemic symbols both in dictionaries and, as is increasingly the case, displayed in tabular form in classrooms. The perception often is that this is yet another alphabet to be learned and, like Russian or Greek, for example, this is something difficult. And if it is difficult for the teacher, how much more difficult will it be for the learner? In addition to the somewhat negative feelings often expressed about the 'theory' and the difficult nature of phonology, there is also a fairly widely held view that pronunciation is much less important than other aspects of language learning and does not therefore deserve to have a more prominent role in the classroom.

Do you consider yourself to be a teacher who devotes adequate attention to different aspects of pronunciation or do you sometimes avoid it for some of the reasons mentioned above?

Task 3

The pronunciation teacher's questionnaire

Tick the boxes that apply to you:

☐ I regularly work on the pronunciation of my learners.

☐ I know which aspects of English pronunciation are difficult for my learners.

☐ I am informed about the major phonological differences between the L1 of my learners and English.

☐ I try to integrate pronunciation work into other aspects of teaching.

☐ I know and use a set of phonemic symbols.

☐ I encourage my learners to keep a record of the pronunciation of new lexical items.

☐ I know where and how the phonemes of English are produced.

☐ I know how to work on typical errors made by my learners.

☐ I try to affect my learners' awareness of aspects of English phonology.

☐ When using dialogues and other recorded material, I regularly focus on pronunciation.

Commentary ■ ■ ■

If you scored 8–10, then you are clearly a committed pronunciation teacher, one who includes pronunciation work regularly as an integral part of your overall teaching. You will probably need no further convincing of its importance!

If you scored 5–7, then you are fairly enthusiastic, without being a single-minded devotee. You probably do enough and are relatively satisfied with the amount of pronunciation teaching that you do.

If you scored 2–4, then you are fairly lukewarm about pronunciation teaching and are probably less than totally convinced of its value. You may well react extremely negatively when you see a phonemic symbol!

If you scored 0–2, then you are either desperate to avoid all contact with or mention of pronunciation in your classroom, or you are intimidated by the notion of theory and prefer to avoid the issue rather than opening a potentially destructive can of worms. ■

Task 4

To compare your kind of pronunciation teaching with that of others, here are some comments by practising teachers that reflect their views on pronunciation teaching. Read through the list and make a note of any which broadly coincide with your own approach to the teaching of pronunciation.

*a   I don't bother much with pronunciation. I don't see the point. I simply
     let it take care of itself.*
     (LISA, UK)

*b   The problem is simply that I don't know if I'm right myself. So how
     can I correct my learners?*
     (MARGARET, GERMANY)

*c   I know where the problems are, but I simply don't know what to do about it.
     I don't know enough theory.*
     (ISABEL, SPAIN)

*d   There are much more important things in language learning than pronunciation.
     Grammar, for example. I simply don't have the time for pronunciation work.*
     (SUE, FRANCE)

*e   My students aren't interested in pronunciation. They don't like it,
     so I don't work on it with them.*
     (MIRO, SLOVAKIA)

*f   I do a lot of pronunciation work. I think my role is to give an accurate model
     If I say it often enough, they'll get it right in the end.*
     (GUY, UK)

*g   I inform myself about typical problems a particular nationality is likely to have
     (the /p/ /b/ distinction for Arabic learners, for example), and then I just work on
     these for a few minutes each day. I try to give them practical hints.*
     (STEVE, UK)

*h   I work on making them aware of the main differences, between, say, the English
     and German pronunciation of place names. This makes them realize some of the
     principal contrasts between the two languages.*
     (ULI, GERMANY)

*i   In terms of sounds, I try and outline the three or four sounds I think they need to
     work on. They can do most of the English sounds. I think that narrowing it down
     gives them a clearer sense of direction and achievement.*
     (PETRA, GERMANY)

*j   I think pronunciation work makes a welcome break from grammar, vocabulary and
     so on. If you work on intonation, you're bringing the language to life in a way.*
     (PHIL, USA)

Commentary ■ ■ ■

Those teachers quoted above who do not favour pronunciation work cite five main reasons: lack of time, lack of necessity (it takes care of itself), lack of theoretical knowledge, lack of practical knowledge (including uncertainty about whether a model is right or wrong), and lack of interest on the part of learners. Naturally, the feelings that underlie these statements are perfectly understandable, but

5 Say the diphthong /aʊ/ as in *now* very slowly. Notice the lip and jaw position at the beginning of the diphthong and observe the movement in both as you continue. Repeat the process with some more diphthongs, eg /eɪ/, /aɪ/ and /eə/.

6 Place your fingertips lightly either side of your Adam's apple. Whisper /iː/. Notice the absence of any vibration. Keep your fingertips in the same position and now utter the sound /iː/ aloud and hold it for some time. What can you feel?

7 In the same way, place your fingertips lightly either side of your Adam's apple and say the sounds /s/ and /z/ alternately several times. Hold each one for a few seconds. What differences do you notice?

8 Mime the sounds /p/, /b/, /m/. Can you *see* any difference between them? Now say each one aloud in turn several times. What differences are there? Hold the palm of your hand a couple of centimetres in front of your lips and repeat the exercise. Can you feel any difference?

9 Say the sounds /p/, /b/, /t/, /d/, /k/ and /g/ carefully several times. What do they have in common? Now divide them into three pairs: /p/ and /b/, /t/ and /d/ and /k/ and /g/. Say each pair again. What is the relationship between the sounds in each pair?

10 Say *hot*. Notice the position of the tip of your tongue when you pronounce the final 't'. Is it making contact with your teeth? Probably not. It is probably touching the ridge behind your teeth.
Now try saying *hot* again. This time make the tip of your tongue touch your teeth as you pronounce the final 't'. How does this sound? Does it sound right? Does it sound English? Does it sound 'foreign'? If it sounds foreign, what language does it sound like?

11 Say /t/ again. Now say the sound /θ/ as in *thin*. Where is the tip of the tongue now? Say the two sounds alternately several times in quick succession. Notice the contrasting tongue position.

Commentary ■ ■ ■

In a sense, all of this is theory. It is intended to promote awareness of a number of factors relevant to pronunciation. As far as vowels are concerned, for example, it is intended to make the point that jaw position, lip position, tongue position and voice all play an important role in the production of vowels. Of course, it is possible to read this information and, similarly, to pass it on in one form or another to one's learners. It is also perfectly possible to be much more complicated about it and to use more technical jargon (in the case of the example of /t/, for example, one could mention that the ridge is called the *alveolar* ridge). The question is whether complicated 'theory' and complex jargon are necessary. Naturally, they are both there if an individual teacher requires them, but it is also possible to proceed perfectly adequately without more detailed theory and terminology and to deal with pronunciation problems at a practical level without exposing the learner to difficult and potentially demotivating jargon. What we feel that the teacher does need is an awareness of how and where the sounds of English are produced, for without that awareness it is rather difficult to see how he or she can take concrete action to remedy learners' persistent errors with the production of particular phonemes (where to place the tip of the tongue for the English 't' sound as opposed to the Russian 't' sound, for example). Thus, *some* theory is necessary. It need not, however, be difficult and it can be mastered by teachers themselves through simple self-discovery exercises along the lines of those outlined above. ■

6   I don't know whether it's right or wrong myself

We have frequently heard this fear expressed by non-native teachers of English and it is a perfectly understandable one, given the vagaries of English pronunciation and the sheer range of demands placed on the non-native teacher. One would not, however, normally find such statements attached to grammar or vocabulary. At the very least, one would expect teachers to be 'one jump ahead' of their class and to be prepared accordingly. The same principle, however, can surely be applied to questions of pronunciation. This is where a knowledge of the forty-four phonemes of English can prove so practically beneficial. Armed with such knowledge, the uncertain non-native teacher can at the very least check the pronunciation and word stress of an unfamiliar lexical item in a good learners' dictionary and present to his or her learners a perfectly adequate model on that basis. Without such knowledge, any help on the part of the teacher is likely to be based on guesswork and may, consequently, be misleading. Thus, once again, a little theory is called for. How much may well depend on the L1 of the teacher and how many phonemes in English are more or less equivalent to phonemes in that L1. The task for the teacher will be to identify and master those phonemes which are either perceptibly different in English from the L1 or exist as separate phonemes in English while not existing in the L1. Perhaps, too, if teachers perceive pronunciation questions in much the same way as grammar questions and accept that perfect knowledge is not required and that there will be times when they have to resort to a dictionary to check pronunciation, they might feel more confident in their ability to deal with their learners' pronunciation problems.

7   My learners aren't interested

Where is the learners' lack of interest? Is it in improving their pronunciation or is it in the way or ways in which the teacher has attempted to deal with pronunciation in the past? The former is certainly possible, but it is rather unlikely, given that the motivation of most learners is to improve and that improving pronunciation, as part of the spoken language, is clearly one aspect of improvement. It is comparatively rare to meet a learner who has no interest whatsoever in improving their pronunciation – it is almost like saying that one does not want to increase one's vocabulary, or improve one's writing ability. Lack of interest amongst learners may well be brought about by a lack of interest in pronunciation as a topic. Perhaps it has been presented to learners in an over-theoretical way. Perhaps the method used is repetition and more repetition. Perhaps it has been over-emphasized, singled out rather than integrated into other aspects of teaching. Perhaps the lack of interest is actually in the teacher and stems from his or her inability to incorporate pronunciation work painlessly into the kinds of areas outlined above in Section 3 of this chapter.

Improving pronunciation may not simply be a case of doing repetitive pronunciation drills in order to work on a particular sound. It can also include promoting
awareness – awareness of the way in which sounds are made in English, awareness
of the relationship between sounds and spelling and awareness of the links between
intonation and meaning. These aspects need not be presented in an uninteresting
drill-based way, but can be introduced in the form of discovery tasks that engage
the learner in finding out about English pronunciation and the differences between English pronunciation and the pronunciation of their own L1.

8   Making a start

The comments by the last five teachers quoted in Task 4 (p 63) are all broadly in
favour of teaching pronunciation and they all, in their own way, highlight certain
important aspects of pronunciation teaching. Comment **f** highlights the need to
provide a pronunciation model of some kind and the teacher in question clearly sees
his role as the provider of this model. He also feels that repetition will help learners
'get it right in the end'. Clearly, a model will often be necessary for learners either
to copy or at least to aspire towards. They will look to the teacher to provide this
model, either personally or via recorded material. There is a case for a guided
discovery approach to phonology, and tasks promoting awareness of the phonological
features of the target language as well as contrastive aspects between the L1 and
the L2 may well be beneficial, but there is little doubt that a great deal of listening
and repetition plays an important role in acquiring a working pronunciation, both
at the level of individual sounds and at the level of stress and intonation.

Comment **g** refers to the need for teachers to prepare themselves for the kind of
pronunciation problems their learners are likely to meet when speaking English.
In the monolingual classroom where the teacher shares the mother tongue of the
learners, this is clearly a much simpler task for the teacher as he or she will probably
have experienced the same problems as the learners and will thus be aware of
exactly which problems to work on. Similarly, such teachers will know which
areas do not need attention, which phonemes, for example, are broadly the same
as their English equivalents. Many native-speaker teachers working abroad and
speaking the language of their host country reasonably well will find themselves
in a similar position and will be aware of contrastive phonological differences
between the learners' L1 and English. They will thus be well placed to take appropriate action and deal with typically problematic areas of pronunciation. Teachers
working with mixed nationalities or with groups whose native language they are
not familiar with are in a much more difficult position, and it is tempting when in
such a position to argue that any meaningful pronunciation work is impossible.
There are, however, two aspects to this argument that merit comment. In the first
place, there are many features of English pronunciation that seem problematic
for learners from a wide variety of linguistic backgrounds (the pronunciation of
the phonemes /θ/ and /ð/, for example, phonemes which exist in only a handful of
European languages, including Icelandic and Albanian; or the use of a typically
falling intonation pattern in *Wh-* questions, where in many languages a rising tone
would be used). These can thus be dealt with as generalized difficulties within the
English phonological system itself that are of interest and relevance to learners
from all linguistic backgrounds. The second factor is that a serious teacher should

perhaps learn about typical areas of difficulty for learners from particular linguistic backgrounds, even when he or she is completely ignorant of the mother tongues of the learners in question. Enough well written and easily accessible material now exists for teachers to be very well informed about the main pronunciation problems experienced by speakers of the world's principal languages (for a very clear report on over twenty major languages, see *Learner English*, Smith and Swan, 1987).

This contrastive aspect of pronunciation is taken further in comment **h**, where the teacher in question refers to the need to appreciate some of the differences between the pronunciation of the L1 and English. To illustrate the validity of this approach, compare the English and French pronunciation of the word *Paris*. There are several differences, of course, but perhaps the most striking are the different quality of the 'r', the different vowel sound in the second syllable, the pronunciation of the final sound in English as compared to the silent final letter in French, and the different stress patterns in the two languages. Similar comparisons can be made between English and other languages (eg English/German *Hamburg*; English/Spanish *Barcelona*). It is also possible to compare and contrast the articulatory setting of English and the learners' L1 in this way, by getting learners to pronounce a list of international words (eg place names) in their mother tongue and then in English and to notice the different positions of lips, jaw and tongue in the two languages. Another way of doing this is to ask the learners to speak to each other in pairs in their mother tongue as an English speaker of their language would speak it and to observe what happens to the speech organs in the process.

Comment **i** is a significant one in that it draws attention to the question of setting targets. It is related to the contrastive questions mentioned in both **g** and **h** and it also brings out the question of not working on sounds (and other features of pronunciation) that are already familiar to the learners, either through their own mother tongue or because, for whatever reason, they are not particularly problematic. By targeting those sounds that are problematic (four, six, eight out of the total of forty-four phonemes), the teacher enables the learner to have a clear, and possibly, achievable goal in an area of language learning that may otherwise seem horribly arbitrary and random.

The final comment focuses on the fact that working on pronunciation can bring another dimension to language learning. Pronunciation work need not be theoretical or dull. If integrated well into other activities, it can become simply another aspect of the language-learning process, and can be accepted as such by the learners, much as they accept copying down new vocabulary or doing grammar-based exercises.

9   What does it mean to teach pronunciation?

When we work on learners' awareness of aspects of pronunciation on the one hand, and on their active production on the other, we have found a certain basic awareness on the teacher's part essential. This awareness need not, however, be based on a complete mastery of the extensive theory underlying the field of phonetics and phonology. In a practical sense, it can be based on a basic awareness in five areas of pronunciation:

- an awareness of what happens when sounds are produced;
- an awareness of what happens to sounds in rapid speech and when they come into contact with one another;
- an awareness of what it is that makes a stressed syllable stressed;
- an awareness of the relationships between tonic prominence placement and meaning;
- an awareness of the basic intonation patterns of English and how they relate to meaning.

Sounds

At a basic level, we suggest that a teacher who intends to deal with pronunciation will need to understand the fundamental distinction between a vowel and a consonant and to appreciate that a diphthong is a glide from one vowel to another. Similarly, he or she will need to appreciate the use of voice, tongue, lips and jaw to produce vowel and diphthong sounds. As far as consonants are concerned, an awareness of whether a particular consonant is voiced or not, which of the speech organs are used to articulate this consonant and what kind of consonant it is (eg a 'stop' or a 'continuant') will all be relevant knowledge. The kind of awareness necessary to operate constructively in this area can easily be gained by using activities of the type suggested in Section 5 of this chapter. Allied to this is an understanding of the fact that there are forty-four phonemes in standard RP English, that twelve of these are vowels, eight diphthongs and the remaining twenty-four consonants, and that these are *standard* forms intended as a general reference point, rather than a prescriptive model that has to be followed. An appreciation of the fact that numerous allophonic differences (ie sound variations that do not affect meaning) exist for most phonemes and that many native-speakers operate totally effectively with a phoneme bank of fewer than forty-four phonemes is also helpful. (Neither of the authors of this book speak 'standard' RP English.)

With this basic awareness of the nature of the sounds of English comes the need for an ability to pass on this knowledge to learners. One way is simply to use the type of discovery activities exemplified in Section 5 of this chapter. We find the use of phonemic symbols of immense practical value. Examples of these can be found in most good learners' dictionaries (*Longman Dictionary of Contemporary English*, *Oxford Advanced Learners' Dictionary*, COBUILD dictionaries, etc). We regularly use a chart illustrating the phonemes in tabular form, as do many other teachers. One of these that is widely used is Adrian Underhill's phonemic chart, which groups vowels, diphthongs and consonants according to place and manner of articulation and which is thus extremely valuable as a classroom reference point.

iː	ɪ	ʊ	uː	ɪə	eɪ	X
e	ə	ɜː	ɔː	ʊə	ɔɪ	əʊ
æ	ʌ	ɑː	ɒ	eə	aɪ	aʊ
P	b	t	d	tʃ	dʒ	K	g
f	v	θ	ð	s	z	ʃ	ʒ
m	n	ŋ	h	l	r	w	j

Phonemic chart © Adrian Underhill

Learning the symbols may seem an unattractive proposition at first for both teachers and learners alike, but in our experience the merits of doing so far outweigh the disadvantages. A knowledge of the symbols can enable learners to discover the pronunciation of new lexical items independently through the use of dictionaries, and also to keep a pronunciation record of lexical items in their vocabulary store. By having their own 'mini-copy' of a phonemic chart and shading in, with the help of the teacher, those phonemes which they can already produce reasonably accurately (approximately the same sound as in L1 or not a problem for speakers of a particular language), learners can be left with a clear idea of exactly which phonemes (the unshaded ones) they need to work on. In this way they will have a clear and identifiable goal as far as the pronunciation of individual sounds is concerned.

Sounds in contact

Unfortunately, however, sounds are rarely produced in isolation in 'real life' and what happens when sounds come into contact with one another and are produced in rapid speech is consequently of considerable significance to both teachers and learners. The stress-timed nature of English produces a lot of reduced or 'weak' vowel sounds, typically rendered as /ə/, /ɪ/ and, sometimes, /ʊ/. This can cause numerous difficulties for learners, both with production, but, often more acutely, with reception – they simply cannot hear the weak forms and may not understand whole utterances as a result. An awareness of this feature of English and of the importance in English of the phoneme /ə/ is therefore crucial. This awareness can be promoted by a knowledge of the types of words affected by this feature, namely articles, conjunctions, prepositions, auxiliary verbs and modal auxiliary verbs. The relationship with the placement of tonic prominence on 'content words' is also extremely important in this respect. One way of drawing learners' attention to this particular feature of English is to compare and contrast English with their own language. The pronunciation differences between English and a syllable-timed language are likely to be considerable, but any differences between English and other stress-timed languages are also of interest.

In the same way, it is also possible to draw learners' attention to other features of connected or rapid speech, such as elision and assimilation. Such features are not confined to English, of course, and it can be very illuminating to discuss whether changes such as the disappearance of the 't' in *last chance* or the assimilation of 'd' to something like 'b' in *good morning* are found in the learners' mother tongue too. This is not to suggest that features of the language such as these need to be *taught*.

No doubt it is possible to teach them actively in a systematic way (eg giving learners a complete list of all the possible assimilations in English and then practising with examples and testing this knowledge), but this would probably be inappropriate for many learners. What we have found personally useful, however, is to have a basic awareness of these features and to be in a position to pass on this awareness where interest or curiosity are expressed (eg *Listen to that phrase on the tape again and notice what happens to the final sound in 'last.'*).

Word stress

It is sometimes argued that incorrect word stress placement is a greater barrier to communication than incorrectly articulated sounds. A passenger asking for a ticket to Bris'tol as opposed to 'Bristol might find his or her request met with a bemused stare. The placement of primary stress on a syllable upon which it is not normally placed can result in a radically different sound to the word in question, and possibly in a misunderstanding or breakdown in communication. In order to appreciate the importance of word stress and to be in a position to help learners develop an awareness of this phenomenon, teachers will need, first of all, to be aware of the notion of the syllable and of syllabic division. Recognizing the number of syllables in a word is clearly the first stage in attributing to one of these syllables a primary stress and to others secondary stress or unstress. Then they will need an awareness of what constitutes a stressed syllable, ie a higher pitch than that of surrounding syllables, a slightly greater length and greater breath effort or muscular energy (usually manifested for the listener as loudness).

A knowledge of the fact that many multi-syllable words (particularly those of Latin origin) bear a secondary stress in their prefix may also be of benefit. Likewise, familiarity with the set of words that have a different stress pattern in their noun and verb forms (eg 'contract/con'tract) can have practical applications. In the case of compounds, an awareness of some of the different ways of forming compounds (eg noun + noun, as in *tissue paper*; adjective + participle, as in *easy-going*; and gerund + noun, as in *swimming pool*) and the stress patterns typically associated with these different types of compounds could be of substantial practical value. Once again, if you feel uncertain about the stress pattern of a particular word or compound, then recourse to a good learners' dictionary should provide the answer, as such dictionaries normally carry the stress patterns of words as well as their phonemic transcription.

Emphatic stress

Whereas many highly inflected languages (languages where nouns have varied case endings to indicate grammatical functions, such as Czech and Russian) can achieve emphasis by changing word order to place the emphasis on a particular word or group of words, English can achieve a similar effect by placing the tonic prominence on a particular syllable of a given word. This phenomenon is by no means confined to English, nor is it excluded in languages like those cited above where other methods can also be used to achieve this effect. An awareness of how flexible this can be and how it can affect meaning is, however, arguably of some significance to both teachers and learners. To take a simple example:

a She went to Paris last week on **business**.   (not for pleasure)
b She went to **Paris** last week on business.   (not to Brussels)
c She went to Paris last **week** on business.   (not last month)

One way that we have used to sensitize learners to this phenomenon is to show them examples of authentic recorded English (news headlines are particularly suitable for this) and ask them to predict which syllable in each tone group carries the tonic prominence. They may then compare their predictions with the original version. Recognizing which syllable is stressed is an important stage on the way to recognizing and interpreting the function of intonation patterns, as it is on the tonic syllable that the glide in pitch begins.

Intonation

The final area of awareness for the committed pronunciation teacher is that of intonation. A great deal has been written about this topic and much of it has only served to complicate and obscure rather than to simplify and to clarify. At the one extreme, detailed analysis is carried out on thousands of authentic utterances and these are then divided into intonation patterns and matched with functional equivalents (eg polite enquiry, tentative apology, etc). No doubt such efforts are extremely worthy but they are of little practical help to the learner because in many situations the choice of intonation pattern does not depend solely on context but on other, related factors such as the speaker's intention and mood. This can mean that the functional equivalents so neatly attached to each pattern may prove interchangeable and the unfortunate learner becomes even more confused as a result. At the other extreme, but arguably much more usefully, intonation is reduced to two basic functions, proclaiming and referring. The first is a fall or a rise-fall used to give new information or information which has not been referred to previously. The latter is a fall-rise or a rise and is used to refer to previously mentioned information or knowledge shared by the community of listeners. As a general guideline, this reduced version is extremely helpful, but leaves the learner with the mammoth task of deciding whether an utterance contains shared or new information. Time does not usually permit such considerations to be made before speaking.

In practical terms, perhaps all that the teacher can hope to achieve is to pass on to his or her learners the general implications of this reduced model of intonation and to add to this by making them aware of certain generalized rules that are observable phenomena within English intonation. Examples of such generalized rules that we often use ourselves are that *Wh-* questions generally have a falling pattern, while *yes/no* questions typically rise. Likewise, echoic questions generally rise, while statements introducing new information tend to fall. Similar generalizations can be made with other types of questions and various functional areas too. Clearly, this is not a detailed analysis of the myriad intonation patterns and their meanings possible in English, but by helping learners' awareness of certain general tendencies in English intonation and by exposing learners to examples of these tendencies through listening material, teachers can provide a way into what is generally held to be a particularly problematic area of pronunciation teaching.

10 Conclusions

The teaching of pronunciation is a wide-ranging area of language teaching. While a native speaker-like pronunciation might be an ideal goal (just as a native speaker-like command over structure might be a goal as far as grammar is concerned), realistically such a goal is probably unachievable, and possibly even undesirable, for most learners. What is achievable is a comprehensible pronunciation and, within the scope of this goal, the constant possibility for change and movement, in both awareness of features of English pronunciation (and one's own L1 pronunciation) and in the production of those features. The role of teachers could be to teach explicitly all aspects of English pronunciation. It might be preferable, however, to focus on those areas of English pronunciation that are specifically problematic for a given learner or group of learners and to heighten learners' awareness of those aspects of pronunciation that will have a significant effect on the learners' production. In order to achieve this, teachers will need to be open to the idea of affecting their own awareness of pronunciation, both by becoming more informed about the 'theory', and by listening more carefully to their learners and informing themselves about the phonological idiosyncrasies of their learners' native languages.

11 Recommended reading

Sound Foundations by Adrian Underhill guides the reader through a series of practical exercises which develop a comprehensive awareness of the theory underlying pronunciation teaching, and offers the reader a range of innovative and practical techniques.

Teaching English Pronunciation by Joanne Kenworthy deals with a variety of issues central to the topic and contains specific guidance for tackling the pronunciation problems of speakers of a number of major foreign languages.

The *Longman Pronunciation Dictionary* by John Wells is a good example of this type of reference work, containing as it does not only the pronunciation of the names of people, places and institutions which are not found in standard dictionaries, but also full information about alternative pronunciations.

12 References and bibliography

Baker, A. 1982 *Introducing English Pronunciation* (CUP)
Bowen, T. and Marks, J. 1992 *The Pronunciation Book* (Longman)
Bradford, B. 1988 *Intonation in Context* (CUP)
Brazil, D. et. al.1980 *Discourse Intonation and Language Teaching* (Longman)
Brown, A. 1991 *Pronunciation Models* (Singapore University Press)
Gimson, A. 1980 *An Introduction to the Pronunciation of English* (Arnold)
Kenworthy, J. 1987 *Teaching English Pronunciation* (Longman)
Kreidler, C. 1989 *The Pronunciation of English* (Blackwell)
Mortimer, C. 1984 *Elements of Pronunciation* (CUP)
Nickcl, G. 1987 How 'Native' Can (or Should) a Non-native Speaker Be?
In *The Language Teacher,* vol. 9, no. 11
Poldauf, I. 1984 *English Word Stress* (Pergamon)
Roach, P. 1983 *English Phonetics and Phonology* (CUP)
Smith, B. and Swan, M. 1987 *Learner English* (CUP)
Underhill, A. 1994 *Sound Foundations* (Heinemann)
Wells, J. 1990 *Longman Pronunciation Dictionary* (Longman)

Chapter 6

**The glamour of grammar and
the brass tacks of syntax:**

Some views of the significance of grammar

1   What *is* grammar?

It's one of the most common bits of terminology which learners, teachers – and even people who are neither – use in talking about language. But what *is* grammar exactly, and are we all talking about the same thing?

Task 1

Before you read on, write down your definition of grammar, and edit it if need be until you're reasonably satisfied with it.

Commentary ■ ■ ■

Well, here's what one dictionary says. You might like to compare it with other dictionaries – as well, of course, as with your own understanding.

> **Grammar is 1.1** the rules of a language, concerning the way in which you
> can put words together to make sentences. **1.2** the way someone either obeys
> or does not obey the rules of grammar when they write or speak a language.
> A **grammar is 2.1** a book that describes the rules of a language. **2.2** a theory
> that is intended to explain the rules of a language.
> (Collins COBUILD Dictionary)

This gives at least a hint of the various meanings embodied in the word, and the potential for confusion if meanings are not carefully identified and distinguished.

Imagine what a difference it would make if there were four separate words for these four meanings! ■

Task 2

We asked a group of teachers to answer briefly in writing the question *What is grammar?* Here are some of their responses; how closely do they match the dictionary definitions?

▶ *Grammar – rules and patterns which have to be obeyed in order to be communicative and understandable in a given language.*

▶ *Grammar is a set of rules organizing the proper ways the language is written or spoken as far as the form is concerned.*

▶ *Grammar is a group of different kinds of language rules used by people to understand each other correctly.*

▶ *Grammar is a set of rules that govern the way ideas are expressed in a language, both spoken and written.*

▶ *Grammar is a branch of science that explains the rules occurring in the language.*

▶ *Grammar: – a set of rules which helps us to create correct English sentences, expressions, etc.*
  – something that shows us the structure of a language, relationships between particular parts of speech.

▶ *Grammar is something worth knowing but not worth using.*

Commentary ■ ■ ■

The idea of rules, and of obeying them, is well represented here. For some of these teachers, grammar is concerned primarily with form or structure, but for others, meaning, communication and being understood are also a crucial aspect of what grammar is. The role of grammar in analyzing and describing language is also pointed out by some of them. The respondent who made the last comment meant that it's worth knowing grammar because it will help you to understand people when they do follow rules, but that often they don't do so, and learners shouldn't feel obliged to, either!

Most of the above teachers, like the dictionary definition, mention 'rules' which are to be 'obeyed', or which 'govern' the way ideas are expressed in language. We'll have more to say about rules later.

Here is another view, which emphasizes the meaning/form duality of grammar. Grammar is:

> a resource for the adaptation of lexis. But there is no absolute distinction between the two, only a convenient distribution of semantic responsibility. Grammar is a device for indicating the most common and recurrent aspects of meaning which it would be tedious and inefficient to incorporate into separate lexical items. (...)
> So grammar simply formalizes the most widely applicable concepts, the highest common factors of experience: it provides for communicative economy.
> (Widdowson 1990 p 87)

Teachers (including us!) commonly talk about 'grammatical' (or 'structural') words as opposed to lexis or vocabulary, and there's a pedagogical dichotomy between teaching grammar and teaching vocabulary. The 'most common and recurrent aspects of meaning' presumably include things like number, gender, definiteness, aspect, tense and modality, and the 'g-words' are ones which articulate these most abstract elements of meaning – words like *the, of, is, then, her, would,* and so on.

Grammar teaching is often thought of as teaching the operation of these words. But of course *all* words have grammatical restrictions and grammatical implications. *We reached the pub at 10.30, We got to the pub at 10.30* and *We arrived at the pub at 10.30* mean more or less the same thing, but *reach, get* and *arrive* have different grammars.

Grammar is generalizations about how words and groups of words behave. So grammar is an inescapable part of teaching and learning vocabulary, too. In fact, you could say that grammar teaching and vocabulary teaching are two sides of the same coin.

Similarly, there's really no opposition, as we think some teachers suppose, between teaching grammar and teaching language functions. Control of grammar is a prerequisite for expressing functions appropriately. ■

2   Popular wisdom

It appears that *grammar* and *glamour* are cognate. According to *The Concise Oxford Dictionary of English Etymology,* the form with the 'l' probably came via mediaeval Latin and Anglo-Norman into Scots. The meaning developed from grammar to learning, occult learning, magic, spell and magic beauty.

A lot of people, even those without any experience of, or particular interest in, foreign language learning, have got something to say about grammar, and attitudes to grammar vary. Grammar can be a kind of glamorous holy grail of learning, or a lowly mechanical artifice, a bag of brass tacks for cobbling bits of language together – or anything in between.

Task 3

What attitudes underlie people's views about grammar? Firstly, here's what some English speakers say about English grammar.

English hasn't got any grammar.
We say 'who', but 'whom' is grammatically correct, of course.'(Referring to an example like 'Who did you see?')
I've never learned English grammar.
You can only understand English grammar if you've studied Latin.
We don't even speak our own language properly, and they don't teach grammar at school these days.

Commentary ■ ■ ■

People who think English hasn't got any grammar are probably thinking of grammar as morphology, inflection, conjugation – and it's certainly true that

English has less of these than many languages. Maybe they also say this because they can speak English without ever having been taught any grammar, though this doesn't mean they've never learned it, in fact. The comment about *who* and *whom* is an example of the widespread acceptance of a prescriptive view of grammar; the way we speak our language is an imperfect attempt to comply with the way certain shadowy authorities think we should speak it. Having studied Latin will certainly help you understand grammars of English which posit categories such as *nominative* or *subjunctive*; the question is whether such categories give much insight into the workings of modern English. The last comment suggests that there is a form of English somewhat different from the one most speakers use, which is superior or preferable, but which most users fall short of, and it reflects a prescriptive view: if people were taught explicitly how to use language, they might be better at it. ■

Task 4

Secondly, what about some of the things English speakers say about the grammar of other languages?

Russian's a very grammatical language.
Polish grammar's complicated.
I'm making progress with Hungarian but I find the grammar difficult.
You can't really speak German properly without learning the grammar.
Finnish grammar's very logical.
(Names of other languages can be substituted, of course.)

Commentary ■ ■ ■

The first two comments probably refer to the fact that the two languages cited are more highly inflected than English. The fourth comment perhaps implies a contrast with English, but you can't speak any language 'properly' – if this means accurately – without learning its grammar, although the nature of what you have to learn might vary quite a bit between languages, and so might the way you learn it. The remark about logic is made about all sorts of languages but not, usually, about English. Presumably any language must be logical, otherwise it would be unusable, and it's only when subjected to close observation and analysis – eg by a learner – that the logic becomes apparent. The logics of different languages will differ from each other – we are not talking here about any kind of universal or mathematical logic – and maybe logic is easiest to perceive when it's embodied in identifiable morphological inflections. ■

Task 5

And finally, as food for the same kind of thought, here's what some learners say about English grammar:

We don't do enough grammar in our course.
Was, were, was; were, were, were.
Let's go to swimming – ah, no, let's go swimming without 'to'.
The thief or he broke into the house or bedroom.
I just picked up my English working in Britain, so I've never learned the grammar.
I had five years of English at school but we only learned grammar.

Commentary ■ ■ ■

One teacher said:

I think they say these things because of the way it's presented – 'We don't have enough grammar,' meaning 'It isn't hard enough, I'm having a lot of fun here, but I can't see it written down in a form I'm used to, it's not hard enough, it's not tough enough.' Or 'I had five years of English at school ... and we did a lot of formal exercises, transformations, translations, identifying what this or that tense was called – but we didn't learn to use it.'
(ELLIE, UK)

Was, were, was may be a useful mnemonic at a certain stage. The danger arises when a learner feels that learning such things is the aim of studying grammar, and when knowledge of grammar is judged according to the ability to recite such incantations.

The thief or he ... is the language of the walking substitution table, displaying knowledge of a set of possibilities rather than choosing one like most language users.

Let's go ... exemplifies the role of conscious knowledge in shaping performance.   ■

3   Different kinds of rules

A 'rule' can mean a requirement – something you are expected to comply with – or a statement of an observed regularity or tendency. This duality is paralleled in the contrast between prescriptive grammar, which tells you how someone thinks you should use language, and descriptive grammar, which aims to describe how language is actually used. The dictionary definition on p 76 seems closer to the spirit of the first of these. Many descriptive rules are approximate or statistical: *X is usually followed by a gerund* or *Y is countable in more than 95 per cent of cases.*

In the realm of foreign language pedagogy, the distinction between descriptive and prescriptive rules is rather obscured because a description of how language is used by its native speakers is an obvious starting point for recommending or prescribing how learners should use it. Pedagogic grammars are based on available descriptions, with, depending on their exact target audience, deliberate omissions, simplifications and so on. A pedagogic grammar should be 'an interpreter between a number of formal grammars and the audience and situation-specific language teaching materials.' (Candlin 1973, cited in Stern 1983 p 175.) Often, approximate rules are taken, either by the author of the grammar or by the learner, to be absolute ones, and this can give rise to frustration and disillusionment when the exceptions start to appear. Approximate or statistical can also be less than helpful to the learner as a potential language user. It isn't enough to know that X is usually followed by Y; you also need to have a principled way of deciding exactly when it would be appropriate to follow X by Z instead of Y.

A further difficulty is that descriptions made available to teachers and course writers are often unreliable, because they are based on tradition, assumption and prejudice as much as on actual data. This state of affairs is now changing enormously, with the advent of computer-assisted analysis of huge amounts of naturally-occurring language, and the feeding-in of this data to ELT reference materials and coursebooks.

4   Where does grammar come from?

Grammar is continuously remodelled as part of the social history of the community of speakers of a certain language, rather than being handed down in unchangeable form on tablets of stone. So in this sense grammar comes from the collective consciousness and consensus of speech communities. But this data, because it is so diffuse, is not easily available to a learner or teacher of the language, and so these people rely to a large extent on printed 'grammars' which may subordinate description to prescription, but which, even if they sincerely set out to tell it like it is, inevitably fall short of recording the whole truth and nothing but. In this sense, grammar comes, sometimes, from dubious sources.

Some traditional grammars aimed at learners tend to treat formal aspects of grammar exhaustively but to neglect to treat in detail how these forms are used to express meanings in current English, which is left to intuition and experience. And this tendency is perhaps propagated by the terminology traditionally associated with grammar. *Present continuous* is easily associable with *something in progress at the moment of speaking*, but less so with something like *We're starting at 9.30 sharp*, which is neither present nor continuous. Lack of adequate treatment of such issues has led many learners to expect a one to one correspondence between form and function, and a spurious transparency in the names of forms.

So there can be a conflict between authority and authenticity, between what the books say and what the speakers of the language actually do. This can lead learners and teachers, even teachers who've been speaking English their whole life, to believe things about English which observation and introspection would reveal to be fictional. For instance, *You use 'some' in affirmative sentences and 'any' in questions and negatives*, or *There are three possible sequences of tenses in conditional sentences (well, all right, maybe occasionally you do get some different, rogue examples ...).*

Here are some further examples of some fictions propagated by grammars:

* The third person singular subject pronouns are *he, she,* and *it.*
  But what about *If the owner of pink Ford Model T, registration number XYZ 123, is in the building, will **they** please move it, as it is causing an obstruction?*
* The use of the present continuous with *always* expresses annoyance.
  But *Oh, you shouldn't, you're always giving me presents*, for example, may or may not include an 'annoyance' factor; this isn't an inherent part of the form. If it can be shown that a high proportion of instances of this form express annoyance, this would be an interesting finding, and helpful to learners, but it would be a statistical rule, and would not offer any explanation of the use of the form to express other meanings.
* Part of the meaning of *used to* is that the state or habit referred to no longer exists or applies.
  This is certainly often true, but what about *We still get our eggs straight from the farmer, just like we used to,* or *I used to like listening to the Beatles in those days – in fact I still do?*

Even when teachers and materials writers have seen through the falsity of such descriptions, they can find themselves involved in a battle for credibility with learners. If someone has been taught by their schoolteachers and the writers of their grammar books that you express futurity in English by using *will* + infinitive, they may be understandably resistant to younger teachers and more recent books telling them that *will* is only one of the resources for expressing futurity and, what's more, look at all these *other* uses of *will* ...

The solution to this conflict probably lies partly in the development of more reliably data-based materials, and partly in a policy of giving learners exercises which require them to process and analyze real examples of spoken and written English.

5 Grammar in language learning

Some published grammars, and some teaching traditions, focus on formal aspects of grammar to the extent that grammar became seen in some quarters as peripheral to the true concerns of language as actually used for communicative purposes. The advent of new proposals for syllabus design based on functional criteria led to the discrediting of grammar teaching, and a downgrading of the importance of grammatical knowledge in language competence. What we have seen more recently has been heralded as a 'return to grammar'; what this probably means is the increasing realization that grammar, far from being peripheral to communicative language use, plays a vital role in achieving meaning and communication, and that teaching materials and methods need to take grammar very seriously indeed, but giving due attention to its semantic aspects. Through increasing control over grammar, learners can progressively extend and refine their ability to express and communicate meanings clearly and in keeping with their intentions, and their ability to interpret other speakers' meanings more accurately. Meanwhile, many teachers are probably breathing a sigh of relief that they can go back to teaching grammar without a guilty conscience, and many others have probably been blissfully unaware of the shifts in orthodoxy that have gone on!

Task 6

How do you see grammar, and its significance to the language user or the language learner? What do the metaphors proposed here suggest about the nature of grammar? And which other metaphors suggest themselves to you?

Grammar is:

- an algebraic system;
- a scaffolding;
- a skeleton;
- a blueprint;
- ...

Commentary ■ ■ ■

Grammar is an algebraic system, for example, in that it is an abstract system with a certain logic and with certain rules and restrictions, and we can substitute a large number of different items into its structures and equations in order to generate certain values.

It is a scaffolding because it holds the structure of a piece of language up and prevents it from collapsing into a chaotic heap of words whose meaning would be unclear. It is also a scaffolding because its conscious manipulation and extension by the learner provides a framework for building competence in the language; at a later stage, when this competence is sufficiently strong, the scaffolding, or at least a large part of it, can be dispensed with. (Sometimes it may have to be rebuilt to enable repair work to take place.) ■

When we asked a group of teachers *What is the significance of grammar in language learning?*, the responses included the following:

Grammar plays a significant role in language since every single change in any grammatical structure causes a change in meaning. So if there were no clear grammatical rules, the language wouldn't play its role as far as communicating ideas is concerned.

Grammar organizes language structures and makes a language understandable for a learner.

Grammar is the most important thing in learning a foreign language. If you don't know grammar you wouldn't be able to speak or to write in that language.

For these teachers, grammar is clearly a very important component of language learning, and the first quotation, at least, reflects a belief that grammar is important not as something separate from communication, but precisely because it enables, or facilitates, communication.

6 Sample materials, activities and classroom incidents

In this section we offer a glimpse of a cross-section of different guises in which grammar can appear in the classroom.

Task 7

For each example, consider:

- What seems to be the underlying rationale, purpose or assumption?
- What do you think it might be able to achieve?
- What are its limitations?
- Do you/would you use activities of this type, or act in these ways, in your teaching? Why, or why not?

Example 1

Learners are given the following task. They work on it individually for a while, then compare notes with each other in twos and threes. Finally, there's a class discussion in which the teacher also participates, summarizes, and draws learners' attention to anything they've missed.

> These phrases all contain 's' added to the end of a word. Sort the phrases into groups according to the meaning of the 's'.
>
> *two days   two days' travelling   a week's a long time   it starts at six*
> *it's starting   it's started   the Scottish Highlands   rainbow's end*
> *rainbows end   John's here   John's hair   John's gone*

Example 2

Learners are given the task of allotting the following utterances to speech bubbles in six different pictures, and then commenting on the different forms of the nouns *coffee*, *sugar* and *beer*.

> *Two coffees, please.*
> *More coffee?*
> *When you go to the shop, can you buy some sugar?*
> *How many sugars?   Three, please.   Three!'*
> *This beer is brewed according to the Bavarian Reinheitsgebot.*
> *Let's go out and have a few beers.*

Possible extensions:

a They translate the examples into their L1.
b They find other occurrences of these and similar nouns, divide them according to countable/uncountable uses, and begin keeping a record of the determiners that collocate with them.
c They invent similar contrasting pairs of examples for, eg *wine*, *tea*, *cake*, *cheese*, *ice cream*, *chocolate*.

Example 3

A coursebook, or grammar reference/practice book, introduces a section on the passive voice by giving an explanation of how to form the passive equivalent of an active sentence, providing tables of passive verb forms in various tenses, and asking learners to work through exercises in converting active sentences into passive equivalents.

Example 4

A different book contains a section titled *Possibility*, which begins with a set of sample texts including instances of the following items, which are highlighted: *can*, *could*, *might*, *may*, *maybe*, *possibly*, *perhaps*, *it's possible that ...*, *it's conceivable that ....* There follow some observations on semantic restrictions and distinctions and on the syntax of the items introduced, before learners are asked to compose their own texts based on given scenarios.

Example 5

Using Cuisenaire rods or other similar coloured building blocks, the learners and the teacher together build visual representations of sentences in the various forms of the past simple tense, which the class are already fairly familiar with, so that, for example, yellow rods represent the past tense form, pink rods represent the infinitive, green rods represent *did*, white rods represent *n't* and red rods represent all other words. So the family of sentences on p 85, for example, would be represented by the rods above each one:

How did they do?

They won.

They didn't win.

Did they win?

Didn't they win?

Yes, they did.

No, they didn't.

They won, didn't they?

They didn't win, did they?

They did win.

Example 6

Learners are asked to determine which of the following sentences are correct.

(*look after* = take care of)
Who's going to look after the kids?
Who's going to look the kids after?
Who's going to look after them?
Who's going to look them after?
Who's going to look after?

(*bring up* = mention)
Thank you for bringing up the matter.
Thank you for bringing the matter up.
Thank you for bringing up it.
Thank you for bringing it up.
Thank you for bringing up.

Example 7

Learners identify what the italicized words in the following text refer to.

> After *they* saved a little money, Howard and Ellen wanted to buy a house.
> So they *did*. The floor plan was almost exactly the same as *that* of Ellen's
> parents' home, where *she* was reared. Buying *it* was not easy for *the young
> couple*, but Ellen was determined to go through with *it*. *She* couldn't stand
> living in *their* small apartment any longer.

(taken from Rutherford 1987)

Example 8

Learners have to rewrite the answers in conversational exchanges, so as to make
a complete sentence. For example:

'Where did you learn your English?' 'At school.' ➜ I learned my English at school.

Example 9

Learners do some work on different uses of English definite articles. They are then
asked to translate certain of the examples into their L1 (which also has definite
articles) and note similarities and differences in article use. In the following
lesson they are asked to translate a specially constructed text which focuses
on these similarities and differences from the L1 into English.

Example 10

A teacher corrects a learner's utterance *He can't did it* to *He couldn't do it*.
It subsequently becomes clear that what the learner meant was *He can't have
done it*.

Example 11

A learner in an 'elementary' class asks *Can I say 'I **did** come by bus?'* The teacher
answers *No*. The learner says *Never?* and the teacher replies *No. Well, yes, you
can sometimes, but you'll learn about that later.*

Example 12

The class play 'alibis', in which they have to invent stories about their activities
the previous evening. The teacher interrupts and corrects all misuses of the past
continuous tense, and tries to elicit further examples by intervening in the game
and asking *And what were you doing at 9.25?* and so on.

Example 13

The same activity as above, but the teacher does no correcting or other
intervening in the activity.

Example 14

Learners are asked to imagine a likely context for each of the following items, and translate them into their L1 in such a way as would be natural in that context. They then compare, and make generalizations about, the L1 grammar they have used in their translations.

> Customers are requested not to park in front of the building.
> This door must not be left open.
> English spoken here.
> But *Wuthering Heights* was written by <u>Emily Brontë</u>!
> Trespassers will be prosecuted.
> Applications should be submitted by December 31st.
> The doors are closed at midnight.
> This year's Nobel Prize for literature has been won by the English
>   poet John Cooper Clark.

Selective commentary ■ ■ ■

Example 1

These items are usually treated disparately. Bringing them together can be a useful way of getting learners to sort out which is which – or perhaps to see for the first time how many uses there are.

Example 2

This could be used to get learners to pay conscious attention to, and make judgements about, uses of language they have become more or less familiar with, as a way of strengthening their understanding and preparing them to extend it to new material.

Example 3

The message here is: The passive is dependent on the active for its existence, functionally they are equivalent, and any active sentence has a passive version which is of exactly equal value. And learners are helped by being given passive forms of all possible tenses (cf 14 above).

Example 4

This grammar seems to be organized according to semantic, rather than structural criteria. It aims to show learners what resources English has for expressing certain meanings, to show examples of how this has been done, and to provide learners with opportunities of doing similarly.

Example 5

Non-linguistic illustration – here, the use of colour – highlights features of form. In particular it shows up the prevalence of *did* and the infinitive, and the relatively restricted occurrence of the actual past tense verb over all the sentence forms. ■

7   Conclusions

These examples reveal quite a range of understandings of grammar, and grammar teaching, on the part of teachers. What attitudes do teachers hold explicitly? We asked teachers the question *Do you think grammar's ever been away?*

Not in my teaching. Partly to give the students a chunk of something that they think they're learning – what they're asking for. I think many students do need that systematization of the language – I do myself – it's the way some people learn. I first started teaching with the idea that you taught it and they knew it. Now I know they don't. So you go back every now and then and deal with it. I deal with it in a much more ad hoc way than I used to. Though I still will do a presentation, I don't expect them to know it. Experience. The second year I taught they came back and they didn't know anything I'd taught in the first year. And they forget it if you don't revisit it.
(KATE, UK)

I think that what people have said and taught about teaching has changed. I was trained to do situational presentations, and the idea was that the students were the ones to find the grammar in it. Since then I've become aware that there's lots of other ways of teaching grammar. Some teachers felt that if grammar teaching was the explanation by the teacher of the rules, then they weren't supposed to do it, so they felt they shouldn't teach grammar. Now there are a lot more varied materials available for teaching and practising grammar, so those teachers can feel that they can *teach grammar and there are some more ways of doing it.*
(LIN, CZECH REPUBLIC)

The fortunes of grammar have been subject to as many swings of the pendulum as any aspect of language teaching. Perhaps, in line with general developments in thinking about language teaching, the emphasis has shifted from the teacher's task in teaching grammar to the learner's task in learning it and putting it to use – and not necessarily in that order! So how can we help them to do this? Language consists of words. Grammar is an attempt to make generalizations about how words are used in combination to produce meanings. So there's actually no distinction between learning grammar and learning the language. It would be pointless to 'just' learn grammar, but it would also, luckily, be impossible. Depending on the items concerned, and depending on the learning style of the individual, any or all of the following broad approaches, some traditional and others not, may be effective:

- Select the language the learners are exposed to on the basis of a grammatical progression.
- Don't select language, but expose students to a rich mixture.

- Instruct and give directed practice.
- Let learners draw conclusions from their own observation and experience.

- Focus on grammar by extracting it from contexts of occurrence.
- Focus on grammar and then apply it to contexts of occurrence.

- Expect accuracy from the start.
- Expect accuracy to develop gradually.

- Draw comparisons with the L1.
- Avoid reference to the L1.

But whatever we do in the classroom, and however well grammatical items seem to be mastered in the practice contexts we devise, the learning of grammar, in the sense of making it as automatic as it is for the native speaker, will need lengthy and extensive experience of understanding, creating and exchanging meanings in contexts.

8 Recommended reading

Readers who wish to explore key background issues and their possible implications might like to consult William Rutherford's *Second Language Grammar: Learning and Teaching*.

As for grammar reference books themselves, we have found the following particularly interesting and useful: *A University Grammar of English*, *A Communicative Grammar of English*, the *COBUILD English Grammar* and *Practical English Usage*.

9 References and bibliography

Harmer, J 1987 *Teaching and Learning Grammar* (Longman)
Leech, G. and Svartvik, J. 1975 *A Communicative Grammar of English* (Longman)
Quirk, R. and Greenbaum, S. 1973 *A University Grammar of English* (Longman)
Rutherford, W. 1987 *Second Language Grammar* (Longman)
Stern, H.H. 1983 *Fundamental Concepts of Language Teaching* (OUP)
Swan, M. 1980 *Practical English Usage* (OUP)
Widdowson, H.G. 1990 *Aspects of Language Teaching* (OUP)

Chapter 7

What's in a word?

Some approaches to teaching, learning
and remembering vocabulary

1 Introduction

Language teaching has always been characterized by the arrival and subsequent
departure of 'new' methods and approaches, some more immediately appealing
than others. The central aim of each method and approach may differ (to promote
oral fluency, to provide learners with a solid grammatical base, to enable learners
to generalize on the basis of rules), but their overall purpose is generally the same,
namely to enable learners to acquire a sufficient amount of language to function
at some level in the target language. If we analyze what it means to function in a
foreign language, we will find, at the most basic level of all, that what is required is
a working vocabulary. It is interesting, therefore, that as the twentieth century nears
its end, the notion of the lexical syllabus is growing in currency and now, for the
first time, with the COBUILD project, we have coursebooks and materials based
directly on the frequency and range of lexical items. Vocabulary, often neglected
in methodological terms in the past, now occupies the centre stage.

This is what some of the experts say on the subject of the importance of
vocabulary:

> The belief that vocabulary acquisition can be delayed until a substantial pro-
> portion of the grammatical system has been learned is tenable only where the
> learner is not likely to have a pressing social need to use the language. (Wilkins)

> ... there is not much value ... in being able to produce grammatical sentences if
> one has not got the vocabulary that is needed to convey what one wishes to say.
> (Wilkins)

> Students not only have to learn how information is conveyed or elicited, or how
> requests are made: they also have to learn the words and expressions which are
> used to refer to the things in the world they want to talk about, ask about or
> request. (Swan)

> Vocabulary has been a neglected area in English language teaching in recent years. In concentrating their efforts on grammatical accuracy or authentic communication, teachers can easily overlook the fact that the source of many mistakes or of students being unable to express themselves is quite simply that they do not know the right words. (Fowler)

> The importance of words in verbal communication hardly needs stressing, yet no other language component has been more neglected in foreign language teaching than the lexicon. (Rudzka et. al.)

> In recent years vocabulary has not received the recognition it deserves in the classroom. (Gairns and Redman)

It is rather difficult to argue with the first main assertion there. It is self-evident that even if you know the grammar and the rules of communication of a given language, if you do not know enough vocabulary you will not be able to express yourself adequately. An analogy to this would be to know everything there is about riding a bicycle without actually being able to ride one, thus rendering the knowledge futile. The second general assertion that there has simply not been enough attention given to vocabulary over the years is arguably true in terms of the attention given to vocabulary in coursebooks and in methodology as a whole, but one wonders whether it has been neglected *in the classroom* to the extent that some of those quoted above seem to suggest. What emerges from the above statements, however, is that the spotlight has now fallen on vocabulary and more interest is now being taken in how it is taught, learned, acquired, stored, memorized and recalled. If this is the case, how does this growing interest reflect the views of learners and teachers on the subject of vocabulary?

Here are a few comments we got from learners:

This was really a terrible day – only two new words.

The lessons are best when the teacher gives us many new words.

I need to learn words and I need to know the translation. If I don't have the translation, I can't be sure if I have the correct meaning.

Sometimes the teacher doesn't tell us the meaning. He asks us to guess it. don't know why he does this.

I keep words in my notebook. I read them every day. Then I will learn.

It's clear to me. If I don't know the words, I don't understand.

Such comments are perhaps unsurprising. When asked about their language-learning needs, most learners refer to improving their speaking and listening and to learning grammar and vocabulary. Because progress can often be seen more clearly in terms of the number of words learned than in, for example, an unquantifiable ability to speak a little more fluently, vocabulary expansion is often cited by learners as their central interest. The learners quoted above (a group of young adult learners from various countries) seem to share the conviction that their basic need is vocabulary, and also share the same kind of frustration when they are not presented with the opportunity to 'learn' vocabulary. Progress and goals seem to be seen in terms of the number of words learned (and, by implication, taught). Apart from the desire to learn vocabulary, the above quotations also point to the individual nature of vocabulary learning, with one learner referring to the importance (for her) of translation, another referring to his dislike of guessing meaning, and a third indicating that her preferred learning method is repetition and reviewing vocabulary items. Even within such a small group, significant differences in learning preferences are revealed, pointing in turn to a number of considerations to be made when teaching vocabulary.

2　What kind of vocabulary teacher are you?

If, as suggested above, vocabulary is at the centre of attention in language teaching at the moment, and if this is clearly where many learners see their learning priorities as being firmly based, how then do we as teachers help our learners to acquire/learn/remember/use items of vocabulary? Where do we fit into the vocabulary-learning process? As a starting point, it might be worth reflecting on teachers' attitudes to vocabulary teaching.

Task 1

We talked to a number of practising teachers about vocabulary teaching in general. These are some of the comments they made. Make a note of those you identify with and those you disagree with:

a　*I always try to present new words in every lesson. I think my learners expect it.*
(ULI, GERMANY)

b　*I give my students a translation of every new word. They need it for their notebooks.*
(URSULA, GERMANY)

c　*I present vocabulary in a context wherever possible.*
(DOUG, USA)

d　*Wherever possible I present words with their collocations. I think this makes it more likely that my students will use the words correctly.*
(SABINE, BELGIUM)

e　*I often show my learners the relationships between particular items of vocabulary like opposites or synonyms. They seem to appreciate this.*
(HELENA, CZECH REPUBLIC)

f　*I think affixes are really important and we spend a lot of time working on word-building in general.*
(MARTIN, GERMANY)

g　*If I use a text in class, I usually exploit the vocabulary in it. I think texts are an excellent vehicle for introducing and recycling vocabulary.*
(JÜRGEN, GERMANY)

h　*I try to encourage my students to become more independent by making them guess the meaning of unknown words.*
(MARIA, SLOVAKIA)

i　*I encourage my learners to use dictionaries as much as possible. I think it really helps in vocabulary development and it can also make them much more autonomous in their learning.*
(NEIL, UK)

j　*I spend a lot of time giving stdents advice on how they can work on expanding their vocabulary in their own time.*
(HELEN, UK)

Commentary ■ ■ ■

a I always try to present new words in every lesson. I think my learners expect it.

An interesting comment in the light of the student comments cited earlier. Clearly, this teacher is concerned about the expectations and wishes of his students. In their perception, it seems, each lesson requires an element of *new* vocabulary, and the teacher teaches in a way that meets this need. It is worth pausing for a moment here, however, to consider the types of lessons in which you might consciously avoid teaching new vocabulary. A fluency-based lesson, perhaps? A discussion or debate? A roleplay or simulation? A reading lesson where your focus was fairly and squarely on reading skills and strategies? Possibly. Consider, too, the need to recycle known vocabulary and, perhaps more importantly, to reactivate previously learned vocabulary items that are lost somewhere deep in the recesses of the brain. As a rough guide, a regular dose of 'something new' seems to motivate most learners, but if everything is new and nothing is recycled or reactivated, then overload becomes a real possibility.

b I give my students a translation of every new word. They need it for their notebooks.

There are numerous (probably apocryphal) stories about teachers crawling about on the floor to illustrate (to a monolingual class) the meaning of some abstract term like *humiliating* or *exaggerated* and spending (or wasting) twenty minutes in the process. Translation seems another guilt area for some teachers. Someone, somewhere (probably in a position of some influence) suggested that translation was somehow a bad thing, to be avoided at all costs. This unwritten law then passed into the subconscious folklore of the language-teaching profession. Unfortunately, it takes no account whatsoever of the fact that most English teachers in the world share the same mother tongue as their learners. Avoiding translation at all costs is thus as absurd as telling teachers they have to wear green socks or that they should never sit down. Clearly translation is there as a useful tool when it is appropriate and constructive to use it.

In the case of an abstract word, when other means have failed or would be too time-consuming, translation is useful as a means of ensuring that learners leave the classroom with a correct understanding of the word in question. Some learners operate particularly effectively by relating lexical items to their L1 equivalents. This is their preferred way of learning vocabulary, the memory 'peg' on which they hang each new word. Attempts by teachers to interfere with, or even prohibit, this bilingual approach could have extremely negative effects on the motivation of such learners. On the other hand, we sometimes find that if translation is over-used as a technique for all the learners in a particular group, it can make them over-reliant on the teacher's translation, and thereby prevent them from experiencing the potentially valuable cognitive stage of discovering the meaning for themselves with the help of various clues.

c I present vocabulary in a context wherever possible.

Presenting vocabulary in context can be seen as important for two basic reasons. Firstly, the context itself can present an association for the learner that may help to trigger the recall of lexical items linked with this context. There is considerable evidence that many language learners are able to recall vocabulary by making mental associations with situational or contextual images. Research into memory has also shown that many people are able to recall lexical items more easily by association with a topic area. A second point in favour of contextualizing vocabulary is that it presents learners with a means of physically storing vocabulary items under a topic category, rather than in random or alphabetic lists.

d Wherever possible I present words with their collocations. I think this makes it more likely that my students will use the words correctly.

This, of course, will very much depend on the word. For a word like *large* this would clearly be an impossible task as it has so many collocations, but for a word like *petty*, this approach might be appropriate. When words have restricted meanings they are often only useful in conjunction with the words they actually do collocate with. In the case of *petty*, it has the meaning of *small* in a negative sense and collocates with a few nouns only, eg *cash*, *details*, *crime* and *thief*. It can thus be argued that if you are going to teach the word *petty*, then it is no use in isolation as it cannot be used to replace *small* with *any* noun. There is a case for teaching the more common collocations of certain words, particularly the nouns that go with certain adjectives, as well as the adverbial particles that go with particular verbs to form phrasal verbs and the prepositions that go with particular adjectives or nouns, eg <u>*heavy*</u> *smoker*, *note* <u>*down*</u> and *interested* <u>*in*</u>.

e I often show my learners the relationships between particular items of vocabulary like opposites or synonyms. They seem to appreciate this.

Some learners seem to thrive on opposites and synonyms. It's one way of categorizing items of vocabulary and giving then a reference point. In that respect these basic relationships serve a useful purpose for some learners. If you know the word *hot*, you might recall, through association, the word *cold*. They may be learned and remembered as a pair rather than as two random items of vocabulary. If you know *heiß* (hot) in German, you may recall *kalt* (cold) through association with *heiß* or through some other association, an association with *Eis*, for example, or with the English word *cold*. Although there may be some problems with both antonyms and synonyms (is *drunk* the true opposite of *sober*? Is *amazed* the same as *astonished*?), on balance presenting and storing words in pairs of some sort may well have a beneficial effect on memory and recall. (See Section 3 of this chapter for a discussion on the nature of synonyms.)

f I think affixes are really important and we spend a lot of time working on word-building in general.

English is particularly rich in affixes and a knowledge of their meaning and function can be of great benefit to teachers and learners alike. Such knowledge can help learners to generalize about the meaning of previously unknown words. For example, if a learner knows that the prefix *mis-* indicates *wrongly* or *incorrectly* and learns the word *misunderstand* on that basis, then he or she is in the position to deduce correctly the meaning of verbs such as *misspell*, *mishear*, *misinterpret* and *misinform*.

g If I use a text in class, I usually exploit the vocabulary in it. I think texts are an excellent vehicle for introducing and recycling vocabulary.

This may well be a question of learner perceptions. What is the average learner's perception of the use of a text in class? Learners will often see the text as a vehicle for the teaching of linguistic items – words, structures, functional exponents. It is just possible that they may see the text as a means of acquiring factual information (rather than linguistic information) and nothing else. It is also possible that they may see the text as a means of practising their own reading skills and strategies to the exclusion of any linguistic input.

The problem here appears to be twofold. In the first place, many teachers want their learners to read 'naturally' in the foreign language. And what is reading 'naturally'? Reading a text to extract 'real' information from it and not getting bogged down in the linguistic niceties of the text. How often have you caught yourself saying *Don't worry about the vocabulary. Just read the text*? Unfortunately, learners *do* worry about the vocabulary, as their own perception of the purpose of reading may well be linguistically-based.

The second problem is that learners will generally attack a text in the way that seems most appropriate and purposeful to them, rather than the way in which the teacher suggests they read the text. When you ask them to scan, they immediately take out their dictionaries and start looking up the meanings of words. Invite them to skim and they read intensively. Use a text for skimming and scanning exercises only and they 'home in' on all the difficult items of vocabulary you were praying inwardly they would not notice. A question of failed best intentions? Possibly. What often happens is that learners, quite justifiably, see a reading text as a particularly rich source of new vocabulary and react accordingly. Clearly, this can be a highly efficient way of exposing learners to new vocabulary items. Traditional it might be, but it is still extremely practical.

h   I try to encourage my students to become more independent by making them guess the meaning of unknown words.

The rationale behind this approach appears to be entirely sound. The learner 'arrives at' the meaning by working it out through contextual clues, morphological clues (see the discussion of statement **f**) and any other means at his or her disposal. A valid process and, possibly, a memorable one too. It can, however, be a frustrating process. It can produce either the wrong answer or no answer at all, and, if the latter is the frequent result of the over-zealous application of this technique by the teacher, a severe falling-off in motivation can follow. It is worth putting yourself in the learner's position to judge the impact of this approach. Try reading a text in a foreign language you know adequately but not well. Do not use a dictionary. Every time you encounter a new word, imagine a teacher asking you to work it out for yourself, guess the meaning or ignore the word because it isn't important. Note down how long it takes before you have to stop reading.

i   I encourage my learners to use dictionaries as much as possible. I think it really helps in vocabulary development and it can also make them much more autonomous in their learning.

As with translation, someone, somewhere deep in the mists of time began to broadcast the idea that it was somehow wrong to use dictionaries and that it was virtually a capital offence for learners to use bilingual dictionaries. Teachers should mime, draw, explain, illustrate, elicit, question, contextualize, but never translate and never allow learners to use bilingual dictionaries. They might a) get the wrong answer and b) become over-reliant on their mother-tongue. In the name of this dogma, dictionaries have been dashed from the hands of learners with enquiring minds! The anti-dictionarists overlook the fact that learners might also get the correct answer from using their dictionary and that contrastive elements may be important for certain learners in their own process of making sense of the foreign language. They also overlook the fact that dictionaries enable learners to be more autonomous. Monolingual dictionaries clearly have an important role to play and the better ones illustrate meaning clearly and carefully, but it is still asking a lot of an elementary level learner to rely solely on a monolingual dictionary and never to have recourse to a bilingual one. Anything that helps the learner learn in his or her own way is surely an asset. Next time you feel irritated when you see one of your learners leafing through a dictionary when you feel he or she should be listening to you, scanning a text or something similar, ask yourself what the learner is actually doing before you ask them to put their dictionary away. If you ask yourself the question, you'll probably leave them in peace.

j I spend a lot of time giving students advice on how they can work on expanding their vocabulary in their own time.

Some learners are quite happy to keep lists of words with the translation noted down beside each one. Others use word pools, mind maps, labelled pictures, random notes, word cards carried around in pockets, dictionaries, mnemonics, charts, diagrams, vocabulary exercises, word tables, synonyms and so on. How often do you look at their notebooks? Do you know the techniques they employ? You can help up to a point by making them aware of the different options (some of which are mentioned above). You can easily incorporate these into a vocabulary lesson and encourage learners to experiment and find the ones that suit them best, bearing in mind that they might continue to use word lists with translations!

So, what kind of vocabulary teacher are you? Do you deal with vocabulary as it arises in the classroom, responding to your learners' needs and explaining meaning where necessary and acting as a valuable resource for your students? Or do you take a systematic approach to vocabulary teaching and present items in particular groupings or in a certain order? Perhaps you steer a middle course, sometimes presenting vocabulary items in an interrelated way and at other times simply following the flow. If you do, however, adopt a more systematic approach, either consistently or occasionally, what are your criteria for grouping words together and how do you make sense for your learners of the mass of seemingly unrelated vocabulary that is the English language? ■

3 Patterns and relationships within the lexical system

How is the learner (and, for that matter, the teacher!) to make sense of the hundreds of thousands of words within the English language? How on earth can anyone begin to learn anything from what seems, at face value, to be a huge and random lexis? One approach is for teachers to enable learners to build on the many relationships that exist within the lexical system of English. In a sense, learners are already doing this when they ask whether a word is 'the same as' another word, or when they ask the teacher for an opposite. They themselves are seeking pegs to hang associations on, patterns within the language, stepping stones through the mire.

We designed the following task in order to bring out some of the relationships that exist between words. We have used it profitably with learners at an intermediate level and above and we have also found that it can raise a number of issues for teachers themselves.

Task 2

What vocabulary features are exemplified in the following groups of words?

a stride, walk, saunter, stroll, amble, stagger, trudge;
car, van, ambulance, bus, taxi, vehicle, jeep;

b blew/blue; bare/bear; peer/pier; break/brake; plane/plain; horde/hoard;

c issue; quarry; rest; return; miss; grip; fell; favour; cut;

d lead; wind; bow; record; suspect; rebel;

e difficult, hard, tough, exacting, demanding;
cross, irritated, furious, angry, apoplectic;
slumber, sleep, nap, kip;
friend, mate, colleague, comrade;

f drunk/sober; hot/cold; long/short; alive/dead; absent/present; buy/sell;
teacher/student; come/go;

g sense, nonsense, senseless, sensible, sensitivity, sensor;

h heavy smoker, big eater, hard drinker, keen sportsman;

i bookshop, car park, teapot, guitar string, matchbox, long-distance lorry driver;

j ship, anchor, sailor, bridge, porthole, navigate, deck, cargo.

Commentary ■ ■ ■

a The words here represent superordinates and hyponyms. In other words, one word in each group is a general word and all the other words are different types of that general word. In the case of the second group, for example, the superordinate (or headword) is *vehicle* and all the others are types of vehicle. They thus have a relationship with the superordinate (a car is a vehicle, a van is a vehicle, etc) and with each other through the superordinate (they are all vehicles), but they are not synonyms (a car is not a van, for example). One way of illustrating this is to draw a simple diagram:

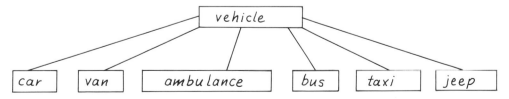

This illustrates the relationship between the hyponyms and the headword. This is also one way for learners to store vocabulary. You can ask them to make similar diagrams for other sets like these.

Another related activity is to invite learners to do exercises like the following:

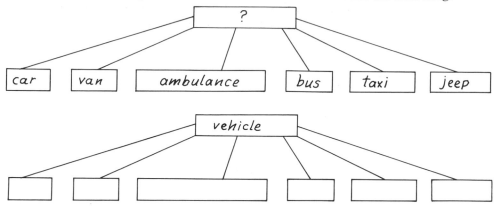

Similarly, you can ask them to find hyponyms for selected verbs, eg *throw*, *pull*, *look*, *think*, and so on.

b These are homophones, words which have a different spelling but share the same pronunciation. There are a large number of these in English and one way of helping learners to cope with the different spellings is to take the pronunciation as the starting point and encourage them to store items thus:

/blu:/   blue; blew
/mi:t/   meat; meet

With elementary level learners, we have also found it quite profitable to give them a list of words which have equivalent homophones and to invite them to guess or look up the homophones in question. This does produce incorrect suggestions at times, but if errors are seen as part of the process, the end probably justifies the means. An extract from the type of exercise we have used might look like this:

steal   _____
way   _____
stair   _____
tail   _____

c These are homonyms, words which share a single spelling but have many different meanings. The word *issue*, for example, has no fewer than ten meanings given in *The Shorter Oxford Dictionary*. One way that we have tried to help learners in this area is by encouraging them to use word pools and diagrams to store different meanings. For example:

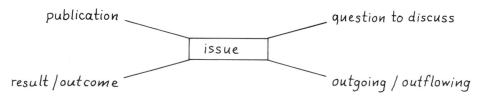

d Words with the same spelling but a different pronunciation are known as homographs. There are, fortunately, a limited number of these in English, and apart from familiarizing learners with the different pronunciations of the most important ones (eg *read* /ri:d/ and /red/), there is not much mileage here. One important area, however, is the noun/verb distinction with certain words, with a consequent effect on stress and on pronunciation. One way we have tried to help learners with this is by classifying them into different groups:

Noun	Verb
■ ▪	▪ ■
suspect	suspect
subject	subject
record	record

e The words in each group in this section are, broadly speaking, synonyms. It can be argued that there is no such thing as a true synonym. Mario Rinvolucri argues quite forcibly in an article entitled 'Concepts that warp me' that 'no word can ever be synonymous with another in just the same way as identical twins are not carbon copies of one another'. If there are two words for something, then they normally indicate, at the very least, a different shade of meaning. This is illustrated in the first set. If something is *difficult*, it is not necessarily *tough*. The latter suggests more physical effort. To help learners clarify the difference, a context or collocation is needed for each one.

In the second group, we are concerned with points on a scale of anger. Clearly, *irritated* and *furious* are not at the same levels of anger. We have sometimes introduced these differences by getting learners to devise their own scales. A scale for heat would look like this:

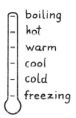

boiling
hot
warm
cool
cold
freezing

Others we have used include degrees of surprise, degrees of pleasure, degrees of sadness and adverbs of frequency, but no doubt a similar procedure can be applied to numerous other adjectives and adverbs.

The third group in this set have the added element of formality. They are, broadly speaking, synonymous, but *kip* is far more informal than *sleep*. Likewise, the *friend* words in the last group are differentiated both by formality and connotation. *Colleague* has working associations, while *comrade* is a friend in adversity or in a struggle of some kind.

f These are all opposites of some kind, but there are distinctions between each group. The first group shows examples of gradable antonyms. These are not 'true' opposites but points on a scale. A test for these is to say, for example, *If something isn't long, is it short?* There are a number of intermediate points on each scale. The only real lesson for learners here is that, while opposites may be useful as a learning 'peg', they may be misleading and other useful vocabulary may lie on each scale line.

If we apply the above 'test', then the second group are true opposites. If you are not alive, you must by definition be dead, except, possibly, in a metaphorical sense! Likewise, someone who is not absent is by definition present. There are very few of these pairs of true opposites.

The third group represents examples of converse actions rather than opposites. Some learners find 'opposites' useful as a means of recalling vocabulary items, so we do not discourage this kind of word association, irrespective of whether the opposites they store are 'true' opposites or not!

g This set of examples shows us some features of affixation in English. Based on the root word *sense* we have a number of new words formed by adding either prefixes or suffixes to the root. This changes both the word class (eg noun – adjective) and the meaning (eg *sense – nonsense*). As mentioned in Section 2 of this chapter, this aspect of vocabulary is often neglected. In our own experience of learning foreign languages (eg Swedish, German, Czech and Polish) there is great benefit in learners developing an active awareness of the meanings and functions conveyed by different affixes.

h These are examples of collocations, words which 'go together'. For a brief discussion of this aspect of the lexical system of English, see **d** in Section 2 of this chapter.

i These are examples of compounds in English. Like other Germanic languages, but unlike Romance languages, for example, English has the facility to form words by adding one word to another. To give some general categories, these are most commonly noun + noun compounds to form another noun (eg *tea + pot = teapot*), various combinations of verbal noun (gerund) + noun to form another noun (eg *sun + bathing = sunbathing*; *spending + money = spending money*), and noun + adjective or participle compounds to form adjectives (*home + sick = homesick*; *law + abiding = law-abiding*).

It is certainly worth devoting some attention to this phenomenon of English, as it can be a fruitful way of expanding vocabulary. This may also help to avoid clumsy constructions such as *a machine for washing*, *the leg of the table* and *the screen of the television*, which tend to be the types of errors made by learners whose mother tongue is French, Italian, Spanish or another of the Romance languages.

We sometimes help learners to practise this aspect of English through simple matching exercises and also by getting them to replace 'clumsy' expressions with more concise compound equivalents. Another useful pointer for learners is to be aware that the stress in compounds where the first element is, broadly speaking, a noun, tends to fall on that first element. For an extensive and entertaining list of different types of compounds in English see Quirk and Greenbaum, *A University Grammar of English*, Appendix 1.

j This last group is an example of a word family or topic area. These are words connected by context or theme. In this case, the words are clearly all connected with the word *ship*, but, unlike the hyponym/superordinate relationship exemplified in **a** above, they are not specific examples of the headword. A *porthole* is clearly not a *ship* and vice-versa!

We have found a certain amount of benefit ourselves in learning foreign language vocabulary in this way, and there may similarly be some profit for certain learners in seeing or being taught words grouped together in a word family. This, after all, is the technique used in picture dictionaries. Some learners appear to learn through visual stimuli and association, so storing words in this way may be of some merit. A practical technique that in our experience usually works well is to present such items in the form of a 'mind map' (a bigger version of the type seen under **c** above), which can be added to and expanded whenever a new word crops up that is related to the word family. We sometimes get our learners to do these in the form of coloured wall posters which are then displayed permanently in class as both a memory aid and a visual stimulus.

It is useful for teachers to be aware of the above relationships within the lexical system. They can also be exploited for teaching and learning purposes and can be used both to generate vocabulary exercises and to form the basis for storing vocabulary in word groups. Focusing on relationships, however tenuous some of these might seem, can give learners *something* to hang on to in the vast ocean of apparently unconnected vocabulary. This is, arguably, particularly important for those learners whose mother tongue differs radically from English and who have few, if any, points of contact to help vocabulary acquisition. ■

4 Learning words – the roles of image, association and memory

If you look at foreign language coursebooks of the more traditional type, eg those used to teach French, German and so on in British secondary schools in the fifties and sixties, you cannot help being struck by the way in which vocabulary is treated in most of these. There are lists. Lists and translations. Random lists. Typically, a text followed by a list of words with their English translations. Sometimes, the words are not even in the text. The words in the list are often juxtaposed for no apparent reason. Here is a typical random example taken from the vocabulary list of a Hungarian coursebook:

távirat	telegram	*mégis*	nevertheless
megbotlik	stumble	*rövidlátó*	short-sighted

One would be hard-pressed to find any link there, although two of the words appear in an associated text. Unsurprisingly, the experience of many learners exposed to such materials and to the list-based vocabulary learning technique is that learning words in a foreign language is a difficult and even painful process. It certainly does not have pleasurable associations. Such memories are often passed on by teachers to their own learners in the form of a rather grudging attitude to vocabulary and, frequently, through the feeling that as it was boring for us, it must be boring for them. Memorizing vocabulary lists, testing memory via the use of gap-fill vocabulary exercises, translating endless lists of words. Little wonder that many learners exposed to such approaches quickly become demotivated.

The main problem we have found with the list-learning approach to vocabulary is that it is based on only one aspect of memory, namely that items are memorized by means of repetition and testing. This approach takes no account of the power of memory and the numerous ways in which the memory may be triggered by stimuli of various kinds. Similarly, like any other universally applied approach, it fails to take account of individual learning styles and whether a particular learner is more likely to respond to methods other than list plus translation. Finally, the typically random nature of such lists tends to ignore the potential of the relationships within the lexical system that could also help learners to remember words through association. In this section, we shall examine some of the associations that may help learners remember vocabulary, in particular the power of images and metaphor.

Investigations into the power of the human memory tend to reveal that the short-term memory is very limited indeed. If you need evidence of this try the following simple task:

Task 3

Think of a friend whose phone number you do not know. Look up the number in the telephone directory and repeat it to yourself two or three times. Then do something else – continue reading this book, for example. Twenty minutes later, try to write down the telephone number.

If you have forgotten the number, you are not alone, and there is nothing wrong with your memory. The same thing happens when, for example, we are given a name or a number on the telephone and we do not have a pen to hand. Often, in the short transition period from completing the telephone call to finding pen and paper, we find that we have forgotten the message. Stevick, in *Memory, Meaning and Method* (pp 23–4) cites the example of a friend taking a message over the phone from a Mr Feigenbaum. Having no pen, the friend committed the name Feigenbaum to memory, only to pass it on in the message as Flaggenheisch. Clearly, he had remembered that the name sounded German, had three syllables and that it began with 'f', but little else. The short-term memory appears to be notoriously inefficient.

The significance of this for language teachers is that testing lexical items shortly after they have been presented to learners may often be a fruitless exercise. The most recently presented words are frequently the ones that cannot be recalled. A certain amount of repetition is likely to be necessary before there is any hope of retention. When a word is retained, and thus passes into the long-term memory, it is highly probable that the learner has been able to retain the word not only as a result of repetition but through some kind of association. The long-term memory is capable of playing some extraordinary tricks. How often do you suddenly remember something, a word, a name, a word in a foreign language, and wonder where on earth that particular word or name came from and how and why you suddenly remembered it? Something, an image, a sound, a context, has triggered the association and unlocked the deepest recesses of your brain, wherein lurks the word in question. Similarly, you will almost certainly have experienced the frustrating feeling of having a word 'on the tip of your tongue'. In this latter situation, the association has been triggered but not completely, leaving you tantalizingly close to the word you are seeking.

If we can identify some of the associations that help us to memorize and recall words, then this may help us to include in our classroom practice ways of making words more memorable in themselves. We may also be able to help learners to store vocabulary in ways that suit their own particular memory styles, as illustrated in the task that follows.

Task 4

Think about the ways in which you memorize and recall words in a foreign language that you know. What associations help you to remember and recall these words?

Commentary ▪ ▪ ▪

We asked a group of teachers on an in-service training course the same questions and this produced the following suggestions:

a By association with a mental image or picture.

The visual element is clearly important in vocabulary teaching. Most teachers will at some stage use pictures or realia to present vocabulary items. Those learners whose learning style has a strong visual element may well also benefit from storing vocabulary in coloured mind-maps or labelled diagrams and from the use of picture dictionaries.

b By association with a situation, topic or story.

Words are often remembered within the context of the particular story or situation in which they were first encountered. The memorability of fairy tales bears witness to this. The presentation of vocabulary items through stories or in a topic-orientated context can be of benefit to learners in terms of memorization, as can storing vocabulary in a topic-based way rather than at random. As a practical teaching strategy, this can be used to work on memory and recall if, for example, learners are asked to write down all the words they associate with a particular topic, situation or story.

c By association with a need of some kind (personal significance).

Words associated with direct personal need are usually memorable as a result of constant use or exposure. Clearly, such words will vary from individual to individual and are likely to differ according to the learning situation (in an English-speaking country or in one's own environment). Basic function words (*push*/*pull*/*exit*/*danger*) and classroom language (*borrow*/*repeat*/*open*/*write*) will probably be recycled often enough for them to pass into the long-term memory. A colleague of ours learned (very quickly) and retained just one word of Czech – *pivo* (beer). Clearly, it was of great personal significance.

d By association with another word (same language; native language).

Such associations may take the form of a link with the word's equivalent in the mother tongue or in a third language, an association with a collocation in the target language (*dense fog*; *fish and chips*), an association with a synonym or opposite, or an association with another word in the same lexical set (*sense*/*sensitive*/*senseless*). Learners may also be able to make analogies with words in their mother tongue, particularly if there is some direct philological link (Czech *sestra*, English *sister*). Words may look or sound similar across the two languages, irrespective of whether they share the same meaning, and this can also be of great help as a memory aid (Czech *peníze*, meaning *money*, bears a strong resemblance to the English word *penny*; similarly, *med*, meaning *honey*, and *mead*).

Word origins can be extremely interesting to some learners, and if the origin of a word is particularly striking for some reason, this too can help memory and recall (for example, *assassin = eater of hashish*; *zodiac = circle of little animals*, association with *zoo*; *creosote = flesh-preserver*). Learners may also be interested in the origins of English words if there are words which originate in their own mother tongue (eg Arabic: *admiral, algebra, alkali, alcohol, magazine, sofa, mohair, sherbet, artichoke, alcove, tambourine, tariff*).

Another productive area for interest, discussion and vocabulary-building is helping learners to identify English words that have passed into their own languages and then looking at differences between them. What are the differences in spelling? What differences are there in the pronunciation in the two languages? Are the words exactly the same in meaning? Are the words 'false friends'? (eg *Büro, Fotograf* and *Spektakel* in German = *office, photographer* and *noise*, respectively and not their more obvious English equivalents). They may be completely unaware of words in their own language derived from English, and focusing on some of these words may help them to internalize the English equivalents, eg Japanese: *sarada* (salad), *songu* (song), *apaato* (apartment), *furai pan* (frying pan), *kabaa* (cover).

Comparing the use of metaphor and idiom across languages can prove memorable to some learners (English *to kill two birds with one stone*, Czech *to kill two flies with one blow*; English *love me, love my dog*, Czech *love me, love my friends*). The sheer vividness of metaphors and idioms in English can in itself prove memorable (*as sober as a judge, looking for a needle in a haystack, to beaver away at one's work*), and a comparison with the images used in the L1 equivalents may be a profitable line to follow.

The suggestion here is that a teacher who bothers to investigate the links and the differences between English and the language of his or her students (not such a difficult task with a good bilingual dictionary and a paperback etymological dictionary) can not only provide his or her learners with some valuable insights, but can also help to provide some associations that might aid memory and recall of vocabulary items in the future. The overall aim of this is to promote awareness of similarities and differences between lexical items in the learner's own language and English, to make the learning load lighter through identifying points of contact, to enhance the learner's appreciation of the diverse origins of English and to exploit any interest in this as a means of making lexical items more memorable.

e By association with a feeling (positive; negative).

Certain words have the power to promote strong feelings and associations. Adjectives, in particular, can often be divided, subjectively, into categories such as positive, negative and neutral in the feelings they engender. As a first stage in the memorization process, it may be of some practical benefit to learners confronted with a reading text, for example, to decide which words in the text they would place in each of these categories. This will not, of course, clarify the exact meaning of each word, but can act as a useful starting point in the process of memorization and recall.

f By association with a smell, sound or movement.

What is the first smell you remember? What smells do you associate with primary school? What smells do you associate with summertime? All the senses appear to have powerful associations and it is possible to make use of these to reactivate vocabulary. Smell and sound seem to be particularly productive in this respect, and the imagery they convey can be channelled successfully into the brainstorming and recall of vocabulary.

Movement too may have its associations. It has been suggested that a poem, for example, which is learned by a group of learners to the accompaniment of physical movements (*look round* and the learners look round) will be remembered more successfully than one learned without any such associations. A classroom technique that can easily be used is that of telling stories with a physical accompaniment to the actions in the story. The association of the movements with both the events in the story itself and with the vocabulary items used to express these events should have a very positive effect on memory and recall. When we tried this with a group of German secondary school teachers, initial inhibitions were soon overcome and the complex (because of their high level of language competence) vocabulary items introduced in the 'moving story' were recalled very quickly and accurately several days later.

g By the word in question being memorable in itself for some reason.

Some words are just memorable in themselves. You probably have a favourite word in a foreign language. It may stick in your memory because it sounds strange or, perhaps, because it sounds beautiful. Its sound may suggest an unusual or vivid image. Here are some examples of memorable words we elicited from a group of Belgian teachers:

sausage	*jeopardize*	*hanky-panky*	*roundabout*
flabbergasted	*hippopotamus*	*rusticate*	*traffic jam*

In this particular case, interest in the sound, and then the meaning, of the word *hanky-panky* led to a very productive discussion of other reversatives in English (examples from the group included *higgledy-piggledy*, *willy-nilly* and *helter-skelter*). The teachers in question liked these words because they 'sound funny'.

Making use of the different kinds of mental associations discussed above can both extend teachers' range of options when presenting vocabulary and also give teachers more chance of being in touch with individual learners' preferred learning styles. Introducing into this an element of comparison with the L1 of the learners (cognates, analogies, words of parallel development, words of similar origin, English words in the L1 and L1 words in English) may also help to enrich learners' vocabulary and enhance their powers of recall.

5 Conclusions

Words are the basis of language, and thus the basis of communication. Without words, it is possible to know everything about the grammatical structure of a language, but yet to be unable to make a single meaningful utterance. In the perception of many learners, learning a language equals learning its vocabulary and they certainly perceive this to be the reason for, for example, reading texts in class, whatever the teacher's perceptions of the reasons may be. Our role as teachers of vocabulary is to help (pointing out patterns and similarities), to advise (helping learners to discover ways of storing and retrieving vocabulary items), to motivate and encourage (applying different techniques and media for presenting vocabulary, making vocabulary memorable), and even to inspire (encouraging in learners an appreciation of the origin, sound and beauty of words).

6 Recommended reading

The Dictionary of Word Origins by John Ayto presents a fascinating and often amusing account of the origins of hundreds of English words.

Working with Words by Gairns and Redman gives a clear overview of theoretical and practical issues with many examples of activity types.

Vocabulary by Michael McCarthy presents a large number of tasks which guide the reader through an exploration of the nature of vocabulary, the ways in which vocabulary is learned and stored, and classroom applications of these issues.

7 References and bibliography

Ayto, J. 1990 *The Dictionary of Word Origins* (Bloomsbury)
Bryson, B. 1990 *Mother Tongue – The English Language* (Penguin)
Claiborne, R. 1990 *The Life and Times of the English Language* (Bloomsbury)
Evans, I. 1990 *Brewer's Dictionary of Phrase and Table*, fourteenth edition (Cassell)
Gairns, R. and Redman, S. 1986 *Working with Words: A Guide to Teaching and Learning Vocabulary* (CUP)
Hendrickson, R. 1987 *Encyclopaedia of Word and Phrase Origins* (Facts on File)
Hoad, T. 1986 *The Concise Oxford Dictionary of English Etymology* (OUP)
McCarthy, M. 1990 *Vocabulary* (Oxford)
McCrum, R., Cran, W. and MacNeil, R. 1992 *The Story of English*, revised edition (Faber)
Quirk, R. and Greenbaum, S. 1973 *A University Grammar of English* (Longman)
Rinvolucri, M. 1993 Concepts that Warp Me. In *Modern English Teacher*, vol. 2, no. 1
Rudzka, B., Channell, J., Ostyn, P. and Putseys, Y. 1981 *The Words You Need* (Macmillan)
Skeat, W. 1978 *A Concise Etymological Dictionary of the English Language* (OUP)
Stevick, E. 1976 *Memory, Meaning and Method* (Newbury House)
Viereck, W. and Bald, W. 1986 *English in Contact with Other Languages* (Akadémiai Kiadó, Budapest)
Wilkins, D. 1972 *Linguistics in Language Teaching* (Arnold)

Chapter 8 **Scanning the horizon:**
Reflections on reading in a foreign language

1 Introduction

Reading in the classroom is a waste of time. I can do it at home.
(ULRIKE, SWITZERLAND)

Millions of people learn to communicate perfectly adequately in all kinds of languages without ever reading a single word. Indeed, this has been the case throughout history, and it is only comparatively recently that the written word has assumed a more prominent role in the affairs of human beings. People have always managed to communicate and even educate themselves without recourse to reading, and still do. Many native speakers of English, for example, would regard themselves as non-readers, even if they are not actually illiterate. They would point out that they can get their information from other media such as television and radio and that reading a novel, for example, would be an activity that they would never even consider. For many native speakers, reading is a peripheral activity and one that they rarely engage in as a conscious process.

The foreign language learner is in a somewhat different position. Of course, it can once again be argued, with some conviction, that there are numerous examples of people who can communicate in a variety of foreign languages without ever having read a word in any of them. Street traders in multi-ethnic communities seem to be able to switch effortlessly from one tongue to another depending on the mother tongue of their clients. Clearly, reading has played no part in their language acquisition process. For those language learners who have learned a foreign language in the more formal environment of a school, however, reading is almost certain to have played some part in their learning. It may simply have been a case of reading language examples written on a blackboard and then copying them into a notebook, or, at the opposite end of the spectrum, they may have studied literature as a part of their language course and read literary extracts or even novels and plays. In such cases reading has been seen as a means to an end, a means of acquiring language, and usually lexis.

In more recent times, learners may have been subjected to a reading programme specifically designed to improve their reading skills and strategies as methodologists turn their attention to reading skills development in the foreign language and attempt to draw parallels with mother tongue skills. It is now difficult to envisage a language-teaching programme without any reading whatsoever, devoid of even such basic elements as a coursebook, a teacher who writes examples on a board, and texts or dialogues to contextualize language items.

There remain, however, a number of grey areas in reading in a foreign language. How similar to the mother tongue reading process is it? Does the added factor of a different linguistic system make the process entirely different? Do we have to teach reading skills and strategies from the very beginning simply because the language is a different one? Is the reading of authentic material a desirable and realistic goal? Are learners (and teachers, for that matter) clear about the purpose of reading in a language-learning programme? This chapter will attempt to address these questions by clarifying the role of foreign language reading and suggesting ways in which it can be incorporated purposefully into the language-learning process as a whole.

2   What kind of reading teacher are you?

Task 1 – Part A

Read the answers to the following question and rank them in order of the priority you attach to each. Add to the list if there are any which you feel are omitted here.

Why do you use text-based activities with your learners?

a To improve vocabulary ☐

b To enable your learners to comprehend coursebook texts ☐

c To improve their all-round language ability ☐

d To show learners examples of language in context ☐

e As a model for writing ☐

f To improve your learners' ability to read authentic texts ☐

g To enable your learners to read particular text types using the strategy or ☐
strategies most appropriate to those text types

h To expand and extend your learners' range of reading skills and strategies ☐

i To encourage your learners to appreciate literature in English ☐

j _____ ☐

Look at your responses to the above task and see whether the emphasis in your use of reading-based activities is on using reading as a means to practise and consolidate language, or whether the main aim is to work on improving your learners' actual ability to obtain information and gain pleasure from reading in English.

Now we shall move on to address the question of whether you actually teach reading at all. What does it mean to *teach* reading in a foreign language?

Task 1– Part B

Read the following questions related to using reading in the foreign language classroom and note down your views on each one.

1 Do you use 'traditional' texts with comprehension questions in your teaching?

2 What do you regard as the main purpose or purposes of such texts and the questions that go with them?

3 Do you set questions before your learners read a text? If so, why?

4 If you select a text for your learners to read, what criteria do you employ for its selection?

5 Do you ask your learners to read graded (ie simplified) reading material?

6 Do you use examples of authentic reading material?

7 Do you work on the development of your learners' cognitive reading skills (eg the ability to predict)?

8 Do you work on the development of reading strategies such as skimming and scanning?

9 If you answered *yes* to question 8, what techniques do you use to work on these strategies?

10 Do you encourage your learners to read outside the classroom?

11 Do you try to develop in your learners an appreciation of literature in English?

Commentary ■ ■ ■

Let us begin by trying to establish what it is that you actually teach when you teach 'reading'. If in Part A you ticked **a, b, c, d** and **e**, but not **f, g** and **h**, and in Part B you have answered *yes* to question **1** and *no* to questions **7** and **8**, it can be argued that you do not actually teach reading directly at all. You use texts in your classes, of course, and your learners read them, answer questions and, probably, do language-related tasks, such as vocabulary exercises based on the text. In a sense, you are enabling them to *practise* reading by giving them the opportunity to do so, and, in a certain sense, you may be helping them to read more effectively in the future by developing their linguistic skills (eg passive vocabulary recognition) to some degree, however small. You are not, however, consciously working on the development of your learners' reading skills and strategies. You are not working on what Nuttall calls *text-attack skills*.

If, on the other hand, you ticked **f, g** and **h** in the first task and have answered *yes* to questions **7** and **8** in the second, it is likely that you pay at least some attention to factors affecting your learners' ability to tackle texts in English in much the same way that they would approach similar texts in their mother tongue. You may, for example, encourage them to read texts such as newspaper articles quickly in order to get the gist or general idea. Similarly, you may ask your learners to make suppositions about what they are about to read on the basis of expectations, previous knowledge, non-linguistic clues and so on. If you do such things, even if it is only from time to time, it can be argued that you are working on the actual skills and strategies involved in reading development. In that sense you are teaching reading.

Is this an important distinction? It might be, both for teachers and learners alike. For teachers, it might be important to be clear about the aims of using texts in class (and outside class), so that they can determine the appropriate balance for individual readers between reading for language development and reading for skills development. If teachers can make the distinction between the two overall aims of reading, then they may be in a better position to judge whether individual learners in fact need any skills development at all and whether time is not better spent on language development such as vocabulary expansion. A case in point would be a learner with a good reading ability in his or her mother tongue, a mother tongue with a similar rhetorical structure to English and the clear ability to apply the mother tongue reading strategies in English. For such a learner, time spent performing mechanical scanning tasks, such as extracting information from timetables, might well be regarded as time wasted.

Similarly, a recognition of the need to work on reading skills and strategies with learners who are unable to apply appropriate strategies to particular text types might also emerge from a recognition of this distinction. A case in point would be a learner with a low level of reading ability in his or her mother tongue, a mother tongue with a radically different rhetorical structure to English (possibly a different alphabet and very different formats for established written forms such as menus or directories), and an inability to apply mother tongue reading strategies in English. For such a learner, the instinctive reaction to a written text in English is to attempt to read it word by word, in other words *intensively*, when such a strategy might be wholly inappropriate.

The above cases are clearly polarized extremes. Many learners are likely to need work in both areas of reading, ie language *and* skills development. The essential question for both teachers and learners is that of emphasis. If this is inappropriate and too much attention is devoted by the teacher to the aspect which the learner does not perceive as a problem, then a lot of frustration will ensue. Thus, both learners and teachers will benefit from a clear realization on both sides of the aims of reading in a foreign language. If there is a plea in the above, then it is a plea for openness, for discussion of the issues between teachers and learners and, ultimately, as we shall see later in this chapter, for learner-centred reading programmes. ■

We asked a number of teachers, native and non-native speakers, the same set of questions. Here is a brief selection of their replies. Read through their comments and compare them with your own comments. Make a note of any responses that you particularly agree or disagree with.

1 Do you use 'traditional' texts with comprehension questions in your teaching?

Of course I do. They are in the coursebooks we use. There's nothing wrong with using them, is there? The students can learn a lot of vocabulary.
(IVO, AUSTRIA)

I do use such texts. I think the students expect it. For me the real problem is that I don't like asking the questions afterwards and I get the feeling they don't like it either.
(JOHN, UK)

Yes. It's difficult to avoid them. They're in all the coursebooks. I think learners like reading them. The only problem is that sometimes the topics are very boring.
(MAGDA, GERMANY)

The texts aren't natural and it isn't normal to ask questions when you read something in your mother tongue. I don't like these texts because they're language-bound. They have nothing to do with real reading and the students don't choose them.
(SEAN, UK)

2 What do you regard as the main purpose or purposes of such texts and the questions that go with them?

Well ... making sure they understand. You need to know the kind of language they can understand, so you know what you need to teach them.
(LOREDANA, ITALY)

Vocabulary and seeing grammatical structures in context. It's reinforcement of both really.
(JOHN, UK)

A different kind of practice. It takes me out of the spotlight and lets them work on their own at their own pace. There's a lot of value in that.
(HUGHIE, UK)

I suppose it's simply to give them more practice. It's a kind of comprehension test too.
(PETAR, CROATIA)

3 Do you ever set questions before your learners read a text? If so, why?

Well, it's the done thing, isn't it? It's what they always tell you to do on teacher training courses! I suppose I do it now almost by instinct. I don't really think about why, but it's better than asking the questions afterwards. The students like it more.
(HELEN, UK)

Yes, nearly always. I try to set a few general questions which will give them an idea of the main theme of the text, the answers I mean, not the questions.
(ROLF, SWEDEN)

Yes, I always do this with texts. It's to give them a reason to read the text. They wouldn't want to read it if there were no questions.
(STEVE, USA)

I make sure the students read through all the comprehension questions in the coursebook before they read the text. Then they sort of 'scan' for the answers. I think that's really important.
(SVEN, SWEDEN)

4 If you select a text for your learners to read, what criteria do you employ for its selection?

I don't usually select texts myself. I use the texts in the coursebook, so t he book selects them for me.
(NIKI, GREECE)

Well, above all, interest. I can deal with complicated vocabulary, idiom, slang and so on. If the text is interesting, most learners will want to read it.
(BARRY, UK)

Topicality. I think it's natural for learners to want to get real information from what they read. News items are the obvious answer. The problem with coursebooks is that the texts are obviously not topical.
(MARCOS, GREECE)

My main criterion is that the learners will understand it without too much difficulty. If it's too difficult, they'll simply give up.
(VERA, CZECH REPUBLIC)

5 Do you ask your learners to read graded (ie simplified) reading material?

Sometimes, but I usually feel a bit embarrassed about it. I mean, the texts are usually a bit childish and I'm sure the learners, even at elementary level, can see that.
(JOHN, UK)

Of course. It's nice when they can understand everything. It helps their confidence. Graded readers are important as a kind of stepping stone to the real thing.
(VERA, CZECH REPUBLIC)

Yes. Such texts usually illustrate grammatical structures in context more clearly than authentic examples.
(LOREDANA, ITALY)

I try not to. I mean, apart from learning vocabulary and grammar, there's no point in reading them. To me Catch 22 *or something in twenty-five pages using two hundred words is a daft idea. Why not wait until you can read the real thing?*
(HUGHIE, UK)

6 Do you use examples of authentic reading material?

I would like to, but I can't find them easily and it takes so long to prepare.
(IVO, AUSTRIA)

Yes, whenever I can. I use newspapers a lot because students are interested in them and it motivates them to buy and read newspapers themselves.
(HELEN, UK)

Sometimes, but I find my learners get fed up trying to read things like small ads and they get frustrated when there's so much they don't understand. A lot of authentic stuff is really boring!
(SEAN, UK)

I try to use a variety of authentic material from adverts and things like that to newspapers and magazines. I think the variety of the language is the important thing. It gives students so much more than coursebook texts can give.
(JOHN, UK)

7 Do you work on the development of your learners' cognitive reading skills (eg the ability to predict)?

I usually ask them to predict content from headlines or pictures and so on. We do this in real life and I think it makes it easier for them to understand the text if they have a rough idea of what it's going to be about.
(BARRY, UK)

I do, but I get the feeling my students don't like it. They expect me to ask them about pictures and so on and build their expectations. I sometimes think it's unnecessary.
(MAGDA, GERMANY)

Of course. I ask them to say what they know about the topic first. This makes the reading easier.
(IVO, AUSTRIA)

I do this at first, but later I expect them to apply these things themselves. When they get used to the idea, I don't see any reason for me to interfere.
(SEAN, UK)

8 Do you work on the development of reading strategies such as skimming and scanning?

Scanning, yes. Especially with authentic texts. We always do this first.
(HELEN, UK)

I do, but it's difficult to stop learners reading everything. They want to know the meaning of every new word.
(NIKI, GREECE)

I try but it doesn't work too well with texts in coursebooks. Scanning maybe, but skimming isn't so easy to organize. Some texts don't have anything to scan for!
(SVEN, SWEDEN)

My students get really bored if I ask them to scan a menu, for example. They don't see the point in it and it's very easy for them.
(IVO, AUSTRIA)

9 If you answered 'yes' to question 8, what techniques do you use to work on these strategies?

With scanning I ask them to find, say, ten pieces of information from the television page in a newspaper.
(HELEN, UK)

For skimming, I usually ask them to read the text quickly and then say what it's about. With scanning it's usually a case of finding the answer to a few questions as quickly as possible without reading the whole text.
(MARCOS, GREECE)

It's a bit of a problem, really. I don't like to set scanning questions, because they are my questions then, not their questions, so why should they want to find the answers to them? Skimming activities are all a bit artificial, like choose a title or match a text with a picture. It's all a bit unsatisfactory as far as I'm concerned.
(SEAN, UK)

We talk about how they would read certain kinds of material in their mother tongue. Then we try and apply the same strategies in English, with things like menus, timetables, newspaper articles and so on.
(ROLF, SWEDEN)

10 Do you encourage your learners to read outside the classroom?

Of course, but I don't think they listen. I tell them it's useful, but they still don't do it. They only read if I give them a text for homework.
(LOREDANA, ITALY)

We talk about the benefits of reading – vocabulary expansion, learning idioms, seeing structures in context and so on, but I think they find reading at home in a foreign language boring. That's the problem.
(IVO, AUSTRIA)

I try to find their interests and then suggest they read magazines and so on in English about these interests. I think it's important that they actually learn something from what they read, something that isn't necessarily language.
(MAGDA, GERMANY)

11 Do you try to develop in your learners an appreciation of literature in English?

Literary appreciation is something I try to encourage. At higher levels they should read novels in English and it will expand their vocabulary as well.
(VERA, CZECH REPUBLIC)

I suppose I do try to do this. Actually, it is probably my ultimate goal in language teaching. If my students can read an English novel easily, then my job is complete.
(ALICE, UK)

I'd like to but there are other more important priorities in my teaching. I feel it would be largely fruitless anyway.
(KURT, SWEDEN)

Commentary ■ ■ ■

The above quotations from a cross-section of teachers working in a number of different teaching environments and with learners of various profiles seem to reveal a few generalizations. Most teachers, it seems, use 'traditional' coursebook texts some of the time, although there appears to be a feeling amongst some teachers that this is not quite 'right'. There is a feeling that, although the use of such texts may have a number of aims, the asking of comprehension questions afterwards is inappropriate. Many teachers appear to get round this by setting questions beforehand and they also do this to encourage students to read for gist or scan for specific information. Interest and topicality are cited as criteria for selecting texts for learners to read, but so are level of language and the fact that texts are in the coursebook. Graded texts are seen as childish and over-simplified on the one hand, but as a means of confidence-building and contextualizing language items on the other. Authentic materials, likewise, are regarded as motivating and a rich source of varieties of language by some, and frustrating for learners and difficult to use for teachers by others. Some teachers appear to regard scanning, in particular, as a rather mechanical strategy but one that nonetheless needs to be practised. Others regard education and training in the application of L2 reading skills and strategies as important. Reading outside the classroom is seen as desirable but difficult to achieve in practical terms.

The above views are intended as a fairly representative cross-section of opinion. Of course, in some cases, they represent opposite sides of a single argument (the use of authentic materials is one example of this), but they do seem to indicate that there are a number of questions in the teaching of reading that leave some teachers with a feeling that something is missing. Perhaps this lies in the fact that whereas teachers can exercise considerable control over what their learners say and write, they have much less control over how they read and what they get from that reading. Helping learners to get the maximum benefit from reading as an activity must surely be every teacher's goal, but the question remains as to how this is best achieved. In the rest of this chapter, we will attempt to suggest some ways of maximizing the potential of reading both as a classroom activity and as an external activity. ■

3 Feelings about the way you teach reading and what you teach

Task 2

Tick any of the boxes that reflect your own feelings about the way you teach reading or use reading materials in your classes:

☐ developmental	☐ haphazard	☐ systematic
☐ random	☐ thorough	☐ progressive
☐ traditional	☐ adequate	☐ unsatisfactory
☐ good enough	☐ uninspiring	☐ purposeful
☐ positive	☐ varied	☐ light

Now write some adjectives of your own:

––––––––––   ––––––––––

Task 3 – Part A

If you have ticked any of the more 'negative sounding' boxes, try to focus on your reasons for doing so and relate your feelings to what you actually do in your classroom practice. For an experimental period (one month, say) keep a 'reading diary'. For every lesson that you teach that includes a reading element, note down in the diary a) the type of reading material; b) the reading activities you asked your learners to do; c) the reaction of your learners to both the materials and the activities, and d) when you yourself felt particularly negative about a certain text or reading activity. Likewise, note down any times when you felt things were especially positive.

Commentary ■ ■ ■

Here is an example of how your reading diary might look:

Date 12.05.94 Class Elem Text CB, p34 Activities Comp/vocab Students Bored Me _ _ _ _ _

Points in the lesson where problems occurred
They found the comp questions dull. Perhaps there were to many of them.
The second vocab exercise was too easy.

Action points/options
Reduce the number of questions.
Find another way of checking comp.
Give the students the questions before they read the text.
Get the students to write their own questions for the text.
Work actively on motivation by setting reading objectives, a simplified short story perhaps.

You can proceed in the same way to analyze how your learners react to the different types of texts you use and the different activities you ask them to do that are based on the text. You can also test in the same way some of the alternative strategies we suggest later in the chapter.

Task 3 – Part B

Here are some of the main types of classroom-based reading activity that you are likely to use already and thus include in your diary experiment. Write up to three points in favour and three criticisms of each one:

1   Scanning

positive remarks: *critical remarks:*

_____   _____
_____   _____
_____   _____

2   Skimming

positive remarks: *critical remarks:*

_____   _____
_____   _____
_____   _____

3   Reading more intensively and answering comprehension questions

positive remarks: *critical remarks:*

_____   _____
_____   _____
_____   _____

4   Focusing on discourse markers/cohesive devices

positive remarks: *critical remarks:*

_____   _____
_____   _____
_____   _____

5   Jumbled reading

positive remarks: *critical remarks:*

_____   _____
_____   _____
_____   _____

We tried an experiment with nine separate groups of students, making a total of thirty-six learners. These were mixed nationality adults on intensive courses in the UK. Their level ranged from early intermediate (ie post-elementary) to pre-FCE (Cambridge First Certificate in English) level. Each group was given a lesson that included each of the above techniques. They were then asked to write comments in favour of each technique and also comments critical of each technique. They were also asked to rank each reading activity in order of a) usefulness to them personally as learners; b) interest to them as learners. Here are some of their comments. Compare their remarks with what you wrote.

1 Scanning (here taken to mean looking through a text quickly to locate information you hope to find there)

Positive remarks:

Useful.
It's what I do in my mother tongue.
It's natural, really.
Practical.
It's what you need to survive in England.
Good with newspapers.

Critical remarks:

Too easy.
I can do this with no problems.
A waste of class time.
Mechanical.
It's over much too quickly.
What's the point?

2 Skimming (here taken to mean looking through a text quickly and getting the gist of the text from key words and other visual clues)

Positive remarks:

It's good to know you don't need every word.
I like reading in this way.
It forces you to read quickly and this is very good.
A simple technique.

Critical remarks:

For me this is frustrating because I want to read more.
I'm not learning anything.
I know the topic of the text but nothing else.
This isn't enough for me.

3 Reading more intensively and answering comprehension questions

Positive remarks:

I like this because I can learn vocabulary.
I like this kind of reading.
I have plenty of time and I can study the language.
I can learn from this.

Critical remarks:

I don't like this text. It's very boring.
Why so many questions?
I can find the answers easily. I know where to look.
The text looks boring.

4 Focusing on discourse markers/cohesive devices

Positive remarks:

This is like grammar. I know it's valuable.
Very useful practice.
This is difficult for us. 'It' is a difficult word.
Systematic practice.

Critical remarks:

This is OK once, but what's the point in doing it again?
Very, very boring.
I don't like these boxes and arrows – it's too theoretical.
Useless – it doesn't help.

5 Jumbled reading

Positive remarks:

This is useful because you have to read the text carefully.
Good fun, like a puzzle.
This gives us good reading practice, and vocabulary too.
I like solving problems.

Critical remarks:

We do this so often that it is now really boring.
I don't see the point.
I want to see the original text. This is just a game.
Frustrating.

Taking all thirty-six in the sample and taking an average of the positions given to each activity, the results of the ranking exercise were:

Usefulness

1 reading and comprehension questions
2 jumbled reading
3 skimming
4 discourse markers/cohesive devices
5 scanning

Interest

1 reading and comprehension questions
2 jumbled reading
3 skimming
4 scanning
5 discourse markers/cohesive devices

Commentary ■ ■ ■

If we consider the remarks made by the learners in the survey and the orders of usefulness and interest they gave, it seems that the perception of these learners, at any rate, was very much that reading in the classroom is a matter of vocabulary learning and little else. They appear to recognize the usefulness of skimming, for example, but appear frustrated by the fact that nothing seems to follow it. Scanning is low down their list of priorities because, in most cases, it seems that this is a strategy that they can apply anyway and they do not seem to want a teacher to instruct them in how to apply it.

It seems that all of the reading activities tried in the survey were judged by the learners in terms of the potential of the activity to provide the opportunity for the acquisition of vocabulary and other aspects of *language* (grammatical structures, for example), and not in terms of whether they helped them to read. The perception of this group of learners was that language comes first. If you have the language, you can read. If you do not know the language, you will not be able to read, no matter what skills and strategies you apply.

Almost all of the learners in the survey said that the basic technique of reading a text and answering comprehension questions was both the most interesting and the most useful activity. Their reasons for saying this seem primarily based on the assumption that reading a text in this way gives them the potential both to practise language (by seeing it in context) and to acquire new language (mainly vocabulary).

A large number in the experiment also said that they found many texts boring and that they were demotivated by the appearance of some texts. This suggests that more attention needs to be given to tuning into the interests of learners. If a text can simultaneously provide the linguistic opportunities learners seem to crave and provide them with interest and motivation, then the text, at any rate, will be successful.

The views expressed on these questions reveal a general sense of dissatisfaction about the way reading is taught, both on the part of the teachers and on the part of the learners. This feeling could well be brought about by confusion in the minds of both teachers and learners about the basic purposes of classroom reading, reading as a means to develop language skills, or reading as an end in itself. Some of the comments reveal that teachers often feel obliged to work on reading skills without having a clear idea of where this kind of work is leading. This may well lead to a sense of frustration in learners, whose expectations are often linguistically-focused, and who may resent peripheral skills-based reading activities.

A solution may well lie in adopting a clearly defined dual approach in which learners are informed of the aims of reading activities, linguistic on the one hand, and improving reading skills with the ultimate aim of enabling learners to read for both pleasure and information in the L2 on the other. If they are aware of this dual purpose, both teachers and learners may be more willing to accept text-based activities for what they are rather than what they think they should be. ■

4 Options for change

The learner survey and the teacher questionnaire earlier in the chapter bring out a number of points about reading and teaching reading. These can be summarized thus:

1 Some teachers may not be happy about using 'traditional' coursebook texts but learners are often less critical.

2 Both teachers and some learners seem dissatisfied with comprehension-type questions, although these are not as unpopular with learners as teachers may imagine.

3 Many learners see vocabulary building as the main aim of reading texts in a foreign language.

4 Scanning is regarded by some teachers and learners as a mechanical skill that is not particularly difficult. Some learners, as a result, see little point in being asked to do it in class.

5 Text selection is regarded by both teachers and learners as a central issue in motivating learners to read.

6 Authentic material is generally regarded as desirable because it provides both 'real' language and varieties of language.

Task 4

If you accept the above six general statements about teaching reading, note down two or three implications that these statements have for you personally as a teacher of reading.

Commentary ■ ■ ■

These are the implications we wrote for ourselves:

1 Coursebook texts are 'there', so we really ought to exploit them.
   Learners expect us to use them.
   I need to think of ways of making them more interesting.
   I need to pay more attention to the ways in which I introduce coursebook texts.

2 I must try to find alternatives to working through lists of questions laboriously.
   I could write my own tasks.
   I could get the students to write questions for each other.

3 I really must explain the purposes of classroom reading to my students.
   If they want vocabulary, I must ensure that they get some.
   Perhaps I can use texts as a 'springboard' to vocabulary-building and storing activities.

4 Maybe I overuse scanning, particularly with learners whose mother tongue has a similar rhetorical structure to English.
   One approach might be to talk about the need to scan and when we do it in the L1.

5 I need to find material that contains real, new information for my students.
   I could find out more about their interests.
   If a text is overtly 'boring' but I still have to use it, perhaps I should stress the linguistic aims of the lesson.
   Maybe I need to go beyond texts and newspaper articles and encourage my students to read more extensively, short stories and possibly even novels.

6 I could try integrating authentic materials into my reading programme alongside coursebook texts.
   I need to explain to my learners the purpose of getting used to reading authentic reading material.
   Well selected authentic material could be in tune with my learners' interests. ■

5   Ideas for experimentation

Here are some suggestions for experimentation in and evaluation of some of the aspects of teaching reading discussed in this chapter. Many may already be familiar to you; some may be new. The suggestions are not intended as 'solutions'. They are intended as options to be tried, tested and evaluated. They may help both to clarify the aims of your classroom reading activities and to give your learners more variety in the reading activities you ask them to do. The suggestions are offered in no particular order and without comment.

Task 5

We suggest the following procedure:

1 Think about the suggested activity or approach and how you could use or adapt it in your own classes.
2 Try it out.
3 Evaluate its usefulness by asking your learners what they think they got from the activity, whether they enjoyed doing it and what they thought its purpose was.

Coursebook texts and similar

Remove a sentence from each paragraph of the text, jumble the removed sentences and ask your learners to replace the removed sentences in an appropriate place in the text.

Remove a sentence from each paragraph of the text and transpose it into a different paragraph randomly. Ask your learners to read the text, locate the 'inappropriate' sentence in each paragraph and replace it in the correct one.

Using correction fluid or similar, blank out every tenth word or so in the text. Ask your learners to find appropriate words to fill the gaps. This can be done as a Cloze test (ie every nth word, irrespective of word category) or by focusing on a particular word type, eg verbs, or possibly by removing all the words you judge to be 'new' for your learners.

Replace a number of 'new' words in the text with 'nonsense words'. Ask your learners to think of synonyms for the nonsense words.

Remove a number of words from the text without leaving blanks. (In this case you will clearly have to retype the text.) List the excerpted words in chronological order. Ask your learners to replace them in the text at any point they judge to be suitable.

Cut the text into sections and jumble it up, ensuring that it cannot be fitted back together in jigsaw style simply by looking at the shape of each section! Ask your learners to decide on the correct order. This can be done either at sentence level or at paragraph level. Usually, there are clear discourse markers to indicate the original order, but where there is more than one possibility, this can lead to a valuable discussion of the most appropriate order.

Talk to your learners about the purpose of their reading the text. If the main aim is linguistic (rather than reading skills development), make sure that this is clear to them. Tell them, for example, that the purpose of the text is to introduce a number of important lexical items.

If your learners clearly want to concentrate on the vocabulary in the text, you may want to encourage this desire by helping them to understand key lexical items and their function, by bringing in related lexis to build up lexical sets based on words in the text, and by helping them to store vocabulary in a way that suits their individual styles.

Questions

Once the topic of the text has been made clear, get your learners to write their own questions for the text. They then read to find the answers to their own questions rather than questions set by the coursebook writer.

If the text contains information which is clearly new to your learners (facts and figures, for example), give them a series of statements relating to the text *before* actually seeing the text, and ask them to decide whether they agree or disagree with the statements, or whether the statements are factually correct or not. They then read to see whether they were right or not.

Divide your learners into pairs or small groups and get them to write questions about the text for other pairs or groups. This can be done with the same text for all groups or a different text for each group. With this activity, they need to see the text first.

Ask your learners to write three or four questions which will focus readers on the main points of the text.

Using correction fluid or similar, blank out different words or short sections containing factual information on different copies of the text. Each learner then receives a copy of the text with, say, ten words or short sections blanked out. These are different for each member of the group. Ask your learners to find the missing information by asking other members of the group questions.

Text selection

To supplement coursebook reading material, try and find material that clearly contains new information for the readers. Good sources for such material are specialist magazines, technical journals, the Education Guardian supplement for secondary schools (now collected in *The Source Book* – see references at the end of this chapter), and, of course, newspapers. The latter need not be expensive imported daily newspapers from English-speaking countries. Local English-language dailies and weeklies often have topical articles and news more relevant to the interests of the learners.

To encourage learners to read autonomously, provide a selection of reading material. Give help and guidance in choosing material appropriate to each learner. Find out each learner's interests (computers, photography, music, cars, travel, etc) and suggest they buy a copy of a magazine in English that deals with their interests.

Authentic materials

Spend some time discussing with your class what exactly they read in their mother tongue. The list of reading matter will probably be quite extensive. Point out the variety of material normally read and contrast this with the type of material often used in language teaching. Discuss with your learners the value of reading different types of material. Discuss, too, the aims of reading such material and compare and contrast it with the aims of reading graded reading material.

Introduce your learners to different examples of authentic written English. Bring in advertisements, menus, newspapers, recipes, instructions, notices and so on.

Prediction

Discuss with your learners the importance of context, expectations about content, prediction and reading for confirmation of predictions. Give them a text without any prior discussion of context and find out how long it takes them to work out the context. Then repeat the experiment, this time giving the context first and having some prior discussion of the content. Ask them which text was easier to understand and why.

Give your learners time to think about the topic before they read. Get them to 'brainstorm' first vocabulary, then ideas related to the theme.

Ask your learners to discuss the answers to pre-set questions before they read. Get them to speculate about content before they start reading.

Scanning

As with the discussion on authentic material, discuss with your learners *how* they read certain types of material in their native language (directories, menus, timetables, small advertisements, etc). Focus on the point that when reading such texts they would normally expect to know what they are looking for beforehand. Point out that most of the text does not need to be read and that location skills are used.

Try a few simple scanning activities with a suitable piece of material (eg the television programmes list from a newspaper). Ask your learners to find certain information as quickly as possible. Discuss with them afterwards the strategies they applied to find the information. Ask them how easy or difficult it was to apply this strategy to an authentic English text.

Now apply similar scanning strategies with a coursebook text or similar that contains a certain amount of factual information (numbers, dates, etc). Again, ask your learners to find information as quickly as possible and discuss with them the strategies they used and the degree of difficulty of the approach. Discuss, too, the value of the activity.

Newspaper quiz. Divide your class into small groups and give each group a newspaper (or, at least, one or two pages from a newspaper). Ask them to devise a quiz for the other groups in the class. They have to write five to ten questions based on facts they find in their newspaper or section of newspaper. They then exchange newspapers and find the answers to the questions as quickly as possible.

Discuss with your learners the value or otherwise of doing more scanning activities in class. They may say that such activities are superfluous because they can transfer this L1 strategy to the L2 quite simply. They may, on the other hand, find this strategy difficult and request more practice. Try to encourage them to apply the technique whenever they read material that needs to be scanned for information rather than read intensively.

Skimming

Ask your learners how they read newspapers in their mother tongue. Ask them whether they read articles intensively or merely skim through them to get a general idea of what each article is about. If they usually do the latter, ask them what it is that gives them this general idea or 'gist'. Emphasize the importance of key words and phrases in getting the gist of an article or text. Discuss with them whether it is necessary to read intensively to get a general idea of something and when they would read something intensively (eg when they are interested in something having already skimmed it to get the gist, when they have to read something important such as instructions).

Find a text and decide which are the key ten or so words or phrases which give a general idea of the topic or theme of the text. Write them up on the board in chronological order and ask your learners to discuss what the text they are taken from is about. When they have done this, ask them to imagine these words highlighted in a text. Would it be necessary to read the rest of the text to get the general meaning?

Ask your learners to underline key words and phrases in texts.

Find some short newspaper articles with headlines (ten reports and ten headlines, for example). Separate the headlines from the stories and stick both headlines and stories in random order on a sheet of paper. Ask your learners to look at the headlines and the stories and match the correct headlines with the correct stories as quickly as possible.

Find some short newspaper articles (six to ten should be sufficient) and remove the headlines. Write one word which summarizes each text. Ask your learners to match the words with the texts. The same activity can be done by getting the learners to write the words in groups and then trying out the activity on other groups in the class.

After your learners have completed a skimming task (with a newspaper, for example), ask them to read a short section of the text intensively. Focus on details in the text and on items of language (vocabulary, in particular). In this way you can integrate skimming with other reading activities and avoid the feeling that the text was only touched upon rather than dealt with thoroughly. (The same principle can be applied to scanning.)

Extensive reading/reading outside the classroom/reading literature

Ask your learners to buy a copy of a local newspaper in English (eg *The Athens News*, *The Warsaw Voice*) and to write a brief summary of the main news stories in it.

If your learners have access to the daily press in English, ask them to monitor the press for a week and keep a 'news diary' of the main stories.

Find out the reading interests of your learners in their native language. Discuss with them their reasons for reading what they read and explore the extra dimensions that reading comparable materials in English would bring.

Discuss with your learners the advantages to be gained from reading short stories and novels in English. Get them to talk about what they have read in their native language. As a starting point stories read in the L1 can be summarized or briefly described in English.

As a way into encouraging learners to read and appreciate literature, you can adopt a topic-based approach and select short extracts by two or three authors on the same topic (schooldays, falling in love, a disastrous journey and so on). You might even consider adding a poem related to the same topic. Ask your learners to identify the different ways the authors treat the same topic.

Try and make available a selection of extensive reading materials in English (short stories, novels, longer magazine articles and so on). Encourage your learners to borrow materials and to keep a record of what they read. If your learners are all reading the same book, this has obvious benefits. You can give them the opportunity to discuss briefly in class what they have read, by reporting on plot, describing the progress of individual characters and summarizing incidents in the story. You can also encourage them to speculate on what happens next. If learners are reading different books, then clearly the scope for discussion is greatly reduced, but you can ask each learner for a brief progress report. In the latter situation, at some stage you can also ask learners to describe the book they are reading in such a way as to encourage others in the group to read it.

As another 'way in' to literature, select a short novel which has recently been made into a film or a TV series with which your learners are familiar. Knowing the main storyline should help with general comprehension and also with motivation, and a comparison of the treatment of the story in the two different media can provide a fruitful area for discussion.

Remind your learners from time to time of the benefits to be gained by skimming texts. Emphasize once again that it will probably not be necessary to understand every word to get enjoyment and a sense of achievement from reading an extended piece of English. At the same time, remind them of the linguistic benefits to be gained by reading sections of novels, for example, intensively. Encourage learners to keep vocabulary records, word pools, lexical sets, etc (see Chapter 7 on Vocabulary).

Consider introducing your learners to the delights of poetry in English. From the very basic level of using limericks for rhythm and pronunciation, through to using poetry for imagery and association, this area of literature can prove very rewarding to learners. In addition, poetry such as that of the 'Mersey poets' (Henri, McGough and Patten), which is humorous and uses everyday contexts, can both provide amusing and entertaining reading and act as a model for learners' own experimentation with writing verse.

6 Conclusions

In foreign language reading, many learners are slow to apply the kind of skills and strategies they apply in their mother tongue. There may be a number of reasons for this: poor linguistic skills, lack of motivation, lack of interest in the text, a negative perception of the purpose of the reading exercise, and an over-anxious desire to understand each and every word in the text. To overcome such problems, we suggest two basic solutions: talk to learners about reading, and develop individualized learner-centred reading programmes, leading up to, if appropriate to the learner, the reading of literature. Most of the activities described in this chapter come under these two basic headings. If learners are aware of the purposes of reading in the foreign language, if they understand the processes involved in successful reading and the skills and strategies they can employ, if they can see clearly that they can obtain real information and pleasure from reading in the foreign language, and if they have some say in the choice of what they read, then there is every likelihood that they will develop the habit of reading in English and derive considerable benefit to their all-round linguistic ability from so doing.

7 Recommended reading

Developing Reading Skills by Françoise Grellet presents a very clear overview of the rationale behind different types of reading exercise and copious examples closely related to this rationale.

Reading by Frank Smith is an entertaining, enlightening and occasionally provocative discussion of many of the main issues related to the theory and practice of reading.

8 References and bibliography

Alderson, J. and Urquhart, A. 1984 *Reading in a Foreign Language* (Longman)
Bowen, T. 1991 *The Development of Reading Skills in a Foreign Language – The Views of Practitioners and Participants* (unpublished M Phil thesis, University of Southampton)
Gower, R. and Pearson, M. 1986 *Reading Literature* (Longman)
Grellet, F. 1981 *Developing Reading Skills* (CUP)
Guardian, The 1991 *The Source Book*
Henri, A., McGough, R. and Patten, B. 1980 *Penguin Modern Poets 10*, 13th edition (Penguin)
Mackay, R., Barkman, B. and Jordan, R. (eds.) 1979 *Reading in a Second Language – Hypotheses, Organization and Practice* (Newbury House)
Maley, A. and Duff, A. *The Inner Ear* (CUP)
Nuttall, C. 1994 *Teaching Reading Skills in a Foreign Language*, new edition (Heinemann)
Smith, F. 1978 *Reading* (CUP)
Williams, E. 1984 *Reading in the Language Classroom* (Macmillan)

Chapter 9 Hear and now:

Listening in the classroom

1 What counts as 'listening' in the classroom?

Task 1

Which of the following are listening activities?

1 The teacher elicits spoken answers to a written exercise.
2 Learners complete a task while listening to a conversation on cassette.
3 The teacher explains some special arrangements for next week's lesson.
4 A learner asks the teacher a question about the meaning of a word.
5 The teacher conducts a drill with the class.
6 A learner formulates a sentence silently before uttering it.
7 Two learners carry out a pairwork activity.
8 The teacher tells a story.
9 The teacher converses with the class before the lesson starts.
10 The class are engaged in a pronunciation exercise focusing on two contrasting sounds.

Commentary ■ ■ ■

There are some activities which teachers typically introduce as 'listening' (*Today we're going to do some listening; So I'd like you to listen and ...*). In the list above, numbers **2** and **8** might come into this category. Even though many teachers probably don't usually think of all the remaining activities as 'listening', they all involve at least an element of listening – number **6** is perhaps an odd one out in a way, because the listening in this case is to an internal voice. ■

Task 2

How might you arrange the activities in order from most typical to least typical 'listening' activity?

Commentary ■ ■ ■

It's likely that learners can maximize their learning opportunities in all the activities above if their listening skills are adequately engaged. In **4** above, for example, a question from learner A might lead learner B to realize that their own understanding of the word is not as complete as they thought. In **5**, listening to the responses of the other learners might help an individual in rehearsing their own response, or perhaps in refining their judgement of different qualities of performance. In **9**, even a learner who isn't 'taking part' in the conversation – ie speaking – can benefit from the opportunity to listen in a relaxed way to an extended, informal stretch of English. (Indeed, someone who isn't 'participating' might be able to do this better than someone who is.)

Probably most classroom activities, whatever their ostensible purpose, rely to a greater or lesser extent on the learners' listening faculties. This reflects the importance of spoken language in most language-teaching programmes, the role of speech as a basis for the majority of teaching methodologies, and the pervasiveness of listening in life in general. Most people spend a large part of their waking hours listening, with varying degrees of attention, to language and other stimuli. So why is it considered important that learners of a foreign language should 'learn to listen' or 'practise listening'? ■

2 Why 'do' listening?

Why is it that listening now has such a prominent place in coursebooks, and that such a wide range of supplementary listening material is commercially available?

Here are some possible answers:

- to give further practice and revision of previously-taught language in new contexts;
- to introduce new language items in context;
- to give learners opportunities to 'pick up' new language;
- to practise the skill of listening;
- to help learners understand spoken English;
- to build their confidence;
- to expose them to different varieties and accents of English;
- to help them realize that they shouldn't panic if they don't understand everything.

Task 3

Which of these reasons are important for you? Are there any others?

Commentary ■ ■ ■

A comparison of the above reasons reveals what we have found to be a widely-accepted dichotomy between doing listening in order to teach and practise language, and doing listening in order to teach and develop listening skills. The first of these general aims is product-oriented, and the material used is likely to be determined by some syllabus of structures, words or functions to be taught; the second is process-oriented, and although teachers will generally try to choose material which they feel is in some way relevant to the learners' needs, the details of the language contained in the material will be of secondary importance. ■

Questions raised by this dichotomy include:

- Do we need to teach people how to listen?
- Do learners actually do listening activities in accordance with the aims teachers have in mind?

Task 4

Interview learners to find out:

a why they think they need to do listening work in the classroom (if at all!)
b what they feel they got out of particular listening activities they have done.

Commentary ■ ■ ■

We have found not infrequently that what learners perceive as the pay-off for doing listening tasks is different from what the teacher intends. In particular, they often refer to the value of listening material as a source of new vocabulary, where this is not the purpose intended by the teacher (or the writer of the material). ■

3   What people do when they listen

Listening is such a familiar part of our everyday experience that it may not be immediately apparent what a complex achievement it is, though we can get a hint of this from cases where listening is difficult or unsuccessful.

Task 5

Which of these propositions about listening do you agree with? They are grouped thematically; some of them contradict one another. Assume that they refer to the processes of listening to language in general, and listening to a foreign language in particular.

a Listening is passive.
  Listening is receptive.
  Listening is active.
  Listening to language is more or less the same as listening to anything else.

b Listening and reading are very similar.
Listening is more difficult than reading.
As foreign languages go, English is particularly tricky for learners to listen to.

c Everybody (unless they lack the physiological or mental requisites) is a competent listener in their own language.
Competent listeners use different strategies depending on their listening purpose and the nature of what they're listening to.

d People tend to use completely different strategies depending on whether they're listening to their first language or a foreign language. They need to be taught how to listen to the foreign language effectively.
Learners will, if given opportunity, automatically transfer the listening skills they use in their L1 to the task of listening to a foreign language, so that they don't need to be taught these skills.

Commentary ■ ■ ■

a *Listening is passive.*

Listening is receptive.

Listening is active.

Listening to language is more or less the same as listening to anything else.

Proficient listening, even when careful and deliberate, is highly automatic, and we aren't normally aware of the processes and sub-processes involved. They include:

- picking out sounds from the stream of speech and assigning them to phonemes (including, for example, isolating consonant phonemes on the basis of the perception of surrounding vowels);
- picking out words from the stream of speech;
- assigning word forms to citation forms, including interpreting assimilations and elisions;
- understanding prosody – rhythm, stress and intonation;
- recognizing prominence – stress and the meanings conveyed by it, especially emphatic stress;
- recognizing the effect of cohesive devices and following the line of thought in discourse;
- assigning coherence to discourse by interpreting the development of the speaker's intention, ie understanding the meaning of words as they are used in that particular context;
- reconstructing ellipsis, ie shortened forms such as *See the match?* for *Did you see the match?*
- constructing meaning from the words heard;
- guessing meanings of unknown words and phrases;
- recognizing known language in unfamiliar contexts;
- interpreting the likely intention behind performance errors, ie errors made in spite of the fact that the speaker knows the correct form;
- filtering out any other ambient language or other sounds, but remaining prepared to filter them in again as and when necessary;

- predicting, comparing what's heard with what was predicted, and revising predictions;
- attending to discourse-organizing elements like *on the one hand* ... and using these to structure listening, but recognizing that the expectations they raise may not be fulfilled;
- paying attention selectively, and constantly varying the level of our attention – perhaps while engaged in other tasks simultaneously – in response to fluctuating levels of information density and perceived relevance;
- recognizing and dealing with redundancy;
- making judgements about which content to select for remembering;
- remembering certain content while letting other content slip by;
- relating what we hear to our previous knowledge and experience; adapting our knowledge to accommodate what we hear;
- constructing and constantly revising understandings of what we are listening to;
- checking what we hear against any accompanying non-linguistic information;
- interpreting implied information, attitude, and intention;
- recognizing where we are having difficulties in understanding;
- (if circumstances permit) checking our understanding, asking for clarification, and influencing what we are listening to.

In general, listening can be regarded not so much as a question of perception and processing of a signal, but rather as a process of parallel construction on the part of the listener: construction of a coherent interpretation which is consistent as far as possible with the acoustic clues and the listener's mental image.

Listening has often been characterized, along with reading, as 'passive' or 'receptive'. This might suggest that in order to listen effectively all we need to do is relax and let it wash over us. But it's clear even from the brief analysis above that, even though the processes may be deeply unconscious, listening entails a great deal of active mental participation on the part of the listener.

b *Listening and reading are very similar.*

What do listening and reading have in common?

- They engage and rely on interest, motivation, purpose and processing strategies, as well as knowledge and expectations of the world, culture, topic, co-text, and the language system.
- They are largely the subconscious application of a variety of sub-skills.
- The listener or reader is actively, though normally unawarely, involved in constructing understanding.
- The listener or reader uses what they've heard or read to draw conclusions, make evaluations, and experiences changes in knowledge, attitude and behaviour.

Listening is more difficult than reading.

In what ways is listening trickier than reading?

- It usually has to be processed in real time, perhaps with the need to respond, and with the expectation of more to follow.
- It's prone to a variety of problems caused by background noise, distance and so on.

- Speech may be badly pronounced or pronounced unclearly. All you get is clues, traces of something that isn't there, or only partly there.
- There's more redundancy – although this may help proficient listeners, it can be confusing for learners.
- Phonetically quite different items can represent the same underlying form.
- You have to tune into features of the speaker's voice as well as the language and content.

And in what ways is reading trickier than listening?

- There's no prosody, ie rhythm, stress and intonation.
- There's less redundancy.
- There's less extra-textual information.
- There's no possibility of direct intervention and negotiation on the part of the receiver.

As foreign languages go, English is particularly
tricky for learners to listen to.

How do learners see the problems of listening to English?

It's too fast.
They eat their words.
They swallow their words.
They don't pronounce words as they are written.
There are too many differences of pronunciation.

- It seems unlikely that any particular language is spoken in general very much faster than any other. Of course, there may be typically faster or slower speakers. But the overall perception of English as 'fast' is probably experienced by learners of other languages, too.
- There are specific features of spoken English, though, which, under the guise of 'too fast', may make it in some ways harder to understand than some other languages.
- A lot of pronunciation teaching is based on the notion of phonemes or 'segments', which are lined up in sequence to form words and longer utterances. But the equally familiar notion of the 'stream of speech' contradicts the expectation of solid linearity (ie separate sounds) and expresses something of the flux and indeterminacy of real speech. The solid metaphor is a more attractive one from the point of view of ease of recognition and production, but learners have to deal with the liquid one if they want to be fluent speakers and listeners.
- It's generally only in stressed syllables that vowels are given their full, ideal pronunciation. Elsewhere, they are reduced in quality or dropped. This can also result in variability in the number of syllables in a word.
- Consonants are likely to be dropped from clusters, or assimilated to adjoining sounds.
- Stress placement within words is rightly considered a useful guide to the identification of words, but when a word isn't prominent in an utterance, this clue isn't available.
- Word boundaries are obscured by widespread linking and the variability of word stress position.

- Although any spoken language is likely to make some use of processes of connected speech, it does seem that English is exceptionally versatile in this respect – and this comes on top of the fact that English spelling is in any case a notoriously unreliable guide to pronunciation. All this has the effect of subverting listener expectations based on written forms, or even on idealized spoken 'citation' forms. It can lead to expressions of hostility towards the material, the teacher, or the English language, on the basis that such speech is careless and substandard. When it comes to learners' own speech, there's quite a lot of scope for individual choice in how far they want to adopt these features of connected speech, but from a listening point of view, there's really no choice: if they're going to listen to English, this is what it will sound like.

c *Everybody (unless they lack the physiological or mental requisites) is a competent listener in their own language.*

Competent listeners use different strategies depending on their listening purpose and the nature of what they're listening to.

In my own language I know more reliably whether I've understood something I listen to, and whether or not it's important to understand. Being a competent listener doesn't mean being infallible. In my L2 I'm not always so sure if it's OK not to understand. I may realize that I only need to understand the most important words, but unless I understand everything, I don't know what the most important words are. I may understand the grammatical words and inflections but not the key content words. If I don't understand something in my L1, I'm more likely to blame the speaker. If I don't understand something in my L2, I'm more likely to blame myself, even if the problem was really not hearing or not paying attention, rather than trying and failing to understand.

Being a good listener entails, among other things, not filling up another speaker's space with your own talk, and recognizing where a certain type of intervention would be appropriate. In L2 it's probably more difficult to recognize these points, and more difficult to formulate an appropriate intervention quickly. But these are skills which are by no means equally mastered by all L1 speakers. It could be that some people will even learn through English to be better listeners in their L1!

d *People tend to use completely different strategies depending on whether they're listening to their first language or a foreign language, so that they need to be taught how to listen to the foreign language effectively.*

Learners will, if given opportunity, automatically transfer the listening skills they use in their L1 to the task of listening to a foreign language, so that they don't need to be taught these skills.

Learners need to achieve in the L2 the same degree of automation of strategies as in the L1, in order to free their attention for higher-level tasks of listening for content and responding, as well as any other tasks they are engaged in simultaneously. There's some evidence that some learners, at least, are reluctant to abandon the strategy of identifying every word and piecing together an under-standing on this basis (or abandoning the attempt if there are too many unknown words). Hence the value of confidence-building activities which show learners that they can achieve understanding despite a high density of unknown items.

It might seem obvious that if a learner can do a listening task successfully apparently without effort, then they don't actually need to do it. But it may be that they're using some kind of approach that requires an inordinate or inefficient expenditure of attention. If this can be brought to light, it might bring an opportunity for the learner to review their approach and perhaps try alternatives. But how could this come to light? Perhaps by interviewing learners about *how* they do activities, rather than simply being satisfied that they *can* do them.

Even if some learners do transfer their skills automatically, this still doesn't mean that they don't need to practise listening to English, which is, after all, a less familiar language. But it does suggest that the activities used in the classroom to practise listening – the means – can resemble the listening that learners will eventually need to do outside the classroom – the end – quite closely. If a more step-by-step approach is needed, on the other hand, the means might look quite different. And a supplementary question concerns the role of conscious knowledge: how important is it for learners to know about the skills and strategies they are practising? ■

Task 6

Reflect on the listening you do in your L1 during the course of a particular day. Note any variables in your approach to listening, and see if you can identify any of the sub-processes described above.

4　What teachers do when they 'do' listening

Task 7

Which of the following do you regard as good recommendations for doing listening work? (Some of them refer particularly to the use of recorded material for classroom listening work.)

- ☐ Don't spend too much time on listening at the expense of teaching new language and giving practice in speaking.
- ☐ When you do listening activities, teach don't test.
- ☐ Encourage learners to listen to each other rather than just to the teacher and cassettes.

- ☐ Use cassettes as much as possible for classroom listening work.
- ☐ Use video as much as possible for classroom listening work.
- ☐ Use authentic listening material as much as possible.
- ☐ Use material that will appeal to the learners' interests and needs.

- ☐ Set tasks or questions before the learners listen, not after.
- ☐ Set tasks which require non-linguistic or minimally linguistic responses (ticking boxes, filling in details on a map, etc).
- ☐ Grade the task, not the material.
- ☐ Work on general understanding before detail.

☐ Don't allow learners to look at the tapescript while they're doing a listening activity.

☐ Prepare learners for their encounter with what they are going to listen to, set the scene, introduce the characters and so on, rather than expecting them to listen 'cold'.

☐ Pre-teach all the vocabulary you think the learners might not know.

☐ Pre-teach selected key vocabulary.

☐ Play the tape a certain number of times – two, say, or four – which you decide in advance.

☐ Play the tape as many times as the learners want.

☐ Allow them to ask you to stop the tape whenever they want, to ask questions, or to ask you to replay part of it.

☐ Give a time limit for completing the listening task.

☐ Ensure that all answers are linguistically accurate.

☐ Explain everything the learners don't understand.

☐ Give learners a copy of the tapescript after they've finished the listening activity.

☐ Use part of the material for detailed pronunciation work.

☐ Follow on with a related activity.

Are there any others that seem important to you and that you'd like to add ?

Selective commentary ■ ■ ■

Don't spend too much time on listening at the expense of teaching new language and giving practice in speaking.

Sometimes teachers and learners may feel that time, especially if there isn't much available, is best spent teaching and practising identifiable language items, so that there's a concrete sense of achievement and progress. But it's worth spending time on the 'receptive' skills because it helps to prepare learners for outside-the-classroom encounters with the language and at the same time provides opportunities to learn and practise language in context.

When you do listening activities, teach don't test.

Of course it's sometimes appropriate – it may be required – to test the 'receptive' skills. But most of the time the aim should be for the learners not merely to find out how well or badly they completed a task, but to feel that they are being given help, support and the opportunity to complete the task as well as they can, and to develop their skills so that their performance will improve.

Encourage learners to listen to each other rather than just to the teacher and cassettes.

There are at least two reasons for this: a pedagogic one – it maximizes opportunities for exposure and learning – and a 'political' one – the teacher isn't the only person in the room who's got interesting and useful things to say, and an important aspect of working together is paying attention to, and respecting, what other people have to say.

Use cassettes as much as possible for classroom listening work.

There are numerous advantages in using taped material:

- It enables the teacher to bring into the classroom a variety of voices: male and female, different ages, different accents.
- In some teaching situations it may be the learners' only opportunity to hear native speakers, and/or to hear English-speaking voices other than the teacher's.
- It enables dialogue to be presented.
- It removes the teacher from the focus of attention.
- It permits an indefinite number of repetitions with absolute consistency.

On the other hand, enthusiasm for cassette material and misgivings about 'teacher talking time' have tended to obscure what a valuable resource the teacher's voice can be. The voice of the teacher is a model not only for learners to imitate, but for them to listen to, and has the following advantages:

- Meaning can be supported by facial expression, gesture and body language.
- The speaker can respond to verbal and non-verbal signals from the listeners, and the process can be interactive.

It seems likely that learners will tend, in their listening, to pay attention to linguistic form to a greater degree than L1 listeners. If this is so, it may be reinforced and encouraged by classroom procedures involving recordings, interactions in which learners are not participants, even in a passive sense, and are deprived of contextual clues.

Teachers who rely on their own voice for a substantial amount of listening work should be especially careful not to perpetuate an unnatural style of speaking, with over-articulation, lack of 'connected-speech' features of pronunciation, and general – rather than specifically chosen – reduction of syntax and lexis.

Use video as much as possible for classroom listening work.

Video allows the inclusion of much more non-linguistic information (ie visual clues) which may act as an aid to comprehension. Of course, such information isn't always present in all listening situations, but it's certainly true that in many cases where it would be available outside the classroom, it is not available when the material is presented on audio cassette. It is reasonable to suppose that this tends to make the listening more difficult, other things being equal.

Use authentic listening material as much as possible.

The attention paid to authenticity of material has been a useful corrective to the dominance of extremely unnatural material for listening work. Nevertheless, there seems no reason to assume that a pedagogic process aimed at developing listening skills, not to mention using listening material for introducing and practising new language, should make exclusive use, right from the start, of the sort of material it is assumed learners will need to listen to outside the classroom. The nature of the material used is certainly one factor that can be graded.

Use material that will appeal to the learners' interests and needs.

This is usually recommended and sounds obvious. But how well do we actually know what their needs and interests are? And can't we assume that they can become interested in something new? And that if they are focusing on practising their skills or acquiring new language, they may be able to transcend a lack of interest in the topic?

Set tasks or questions before the learners listen, not after.

This is usually recommended to replicate the fact that we normally have a reason for listening, and that in the absence of this it's a matter of chance whether or not we'll be able to answer questions posed afterwards, because we may well not have paid attention to those particular points – or even if we did, we may have forgotten.

Set tasks which require non-linguistic or minimally linguistic responses (ticking boxes, filling in details on a map, etc).

It's certainly a good idea to ensure that the demands associated with the mechanics of the task don't inhibit the learners' chances of achieving it. If learners have difficulty with a task which requires them to write answers to questions, is it because their listening skills are inadequate, or is it because they don't have time to write the answers, or even because lack of familiarity with the script and spelling means they can't write the answers?

Grade the task, not the material.

Difficulty isn't an absolute quality residing in material. It's quite possible to use exactly the same material at any level at all, by varying the demands of the task set, and the degree of accuracy expected in achieving it. You could use a political debate, say, with absolute beginners, by asking them to see if they can recognize any words, or by playing it as part of a series of short extracts from similar discussions in various languages and asking learners to identify which extracts are English. On the other hand, there may be some low-level tasks which are so easy and rely on such minimal appreciation of the passage in question that the learners feel they really aren't worth doing.

Work on general understanding before detail.

Not necessarily. It may be that some of the details are easier to retrieve than the overall gist, and the former can be a useful stepping-stone towards the latter. ■

5   Glimpses through classroom keyholes

Task 8

Here are some glimpses of a variety of classroom activities involving listening. Try to identify a rationale behind each of them.

a   The teacher reads a complete, longish narrative passage which the class have previously studied. They don't look at the text. Some of them have got their eyes closed. There's no preparation for listening, no task, no questions and no follow-up activity. After the reading there's an interval of silence, and then a break.

b   The learners listen to a text, and simultaneously follow the printed version in their books.

c   The learners are given a short time to read a transcript before they close their books and do a listening activity.

d   The learners have a printed text. They hear a spoken version of it, and at the same time speak it themselves, following the original voice as closely as possible.

e   The teacher says the sentence *Why didn't you think you'd be able to?* (which is well within what the learners 'know' at their level of English) – once, fast, casually, as it might appear if extracted from an everyday conversation among friends. The learners' task is to determine individually how many words there are in the sentence. (It's been previously established as a convention that a combined form like *didn't* counts as two words.) After a few moments of silence and reflection, the teacher asks for their answers. There's some disagreement – *eight, nine, ten, eleven* ... The teacher says the sentence again and the procedure is repeated. Finally the teacher asks the class to reconstruct the sentence in writing – individually and then joining forces with their neighbours.

f   The teacher gives an instruction which the learners seem not to understand. The teacher immediately paraphrases it.

g   The class are going to listen to the news headlines recorded off the radio. Before they listen, the teacher asks them to predict places, people, events and other key words which they think are likely to be mentioned.

h   The class are doing some listening work with video. The first time the teacher plays the video, the sound is turned off, and the learners' task is to suggest what the characters might be saying.

i   The teacher stops a cassette immediately after *Although this is certainly very good news for manufacturing industry ...*, and asks the class to predict what comes next.

j   After playing a short section of tape, the teacher asks *What did he say?* The learners seem unable to answer. The teacher responds: *Couldn't you understand him?*

k   The teacher gives commands for physical actions, such as *Stand up. Turn to face your partner. Pick up your pen in your left hand and give it to your partner,* which a selected group of the learners carry out.

l A listening passage is accompanied by some comprehension questions. Before the class listens, the teacher asks them to read the questions and try to answer any they possibly can. There's a brief discussion of possible answers.

m A listening passage is accompanied by a task which requires learners to tick the correct boxes according to what they hear.

n Learners A and B compare their answers to questions after listening to a cassette. A has got the answer to question 1; B hasn't, but is told by A. The teacher asks B for this answer. B gives it. The teacher says *Good*, and moves on to the next question.

o A learner answers a listening comprehension question. The teacher says *Yes, that's right*, but goes on to ask why the learner thought that was the right answer.

p The teacher gives the class a dictation.

q Learners respond to a listening task by giving answers in their L1.

6   Summary: Gradable variables in listening work

A scheme for description and experimentation

Variables in the choice of material

- Who chooses it? The coursebook writer? The teacher? The learners – individually or collectively?
- The familiarity of the topic and its cultural background.
- The learners' likely interest in the topic.
- Linguistic difficulty. This isn't an independent variable, though. Which is more difficult – technical or everyday language? It depends on the listener.
- The proportion of cohesive devices to lexical expressions.
- Conceptual difficulty.
- Information density.
- Information organization. Is it chronological – or in accordance with some other principle of organization – or is it more chaotic? Is there a clear preview or summary?
- The explicitness of the message, and the amount of inferring the listener has to do.
- Is it primarily a one-way message or is it interactional?
- Length. Difficulty and fatigue may often increase with length, but on the other hand greater length may help understanding if the important points are spread through the passage.

It would be possible to produce on tape a series of versions of the 'same' piece of listening graded for difficulty according to a mixture of the above criteria, and to use these in turn with a class.

Variables in the before-listening procedure

- The amount of preparation to capitalize on learners' previous knowledge of the topic, or to provide a background to it.
- The possibility of introducing the passage.
- Using some supporting visual material.
- Stimulating a discussion around the topic.
- Asking learners to predict content or vocabulary.
- Asking them to suggest their own questions to be answered by listening.
- Asking them to attempt the listening task provisionally *before* they listen.
- Checking or teaching key vocabulary.

Variables in the listening task

- The role of the listener: participant, addressee or eavesdropper.
- The type of response: cognitive and unobservable, verbal, manipulation of diagrams or symbols, written, physical action.
- Focus: extensive listening for gist or intensive listening for detail. Note that the former isn't necessarily easier than the latter; it may be easier to pick out certain details than to come to an overall understanding.
- Mechanical complexity: ticking boxes, matching content to pictures, writing answers, tracing a route on a map, note-taking, filling gaps, carrying out physical instructions, predicting what comes next when the tape stops.
- Degrees of simulated 'authenticity' of response may be related to different teacher aims or learner motivations. Listening to railway station announcements and noting down the departure time of a particular train may be suggested by a skills-based approach, whereas listening to the same announcements to identify functional uses of grammatical items may be suggested by an approach which highlights listening as a means of access to language data.
- Negotiation: opportunities for the learners to negotiate understanding with each other and/or with the speaker(s), or even to co-determine the content of the listening as it proceeds, asking questions for clarification, amplification, exemplification.
- Depth of processing: do the listeners have to simply identify factual information, or do they have to evaluate what they hear in some way?
- Time allowed.
- The degree of accuracy expected.

Note: The possible added difficulty of interpreting any non-linguistic data needed for the task – reading a map, for instance, isn't something that everybody can do equally well.

There's also the possibility, if you think it's feasible and useful for the learners, of not setting any task at all before they listen, and perhaps not doing any introductory or framing work, and asking them afterwards to reconstruct their understanding, perhaps in the form of a summary. Even groups of learners who claim individually *I couldn't understand anything* will often be able to generate a co-operative version of what they've heard. Of course, it's debatable how valuable this is as an exercise in individual listening, but it may at least reveal to individuals that they did in fact understand more than they thought. Finally, let's not forget the possibility of getting learners to listen to English with no task, no follow-up and therefore, perhaps, no pressure – this has been called 'secure listening'. Some learners might have no opportunity to do this outside the classroom; even those who have may not take the opportunity.

It's obviously advisable, until you have a good idea of what a class will be able to manage, to err on the side of easiness in setting these parameters. Even in our L1 we probably have unequal competence in speaking and listening, and we should bear this in mind in setting our expectations of learners. Sometimes, the demands of the listening task may be determined by any subsequent work you intend to do following on from the listening activity, such as a writing exercise or a problem-solving activity.

Using the above set of variables in a principled way, differentially according to different aims, may enable you to resolve conflicts between the wish for clarity and the need to prepare learners to deal with unclear, messy pieces of spoken language, or between the wish to give as much help and support as possible, and the danger of making learners over-dependent on classroom artifice. However, we should also recognize that learners may well have their own agendas for listening work. They may be sufficiently interested to put a lot of work into a passage that the teacher feels is 'too difficult'. They may want to listen intensively and figure out the exact words being spoken on a cassette which the teacher intended to be used for gist understanding. They may arrive at an interpretation of something they hear which is different from the teacher's or the material writer's but nevertheless, if evaluated objectively, equally plausible.

Finally, teachers and learners could probably benefit from listening to themselves more carefully from the points of view of the language they use and the quality of the interaction between and among them. Audio recording during lessons could be a useful tool for this. Questions for investigation might include:

- As a teacher, do I simplify my language in ways I'm not aware of when I address learners?
- Do I allow reasonable processing time for the learners before I assume their silence means they haven't understood something?
- Do I jump to conclusions in interpreting ambiguous utterances by the learners?
- Do I allow their English to stand alone when they're addressing each other, or do I tend to polish it and paraphrase it?

7 Recommended reading

Teaching Listening Comprehension by Penny Ur surveys the range of possible listening activities, with practical examples, and relates these to our theoretical understanding of listening.

For a more detailed treatment of some of these issues, see *Listening* by Anne Anderson and Tony Lynch.

8 References and bibliography

Anderson, A. and Lynch, T. 1988 *Listening* (OUP)
Underwood, M. 1987 *Teaching Listening* (Longman)
Ur, P. 1984 *Teaching Listening Comprehension* (CUP)
Widdowson, H. G. 1978 *Teaching Language as Communication* (OUP)

Chapter 10 **Write on:**

Some thoughts on teaching writing

1 Introduction

Writing is sometimes regarded as the 'forgotten skill'. Arguably, writing receives the least attention because it is at the bottom of the list of teachers' priorities. With limited classroom time and limited time for correction of written work, anything more than a piecemeal approach will both occupy time that could perhaps be spent on more immediate linguistic needs and, perhaps more crucially for many teachers, make excessive demands on their preparation time. In addition, in the perception of many learners, writing in English is not within the scope of their purpose of attending a language course in the first place. With its associations of homework, written exercises and examinations, writing may seem both 'traditional' (in the negative sense of the word) and irrelevant to learners' immediate needs. From a purely pragmatic point of view, they may not view time spent writing in class as time well spent, preferring the time to be spent on more active aspects of language learning. Like reading, writing is generally a silent, reflective activity and silence is not something that learners (and many teachers) generally associate with a language classroom. Likewise, many teachers may regard writing as some-thing that 'takes care of itself', a side issue that is best taken care of in the form of an occasional homework task. In short, writing gets a bad press, particularly in relation to the other productive skill, speaking.

If we consider some of the reasons for negative attitudes to writing in relation to speaking, some of the following issues emerge:

Feedback on oral production can be instant (correction of errors of syntax, pro-nunciation and so on). Such interaction in class can be motivating, lively, even fun. Error correction may come from the teacher, from other learners or from the speaker himself or herself. If such classroom interactions are skilfully managed, the oral element can be clearly seen to have a direct relationship with performance and improvement.

Feedback on written work, by contrast, usually lacks this sense of immediacy. Error correction comes later, often days or even weeks later, when the original task may no longer have much relevance to the writer. Even if it does come within a single lesson, if correction of the written work is carried out by the teacher, there will necessarily be an interval where the teacher is involved in the correction, and his or her involvement with the learners is consequently reduced. This will often lead to a quiet period when learners are, perhaps, reading or doing more writing. The effect on pace and classroom dynamics can be negative. The hustle and bustle of the 'market-place' of oral interaction and correction is lost.

With written work, correction will tend to come from the teacher. Peer correction, though possible, is, from a practical point of view, often less easy to manage and may not be widely used as a consequence. Simply returning the text to the learner with all the corrections made can have the same effect on the learner as the kind of oral correction where the teacher simply repeats the correct form each time without giving the learner the chance to self-correct. Except in the case of the most committed learners, written work returned to the learner with all the corrections made by the teacher is likely to finish up fairly quickly in the nearest waste receptacle, the learner pausing only to see what mark has been awarded or how many ticks there are on the piece of work concerned. Self-correction of written work seems to be the most favoured method, since it involves more self-discovery and trial and error on the part of the learner, but it also demands a great deal of application. Rewriting the same text following a scheme of error notation introduced by the teacher is, no doubt, extremely beneficial. However, it lacks the freshness of, say, trying to express something orally in a different way, having made an error or errors the first time. Since such rewriting may demand two, three or even more attempts, the question of motivation and application is a central one. By the fourth time of writing, the text may be as unappealing as a sentence repeated orally by the learner ad infinitum until the teacher accepts it as 'correct'.

Many learners simply find writing more difficult than speaking. Of course, this is not true for all learners and there are certain cultures, Japanese, for example, where more emphasis is placed in education on the written word and this, combined with cultural restraints on taking the initiative in conversation, can lead to the impression that such learners are much better at writing than at speaking. For the most part, however, the opposite is the case and writing is associated with difficulty. One of the major reasons for this is that written discourse, almost by definition, requires a greater degree of formal accuracy than oral discourse. Whereas a learner may be able to get his or her message across relatively successfully in an oral form, despite making a number of grammatical, lexical, syntactic and phonological errors, the same message in written form would generally be regarded as unacceptable, even incomprehensible, if accompanied by a similar number of errors (the phonological errors being replaced by corresponding errors of spelling and punctuation). More accuracy is demanded and this may be as frustrating for many learners keen to express themselves fluently in written form as it is for learners struggling to communicate orally and being constantly corrected. The need for accuracy also means a far greater amount of time is needed. Spontaneous writing, unlike spontaneous speaking, tends to be relatively rare. Preparation time is needed, as is follow-up time, probably involving self-correction of some kind. The whole process seems more time-consuming, more demanding and, possibly, less rewarding.

The above argument rests on the basic premise that writing, as part of the language-learning spectrum, is an area where tasks are set, written and corrected (either by the teacher or by the learners), and where accuracy of written form is the ultimate goal. Writing of this kind is generally regarded not as an end in itself, but as a means of practising language items and, ultimately, as a means of testing all-round language proficiency. Later in this chapter this model for writing will be challenged and a different set of priorities established.

2   What sort of writing activities do you use?

Task 1

Make a list of all the types of writing you ask your learners to do. Then read through the writing activities below suggested by a group of teachers.

In an attempt to discover the kind of writing activities commonly employed in general English classes, we asked a group of thirty teachers (fifteen native-speaker teachers, working both in the UK and overseas, and fifteen non-native-speaker teachers, from a variety of countries, mostly working in secondary education, although a few were in tertiary education) to list all the occasions when they asked their students to write. For the purposes of this survey, the teachers were asked not to include examination classes, where students would be preparing for examinations such as Cambridge FCE, with a large amount of formal writing necessarily included as a part of the course. The results were as follows, with the most frequent responses given at the beginning:

1 Copying

All of the teachers questioned said they either asked their students to copy from the board or from books or expected them to do so without being asked (students who did not write were regarded as extremely off-putting by several of the respondees!). Items copied were generally examples of grammatical structures, grammatical rules and items of vocabulary. Occasionally, students were asked to copy a dialogue or short narrative from the board for reference. Most of the teachers questioned stressed the value of a written record of what had been presented in class and the importance of a student vocabulary record. Many said they were systematic in their approach to vocabulary storing and encouraged learners to keep a complete record. The value of a written record in terms of teachers being able to check students' notes was also mentioned by several teachers. Some pointed out the value of copying for those with script and handwriting problems.

2 Written exercises (structure-based)

Once again, all of the teachers in the survey said that they regularly asked their learners to do written exercises. These were taken to mean exercises to practise grammatical structures, taking the form of writing sentences from prompts following a particular structural pattern, answering questions using a particular structural pattern, sentence completion, matching halves of sentences and writing out the complete sentence, and gap-filling using the correct tense or word, for example. Such exercises were frequently set as homework tasks, but, if done in the classroom, many teachers emphasized that they would use pair- or group-work to introduce a degree of communication into an otherwise fairly dry activity. Almost all of the teachers questioned said they regarded such exercises as valuable language practice and, once again, as a permanent record of what had been presented and practised in a particular lesson. A few doubted the value of giving such exercises on a regular basis, but said they did so because they felt that their learners expected to do this type of exercise and would feel uneasy without being asked to do them.

3 Guided writing exercises

Although the types of writing described above formed the major part of the writing teachers asked learners to do, guided writing exercises were used by the vast majority of the teachers in the survey. Most felt that they did not use these enough or only used them sporadically without any real sense of development. Reasons given for this were mainly lack of time and the fact that the coursebooks they used were, for the most part, inconsistent in their treatment of writing. Guided writing was taken to mean writing activities such as reassembling jumbled sentences to form paragraphs, shadow paragraphs, where students write according to a model with predetermined key words replaced in their version, multiple-choice for options to form a coherent paragraph, choice of linking words (multiple-choice or gap-fill) and writing paragraphs around link words, following a basic model. All were done with varying degrees of consistency and the overall feeling was that, while such exercises might be useful, it was generally difficult to convince students of their merits and the interest level was, as a result, rather low. The question of subject-matter, particularly in coursebooks, was raised as an issue in this and it was felt that lack of interest and relevance in the subject matter was a contributory factor.

4 Dictations

The discussion on dictation raised a number of interesting points. Some, presumably remembering the painful experiences of their schooldays, were vigorously opposed to the idea of using dictation in class and questioned its validity as a technique. The main criticisms were that they felt dictation to be artificial, teacher-centred, test-like in nature and basically pointless. The vast majority in the group, however, expressed a quite different view of the merits of dictation. There were two clear strands here: those who felt that dictation was a valid test of all-round language proficiency (grammar, syntax, lexis, phonology, listening and writing), and those who felt that dictation had numerous possibilities for imaginative, communicative work. In the latter case many had been inspired by the ideas in *Dictation – New Methods, New Possibilities* by Rinvolucri and Davis, which questions the traditional model of dictation (given by the teacher, read in short phrases repeated twice, corrected by the teacher and so on) and suggests a number of different approaches based on, inter alia, the learners giving the dictation, dictation and note-taking as opposed to verbatim writing and, in general, a more interactive approach. At the heart of this, however, dictation is still a form of writing and the teachers in the group who expressed favourable opinions about dictation were particularly impressed by the motivation created in their learners by the more imaginative of the interactive dictation activities and some expressed regret that they had no readily available source of similar activities to make other forms of writing, and not just dictation, more motivating for their learners.

5 Dialogues

Almost all of the teachers questioned said that they asked their learners to write short dialogues on a fairly regular basis. Usually this took the form of a shadow dialogue, where students wrote a new version based on a model, following certain restrictions. This was often done as a means of practising functional exponents, particularly at lower levels, and was frequently a prelude to a roleplay or similar practice activity. One or two in the group said they sometimes asked their learners to write completely free dialogues based around a topic or context and then to act them out. In general, however, this approach did not find much favour within the group, the need for excessive error correction being cited as a major weakness. Another criticism of having learners write dialogues, and free dialogues in particular, was that it was a wholly inauthentic activity. This was neatly summed up by one member of the group who wondered how many people would ever be asked to write TV scripts or plays in a foreign language. Despite this criticism, however, the general feeling of the group was that writing short dialogues was a regular feature of classroom practice, whatever the purpose of the activity might be, and that the general response of learners to this form of writing was positive, particularly if it was done as a collaborative task. It was suggested that learners liked this form of writing because, at a certain level, it brought language to life by contextualizing it in a communicative form.

6 Summaries

As with dictation, many remembered précis writing from their schooldays with a sense of undisguised horror and were consequently reluctant to 'inflict' it on their own learners. The merits of summary writing were, however, mentioned and many of the teachers questioned saw it as a useful means of both consolidating language (structure and lexis, in particular) and also of following up a reading or listening activity. Those who used summary writing on a more or less regular basis said that they often asked students to write for homework a brief summary of a text that had been read or a video extract that had been watched and then used the resultant summary as a means of checking both language and comprehension. One or two referred to the usefulness of guided summaries, where key words (particularly linking words) are given and the learners are given a framework on which to base their version.

7 Authentic writing tasks

The starting point for the discussion on this aspect of writing was a definition of what was meant by 'authentic writing tasks'. The definition arrived at, after much discussion, was that such tasks would include the kind of writing tasks normally carried out on an everyday basis by a native-speaker in his or her native language. For the purposes of the discussion, writing tasks related to following a course of educational study (eg note-taking, academic essay writing) were excluded. The 'authentic' native-speaker tasks included were activities such as writing letters, filling in forms, leaving messages, writing notices and taking down messages.

The context of the foreign language writing was then discussed. Most of the teachers in the group felt that only letter writing would be really relevant to students learning English in a non-English-speaking environment, while those in an English-speaking environment for an extended period of time would need *some* practice with the other types of 'authentic writing', defined by one member of the group as 'survival writing'. A great deal of scepticism was expressed by several teachers about the purpose of giving learners practice in filling in forms. They felt that this activity might be of some (limited) interest on one or two occasions, but that it would quickly lose any appeal if done regularly. For most people form-filling was not seen as a particularly pleasurable experience, and several in the group wondered whether it was a particularly difficult task in any case. Taking down telephone messages was generally regarded as both an essential survival skill and as a useful language practice activity. Similarly, some practice in writing succinct messages and notices was considered to be beneficial.

The subject of letter writing produced an animated discussion, much of which centred on the 'chicken and egg' nature of the topic. Some argued forcefully that learners with an adequate language ability would have no problems in writing letters, while others argued, equally persuasively, that learners could be taught to write better letters by attention to form and style. The consensus was that learners would generally need some help with format and convention, and that exposure to different letter types (invitation, application, complaint, inquiry, etc) with their corresponding formulae was of considerable benefit. Few in the group claimed to adopt a consistent approach to letter writing. Most said that they asked students to write letters from time to time and that, when they did so, they devoted some time to format and style. One non-native teacher had arranged for her class to correspond alternately in English and German with pupils from a school in England. She felt that this both motivated her pupils to write and gave them excellent language practice (errors were corrected by the English pupils). In general, however, with the exception of examination classes, like many other areas of writing, letter writing was not felt to be a priority, with time once again being cited as the main reason for this.

8 Essays

The question of writing essays turned out to be the most contentious of all the types of writing discussed. The basic problem for most of the teachers in the group was that for one reason or another (usually associated with formal examinations of some kind) their students had to write essays, but they did not like having to write them and their teachers either did not know how to help them (other than giving them more essays to write, working on the assumption that endless practice makes perfect) or did not want to help them, regarding essay writing in general as a rather pointless exercise. The question of authenticity was raised again. Who wrote essays in their mother tongue? No one in the group declared themselves an habitual essay-writer in their native language and it was difficult to imagine when anyone would, in any circumstance other than an examination, have the need to write an essay in a foreign language. Essay writing was dismissed by most of the teachers in the survey as a wholly inauthentic exercise, far-removed from the real world. But, at the same time, it was reluctantly agreed that it was a necessary evil, because it existed in so many forms in so many examinations in so many educational systems. As an ingrained manifestation of traditional education, the formal essay still occupied a prominent position and, as such, it had to be confronted and dealt with, whether teachers liked it or not.

Having grudgingly (in most cases!) established that essay writing did have to be taught, the teachers then revealed considerable differences in the ways that they 'taught' essay writing. One group took a similar line to letter writing and suggested that all-round language proficiency enabled learners to write adequate essays and they felt that the job of the teacher was to teach vocabulary, iron out structural and syntactic problems and deal with errors. In a sense, apart from providing the topic or the title of the essay, they seemed to suggest that essay writing was best left to take care of itself. Others felt that essay writing could be improved by explicit work on essay structure and style, while recognizing that this was often not particularly interesting for the learners. Several members of the group pointed out the advantages of linking reading to essay writing, with students being exposed to numerous examples of, say, descriptive and discursive essays, and then producing their own examples. The importance of working on cohesive devices was also mentioned in this discussion, and exercises such as reassembling jumbled paragraphs, gap-fill and multiple-choice exercises for linking words, and replacing linking words with alternatives were suggested.

Many people took issue with the 'traditional' descriptive and discursive essay forms as being too restrictive and far removed from the real world. In this sense, a strong preference was expressed for the kind of writing tasks that required students to respond to a 'real' situation rather than write an abstract essay. Here, the discussion returned to authentic writing tasks, and most of the examples of the kind of writing preferred turned out to be examples of extended letter writing of one sort or another. The writing requirements of a number of examinations (including state examinations in the various countries represented) were discussed and the efforts of some examination boards to make their writing tasks more authentic and practical were recognized. The Oxford Preliminary and Higher examinations were mentioned as including more motivating and realistic writing tasks, which were a clear move away from the traditional formal essay.

9 Other writing activities

The above general areas of writing activities were used at some time or other by all of the teachers in the survey. In addition to these categories, however, a number of other writing activities were mentioned, but were only used by a few of the teachers in the group in each case. The most prominent ones are mentioned here:

Story writing

Some teachers asked their learners to write their own versions of well-known stories (perhaps after hearing the original version in class, either on tape or read by the teacher). Students were also asked to write stories from sequences of pictures. In some cases, teachers built up a story on the board (elicited from the students) and then followed this up by asking them to write it out in full.

Diary writing

Encouraging learners to keep a diary has been one of the features of 'learner-centredness' and 'learner independence'. A few members of the group had tried this with mixed success. While recognizing the merits of this in terms of monitoring learner progress and particularly their own perception of and feelings about what they are doing in class, the validity of this as a writing activity was questioned. Was it not more natural for a diary to be written in the mother tongue? Surely a diary was intended as a personal document and not for the prying eyes of the teacher? Could feedback not be obtained in another way - writing a weekly letter to the teacher, for example?

Poetry writing

Even with lower levels, poetry writing had been successful, according to the few members of the group who had tried it. The most practically achievable forms had been those where learners had written poems according to a widely recognized convention (eg limericks) or had written their own versions in the style of a particular poem (substitution).

Student magazines

Given the luxury of plenty of time with an intensive course group, a few teachers in the group had been able to involve their students in a writing project – interviews, short descriptive articles, jokes, even poems, which were then published in the form of a student magazine. An alternative described by one teacher was a poster display of the same type of material.

Summary

The teacher survey covered a number of issues in writing and showed that the teachers in the group, although from a range of different teaching environments, generally used the same writing activity types. Differences, where they did appear, were not so much in the writing exercise categories, but in attitudes towards them (eg dictation) and in the perceived purpose of each activity. In some cases, teachers could find little purpose for particular activities other than the fact that they had always done them. In the next section we shall examine some of the aims of writing activities and assess whether the activities themselves are in tune with those aims.

Task 2

Using your list of writing activities from Task 1 and the list of activities commonly used by the group of teachers in the survey, note down next to each activity its main intended purpose.

3 What are the purposes of teaching writing?

Task 3

Now compare your views on the purposes of teaching writing with the comments of a number of teachers who were asked the question *What is the purpose of asking students to write?* Read through the list and make a note of any which broadly coincide with your own views.

a Writing is a useful follow-up. It helps to consolidate what has been learned.
(IVO, AUSTRIA)

b I see writing as an end in itself. Just as my learners want to be able to speak English, so they need to be able to write it too.
(ISABEL, SPAIN)

c The main purpose of writing is accurate use of language – especially grammatical structures.
(ULI, GERMANY)

d I think one of the most important reasons for having students write is to be able to assess their formal knowledge of the language.
(PHIL, USA)

e I use writing both to practise language and to encourage my learners to be creative.
(ANDREW, FRANCE)

f Writing is just another form of communication. My learners expect to be given writing practice to improve their all-round English. That's why I do it.
(HUGHIE, UK)

g I make my students write things down. They need it as a reference.
(LOREDANA, ITALY)

h Writing is more reflective than speaking. I think it gives learners more time, and they can be more accurate in what they write. I think they expect to do quite a lot of writing.
(MARTIN, GERMANY)

i The purpose of writing is simply to practise language.
(MARIA, SLOVAKIA)

j If you really think you know a foreign language, then you really need to be able to write fluently in that language. And you can only get to that point through constant practice. My aim in giving my students writing to do is to increase their confidence when writing and to improve their written fluency.
(HELEN, UK)

Commentary ■ ■ ■

These comments illustrate a number of different priorities for using writing activities with learners. For some teachers writing is seen very much as a means of consolidating what has been learned, a means of practising language. Similarly, it is seen as a reference point for learners, a written record of what has been learned. In terms of language purpose, writing is seen both as a forum for more accurate use of language and as a means of assessing formal knowledge of the language. Others focus on writing as part of communication as a whole and for them the purpose of writing is to improve written fluency. In this respect, writing is seen as a more reflective process than speaking, and this, in turn, also leads to higher expectations in terms of accuracy.

Some methodologists argue that writing activities in the classroom (or for homework) need to be based on one of two distinct purposes – either their focus is writing to practise language items of some kind (lexis, syntax, structures, functional exponents) or to practise the skill of writing itself (organizing the message, determining an appropriate style). The implicit message behind this is that the two areas are mutually exclusive, that teachers should either be concentrating on one or the other. It is, of course, extremely constructive for any writing activity to have a clearly defined purpose (both in the mind of the teacher and, if possible, in the mind of the learner), and any writing activity devoid of a purpose in either of these general areas would simply be time-filling (eg *For homework write a letter to your parents.*). However, it is also rather difficult to separate the areas of writing to practise language and writing as an end in itself in this way.

Working on language-based activities in writing (such as the written exercises outlined in Section 2 of this chapter) clearly has a language focus (with the aim of practising a particular form), but the very fact that the language is written by the learner is de facto writing practice too. Similarly, it is extremely difficult to see how any work explicitly focusing on writing can be devoid of language. In the latter case, learners are called upon to employ all their linguistic resources to complete a writing task (eg responding to an advertisement). In so doing, they are, ideally, both writing in an appropriate way and using a wide variety of language from their own personal store, ie practising language. Thus writing has a dual purpose and, if the task selected is relevant and within the ability of a particular group of learners, improvement can take place within both areas.

A more pressing question, perhaps (and another raised in the teacher quotes above) is that of accuracy in writing. The need for more formal accuracy in written discourse inevitably demands more concentration, care and application on the part of the writer (apart from other formal considerations such as clear handwriting and correct punctuation and spelling). This, in itself, may have a profound demotivating effect on those learners who find it difficult to apply themselves to a formal task for any length of time and who prefer to spend their time using language in a more fluent, communicative way. It will suit the type of learner who enjoys a more analytical, measured approach to language learning, and they will welcome the opportunity to write in a more formal, accurate way, away from the seemingly anarchic world of communicative fluency activities. The problem lies in reconciling the needs and wishes of both groups. In the next section some suggestions will be offered that may help to achieve this reconciliation. ■

4   Writing in a foreign language and teacher expectations

Two bald statements:

1 Writing in a foreign language is hard.
2 Teacher expectations are too high.

Writing in a foreign language *is* hard. You may, first of all, have to confront a new alphabet (eg Japanese, Arabic). Once you can cope with that, you have to confront syntax and grammatical rules. Then, of course, there are the various lexical quirks of the language. The idiosyncrasies of English have been well documented and this is not the place to go into them again, but, to take a neighbouring European language, most learners would confess to having problems at some time in deciding whether a word is masculine or feminine, and whether it requires an acute, grave or circumflex accent. In addition, there are specific conventions of punctuation, layout and style for different languages that again present problems for the learner. A little bit of writing in a foreign language may not be so problematic, but any kind of sophisticated, extended writing involving all the above factors is, with the exception of those who have attained an advanced level of proficiency in the language, likely to be a time-consuming, laborious and possibly unrewarding process. In short, hard.

Task 4

Think of a foreign language that you know reasonably well. Now make a list of all the types of writing that you regularly do in that language.

Task 5

Now compare your list with the experiences described in the following brief survey:

We asked a group of twenty native-speaker teachers of English as a foreign language (twelve resident in the UK and eight working abroad) the same question. All of them had, or claimed to have, a reasonable working knowledge of at least one foreign language. Some considered themselves to be fluent speakers of one or more languages.

Eleven of those questioned, including four resident abroad, said they never wrote anything (apart from the odd word or phrase) in any foreign language. They said that they probably could write if they had to but that they had no need to do so. For those who did write regularly in a foreign language, the word *regularly* was interpreted as anything from daily (in two cases) to once or twice a year in another case. Perhaps *sometimes* would have been a more appropriate word than *regularly*!

Those who wrote regularly in a foreign language gave the following categories in descending order of frequency:

1 personal letters and cards
2 forms (eg at the post office, registering at police stations, etc)
3 more formal letters (replying to invitations, requesting information)
4 simple messages

When asked about their proficiency in these areas, most modestly declared themselves to be 'average' rather than proficient writers, admitting to making many mistakes and to being, in some cases, ashamed of their lack of ability in writing. Yet in all cases, these were highly educated people, frequently graduates in the languages in question. Asked which of the four skills they found most difficult in their foreign languages, eighteen said formal writing, while the other two hesitated between writing and listening (citing accent and speed of delivery as the main reason).

Task 6

Think of a foreign language that you know reasonably well. Now consider how you would approach the following writing task in that language.

A friend has applied for a course of study at a university and has given your name as a referee. Write a reference for your friend in not more than 300 words, emphasizing his suitability for such a course.

Commentary ■ ■ ■

You probably would not want to do it, of course, but consider the amount of application required on the part of the writer, and also the degree of lexical and grammatical proficiency required to complete the task successfully. The argument here is that the very nature of writing and the time and motivation required to perform more than the simplest of tasks often mean that writing is perceived by learners as being difficult and, as a result, often labelled boring.

As for teacher expectations, there is a case for saying that they are often too high. In many cases, this is because the task the learner has been asked to do is way above his or her level of linguistic proficiency and thus the end result is error-strewn and, ultimately, demotivating for the learner. The negative suggestion of a piece of work returned covered in red ink can be extremely powerful. While recognizing the need for accuracy in writing, perhaps teachers could be more encouraging of attempts at fluency in writing and accept them as a successful (and possibly creative) message rather than an inaccurate piece of writing. If learners are only given simple tasks that they can cope with fairly easily, thereby producing accurate, if limited, results, then they are left with little room to experiment, little room for self-discovery. A more heuristic or discovery-based approach to some aspects of writing, coupled with a corresponding lowering of expectations by teachers and an acceptance of the fact that such writing will necessarily involve a great deal of trial and error in the search for a creative message, might encourage learners to take up their pens and be more creative, in much the same way that teachers supposedly encourage oral fluency by allowing learners to communicate freely in fluency activities, while taking a back seat themselves.

Naturally, adopting this kind of approach requires a certain amount of discussion between teachers and learners as to the nature and purpose of the writing tasks they are given. If learners understand that there are occasions when they need to be accurate (formal letters, for example) and that on such occasions, more writing time will be needed and the task may need to be done more than once, and that there are also times when the message is more important than how it is written, then progress can be made in both areas. If learners are freed from the constraint of always having to be accurate (or, indeed, always wanting to be accurate) and if teacher expectations of the written work of their learners are shifted accordingly, then learners might be more willing to experiment and be creative with writing and use writing at least some of the time for its original purpose – the passing on of information and messages. ■

5   Some writing options

Here are some suggestions for experimentation and evaluation in some of the aspects of teaching writing discussed in this chapter. Many may already be familiar to you; some may be new. The suggestions are not intended as 'solutions'. They are intended as options to be tried, tested and evaluated. They may help both to clarify the aims of your classroom writing activities and to give your learners more variety in the writing activities you ask them to do. The suggestions are offered in no particular order and without comment.

Task 7

We suggest the following procedure:

1 Think about the suggested activity or approach and how you could use or adapt it in your own classes.
2 Try it out.
3 Evaluate its usefulness by asking your learners what they think they got from the activity, whether they enjoyed doing it and what they thought its purpose was.

a Talk to your learners about the purposes of writing activities. Point out the need for accuracy in shorter pieces of written discourse and the possibility of creativity and experimentation in certain writing tasks. Talk to them about the role of errors and how they would like them to be treated.

b Provide only the key words of a short story or anecdote in chronological order. Ask your students to build up the story on the basis of these key words. Get them to compare the different versions.

c Provide only a skeleton structure of a story. For each part of the skeleton, give an instruction (eg *She was wearing strange clothes. Describe the clothes.*). The students elaborate on each stage. Get them to compare their different versions.

d Ask your students to write you a letter on a regular basis (weekly, monthly). You may prefer to establish in advance that you will not be able to reply by letter to each one (if you have six classes with fifteen students in each class, it would clearly be impossible to respond to each one!). The content can be specific (eg about the course) or general.

e Get your students to monitor the national or local press for a fixed period of time (eg a week in the case of an intensive course and a month in the case of a part-time course) and, working in groups, to produce a written report on the main issues.

f Give your students a set of basic information and get them to compose a fax message based on that information. The focus of the writing can be on the effectiveness of the message, the accuracy and appropriacy of the language, or a combination of the two.

g Jigsaw writing. Divide your class into groups and give each group (at random) one picture from a sequence of pictures. At this stage they will not know where in the sequence their particular picture appears. Tell each group to write a paragraph about their particular picture. For the sake of consistency, it may be practical to specify that all the groups write about the past. When the paragraphs are complete, get the whole group to decide on the correct order for the paragraphs and then to work on the language used (removing repetitions, linking the paragraphs, making the use of vocabulary consistent). If time permits, a variation on this is to mix the groups so that if, for example, you have four groups (one to four) consisting of four students each (A–D), then new groups can be formed of all the A students, all the B students and so on. This has the potential advantage of producing four (in this case) final versions, which may be good for comparative purposes.

h Responding to small ads. One possibility here is to use the small ads page from the holiday section of a national newspaper. If time permits, a variation on this is to use whole newspapers, thus simultaneously giving students skimming and scanning practice. The students are asked first of all to select a destination which appeals to them and then to find a specific advertisement which meets their own particular requirements. They then compose a letter requesting further information, a brochure, a booking form, etc. The focus of the writing in this case can be the style and layout of this type of letter and the effectiveness of the message.

i Invitations to a party. The focus of this activity is to get students to describe to a potential guest the exact way to get to their house or flat. One possibility here is to work with town plans, bus maps, timetables and so on and to write the invitation to someone arriving from a different town.

j Writing an information sheet for new students. Working in groups, students can be asked to produce an information sheet for future students of their school. This can consist of a list of *do's* and *don'ts*, suggestions for places to visit, descriptions of facilities and evening activities and so on. The fact that they are being asked to pass on their experience and expertise to others can often motivate students to do this type of task.

k Dialogue writing. Teachers often ask their learners to write short dialogues as a means of practising lexical items, grammatical structures, functional exponents and formulae in context. An extra dimension can be given to this if learners are given the opportunity to be more creative and to produce dialogues that are, in effect, 'mini-plays'. Differing degrees of contextual and linguistic control can be exercised, but it is also worth trying the idea of simply giving each group of learners a context or topic to work around and allowing them to develop their dialogues as they wish. One option is to do this as a workshop activity, with appropriate teacher monitoring, use of dictionaries, student questions and so on. The final versions can be compared, read out, acted out or, perhaps, displayed on the classroom wall.

l Shadow poetry writing. Select a short, striking poem. It need not rhyme but it will be helpful if it has a distinctive rhythm. Ask your learners to work in groups and to produce a version of the poem that retains the structure of the original and scans in the same way, but where the vocabulary and perhaps the ideas in the poem are different. We saw a very impressive example of this activity produced by a group of upper-intermediate Italian students, who had written their own versions of Adrian Henri's poem 'Tonight at Noon'. Where, for example, the original had the line *America will declare peace on Russia*, one group of students had written the line *The Mafia will give out flowers in Rome*.

6 Conclusions

As with all areas of language learning, writing requires a great deal of commitment and motivation on the part of the learner. If learners are uncertain of the purposes of writing, then often they will rapidly become demotivated and unwilling to invest much time and energy in it. If they see its function purely as reinforcement of formal linguistic patterns, then they will be reluctant to perform 'freer' writing tasks, as these will be error-ridden and lacking a clear linguistic focus. If, on the other hand, they favour a more creative approach, they may well become demotivated if asked to perform endless controlled, guided writing tasks that focus on accuracy. Similarly, they will not be impressed if attempts at free writing come back covered in red ink. Perhaps if learners can be made aware that there are times for accurate writing and times for freely expressed writing just as there are in speaking, and if this awareness can be combined with the use of motivating and interesting writing tasks, then the perception in the minds of many learners (and teachers) that writing is essentially a boring activity might change and writing might once again assume a more prominent place in the language-teaching spectrum.

7 Recommended reading

Process Writing by Ron White and Valerie Arndt applies current thinking about writing to practical classroom activities.

Dictation by Mario Rinvolucri and Paul Davis takes a completely new look at one of the most traditional of writing activities and shows how it can be infused with new life and used to include a whole range of linguistic skills.

8 References and bibliography

Byrne, D. 1988 *Teaching Writing Skills* new edition (Longman)
Coe, N. et. al. 1983 *Writing Skills – A Problem-Solving Approach* (CUP)
Halliday, M. and Hasan, R. 1976 *Cohesion in English* (Longman)
Hedge, T. 1988 *Writing* (OUP)
Jolly, D. 1984 *Writing Tasks* (CUP)
Morgan, J. and Rinvolucri, M. 1983 *Once Upon A Time* (CUP)
Pincas, A. 1982 *Teaching English Writing* (Macmillan)
Rinvolucri, M. 1983. Writing to Your Students. In *ELT Journal*, vol. 37, no. 1
Rinvolucri, M. and Davis, P. 1988 *Dictation* (CUP)
White, R. and Arndt, V. 1991 *Process Writing* (Longman)

Chapter 11 Soft chairs and silence:
Humanistic approaches

1 Introduction

The Silent Way, Suggestopedia and Community Language Learning have, for quite a long time now, been lumped together as 'humanistic' or 'alternative' or even 'fringe' approaches. Many teachers know them from introductory workshops or second-hand reports. And in many quarters, any initial curiosity or enthusiasm has given way to cynicism and lack of interest. So what are these approaches (or are they methods, or techniques, or something else?), what have they got in common, how do they differ from 'mainstream' approaches, what have they got to offer, and are they condemned for ever to remain on the fringes, the topic of provocative one-off demonstration lessons?

2 Reports on journeys to the fringe

Task 1

What do you know, if anything, about these three approaches? Note down some key words about them if you can, as well as notes about your own attitude towards what you have heard.

See whether anything you wrote is confirmed or challenged by these reports.

I've been to quite a few beginning seminars on the Silent Way, and it's always 'Here's a rod,' 'It's a red rod,' and just the very basic things, I've never seen how it develops at all. But the basic philosophy is that the teacher is giving minimal input and the students are having to work hard to process that input and develop it and use it, and that the teacher only comes in as a last resource, having given the initial input. It seems to me very controlled.
(KATE, UK)

The message for me [in the Silent Way] was one of accepting, a non-judgmental approach. The teacher would indicate whether the language was right or not, but it was non-judgmental. The teacher wasn't totally silent, but there was a lot of 'You speak, it's your turn,' opening it up to other students to suggest options. Accepting, 'Yes, that's valid, but it's not correct' – the value of the language, not the person.
(ELLIE, UK)

By Silent Way I understand a method whereby the students are thrown back on their own resources, not given instant reinforcement, or often even later reinforcement, as to correctness or incorrectness of their guesses, and really leaving them to find out and come to clear conclusions about the reasons for their decisions. I think it's a very full student responsibility. The teacher's responsibility is clearly setting accessible tasks that can be useful in developing their analysis of whatever it is they're looking at at the time. Suggestopedia: set long dialogues, music, pictures, armchairs, comfort ...
(LIN, CZECH REPUBLIC)

Suggestopedia – the first demonstration of it I ever had was somebody spouting very loud French at me with Wagner playing in the background, and we were so tired we all fell asleep, and that's an abiding memory for me. [In other sessions] we all stood round in a circle, throwing language across the circle. The theory is of relaxation and a comfortable environment – but the actual way it fits together I've never really understood.
(KATE, UK)

CLL interests me more and more. My picture of it is a group of students who are motivated either themselves or by the teacher to start a conversation. They can use the teacher as a resource to express exactly what they want – the teacher's always bilingual or has a very good command of the students' language. They compile a tape of the bits that they're given by the teacher and presumably they go on and study that later.
(LIN, CZECH REPUBLIC)

CLL – You all sit round in a little circle and I suppose the philosophy is that the students are able to say what they want to say. I've only ever had demonstrations of first lessons, which gives you such a quirky view.
(KATE, UK)

3   Descriptions of what it's like out there

Here we offer rough descriptions of three lessons. These are not directions for rigid procedures that 'have to be' or 'should be' followed; they are sketches of imaginary but – we believe – representative lessons conducted in the spirit of each of the three approaches. In visualizing the lessons described, you may recognize something of your own teaching either at the level of observable technique or at the deeper level of underlying attitude or educational philosophy. You may also find yourself confronted with something new at either or both these levels.

Task 2

As you read, you might like to ask yourself:

- Do I recognize anything of my own teaching in these descriptions?
- How do these lessons differ from 'mainstream' ones? What's 'alternative' about them? What's 'humanistic' about them?
- What questions do they raise for me?

Silent Way

A class of elementary learners of English are clustered around a table, some sitting and some standing. On the table is an arrangement of Cuisenaire rods[1]. One learner picks up a selection of the rods and moves them to a different part of the table. After a few moments, another one says tentatively: 'You moved one of the red ones, both of the blue ones and both of the yellow ones.' Another says: 'Yellow ... both?' Another: 'No, because three and he moved two, so "two".' 'Two of the yellow ones?' 'Yes.' 'So, you moved one of the red ones, both of the blue ones and two of the yellow ones.'

The teacher taps out the rhythm x x X x x X x on the table. The learner who built the sentence now says 'you moved ONE of the RED ones,' following this rhythm, and then the whole sentence, with each of the three parts approximating to this rhythm. One of the other learners also has an attempt, comes unstuck halfway through, starts again and this time manages the sentence successfully.

One of the others puts all the rods back together, and selects some for removal, this time including all three of the yellow ones, which leads, through some negotiation, to sorting out when to use *both*, *two* and *all*. Some of the members of the class pronounce *both* with the vowel of *bottle*; the teacher points to the word *both* on a large chart of words posted on the wall, and draws attention to the 'o', which is printed in two colours (the 'b' is another colour, and the 'th' another). The learners now say *both*, carefully articulating the diphthong. The teacher turns to another chart consisting entirely of coloured rectangles on a black background, and points to three rectangles in turn; the learners say *both* with the – incorrect – short vowel. The teacher then points to another sequence of three rectangles – the first and third the same as before and the second different – and they say *both* with the diphthong.

---

1   Cuisenaire rods, named after their inventor, are small blocks of wood with a uniform square cross-section but different lengths (the smallest is really more a cube than a rod). Each length has its own colour.

Questions which teachers have asked about Silent Way include these:

- Why do these particular learners participate?
- What are the others doing in the meantime?
- What is the teacher doing, and how is the progression of the lesson decided?
- What's the significance of the rods?
- Why aren't the learners taught useful everyday language?
- Can this approach work above elementary level?
- Can it work with large classes?
- How, if at all, does it deal with reading, listening, vocabulary and so on?

Suggestopedia

As we enter the classroom, which is bright and furnished with soft, comfortable chairs and a pleasant, deep carpet, the learners are involved in acting out a sketch, which has clearly been prepared and rehearsed, but still leaves plenty of room for spontaneity and creativity. The atmosphere is one of confidence, mutual support and enjoyment. The language is varied and expressive. The learners don't seem inhibited about making mistakes; on the contrary, they seem to take delight in their own and each other's attempts to negotiate communication difficulties. The teacher is an enthusiastic audience, mingling with the actors and encouraging and applauding them. The actors use simple props and costumes – scarves, hats, shopping bags, umbrellas and so on. The walls of the classroom are adorned with charts containing language patterns, with salient features marked out in various colours, but also pieces of writing done by the class, and paintings and photos. The chairs have been moved to the sides of the room for the sketch; when it ends they are pulled into a semicircle, and after a short break during which the heightened atmosphere of the sketch gradually cools down, the learners sit down and the teacher moves to a position standing facing the semicircle. She passes round a set of handouts containing a long dialogue with a parallel translation into the learners' L1, and stands in silence for a while, smiling and making eye contact with each member of the class, matching the energy level of each person and, it seems, bringing them down to a lower energy. Then she begins to read through the dialogue, including the translation of sections containing new items. She also stops from time to time to give a grammatical explanation, or give a model of the pronunciation of a word, or draw an illustration on the board. Sometimes the learners also ask questions of meaning, pronunciation and so on, which she answers. The dialogue is lengthy – five or six sides of A4, and the language it contains is grammatically and lexically rich and varied. It soon becomes clear that it is a continuation of the story which was illustrated in the sketch we saw at the beginning of the lesson – the subsequent adventures of the same characters. The learners laugh at the humour of the story, and as they recognize the characters they have just portrayed. Now the teacher turns and switches on a cassette recorder, from which emerge the strains of a late classical concerto – maybe some of the learners identify exactly what it is. After a couple of minutes, the teacher begins to read the same dialogue, but in a very different voice, a dramatic kind of declamation somewhere in between speaking and singing. Her voice follows the ebb and flow of the music approximately, the rhythm of the words coinciding at times with the rhythm of the music. The learners either follow the text closely, or glance at it from time to time.

After this reading, there is a break of about five minutes, during which everyone maintains silence, some getting up to stretch, others looking through the text, others closing their eyes. When everyone has reassembled, the teacher again comes to the front of the room, this time sitting down, and switches on the cassette recorder. This time the music is quite different – a sequence compiled from the slow movements of baroque concertos. The learners have their eyes closed; the teacher again reads the dialogue, but this time the reading is relaxed and follows the patterns of normal speech. When she reaches the end of the dialogue, she lets the music play on. One by one, the learners open their eyes and gather their belongings together in preparation for leaving the class.

Questions about Suggestopedia:

- What if they don't like classical music?
- What if I can't afford the chairs and carpets?
- How can the learners handle such huge amounts of new language, especially if it isn't selected and graded very strictly?
- How can they just sit there and listen for so long?
- What about letting them *use* the new language?

Community Language Learning

A group of about fifteen adults sit in a circle. They are meeting for the first time. They share the same L1 and they are all more or less beginners in English. In the space in the middle of the circle, on a small table, is a cassette recorder, and, attached to it by a long lead, a hand-held microphone with an on/off switch. The teacher, who remains outside the circle of chairs throughout the following procedure, begins the lesson by greeting the class and explaining, in the learners' L1: 'We're going to make a conversation together, and record it so that we can do some further work with it. You can all contribute as much or as little as you like to this conversation. Whoever would like to begin the conversation should signal to me. I will then come to you, and you can tell me what you'd like to say. I'll tell you how to say it in English, and I'll help you to practise it as much as you need. When you think you're ready, take the microphone, switch it on, record what you wanted to say, and switch it off again. Then the next person who wants to say something signals to me, and we follow the same procedure, and so on, until the conversation seems to be finished, or until we run out of time.'

The teacher lets the initiative come from the learners, both as regards who wants to speak, and as regards how much they feel they need to practise each utterance and/or hear it modelled by the teacher before it is ready to be committed to tape. After half an hour or so of working in this way, there is a short break for everyone to stretch their legs a bit. Then the teacher asks the class if they have anything to say about the work they have done so far, and reflects back to them what they have said, or asks for clarification if necessary (all in the L1, of course):

LEARNER: It was very surprising.
TEACHER: It was different from what you expected? Maybe different from other language courses you've been on, or heard about?
LEARNER: Yes.

LEARNER: I liked being able to repeat my sentence so many times.
TEACHER: You felt that you needed quite a bit of practice, and it was good that you got it?
LEARNER: That's right.

LEARNER: I'd like to know the grammar.
TEACHER: So you feel uncomfortable because we didn't do any grammatical study of the language we were learning?
LEARNER: Yes, I think this is important.

and so on.

The tape of the conversation is now played and the learners again have an opportunity to comment; because only the final, practised version of each utterance has been recorded, the conversation is coherent, accurate and, apart from a few fumblings with the microphone, has a fairly natural flow. Comments include: 'It sounds like real English,' 'I can't understand anything now,' 'It's so short, after all the time we spent!'

The teacher now plays the tape bit by bit. For each bit – a sentence, clause or phrase of manageable length – the learners are invited to identify the speaker, recall the meaning of what was said, and, if they can, reproduce the English version. The teacher fills in any gaps remaining, and transfers the conversation, bit by bit, onto an overhead transparency, with a parallel translation into the L1. She points out, with the help of the learners' guesses, which bits of the two languages correspond to each other, and answers any questions the learners have; they also ask her to say any parts they would like to hear again, and can, if they want, practise saying these themselves. Some of the learners also try to recombine elements from different parts of the conversation to produce novel utterances. The teacher either indicates that these are correct, or gives a model of a correct version, which the learners may use as the basis for practising.

The lesson is now at an end. The teacher calls in at the school office to make photocopies from the OHT, which she distributes to the class before they leave.

Questions about Community Language Learning:

- What if I haven't got a monolingual class?
- What about the learners who are too shy to take part in building the conversation, or who just don't feel like it? Aren't they missing out?
- The language that gets used and studied must be pretty random if it relies completely on what the learners feel like saying to each other. Isn't there a need for a syllabus, a planned progression of some kind?
- How can I use this approach with higher levels?

4   Some answers

The Silent Way was originally called the Subordination of Teaching to Learning, which is actually more explicit about the intention behind it. It sounds less revolutionary than it used to, and there's some common ground with recent recommendations for 'learner-centred' teaching, but Silent Way goes much further in its insistence that learning is the responsibility of the learners, that their powers of observation and cognition are sufficient to enable them to invent for themselves far more of the language than is commonly supposed, and that they are handicapped by reliance on teaching.

Silent Way teachers often use a certain set of tools in putting this into practice. These include Cuisenaire rods, which enable all the grammar of a language to be introduced and practised in a very pure and clear fashion; the word charts, which contain many of the most common words of the language – including the 'grammatical' words – colour coded for pronunciation and available for combination and manipulation, and the sound–colour chart, which contains all the phonemes of the language in the form of coloured rectangles – corresponding to the colour coding of the word charts – so that the pronunciation of the language can be practised and new words constructed by forming sequences of colours and therefore of sounds. These tools and the techniques associated with them form what might be called a Silent Way 'method', but the *approach* represented by the 'Subordination of Teaching to Learning' requires no particular techniques or materials, but rather a certain awareness or attitude. We have sometimes seen ineffective and pointless Silent Way teaching, where the *method* has been used but without the awareness which gave rise to it.

Here lies, too, the answer to the question about level. It's likely that, in classes at higher levels, the *method* will be less visible, with the materials described above being used less, and replaced by any materials which embody the learners' interests. Seeing the Silent Way in action then requires an observer to look through the surface layer of the visible, to see what is going on underneath. In any case, a lesson conducted in accordance with a Silent Way approach will involve the teacher being acutely aware of where the learners are in their exploration of the language, providing a framework for them to take the next step, providing language which they cannot invent or assemble from their previous knowledge, and giving factual feedback on the correctness of their hypotheses. One of the implications of this is that the teacher may not need to say very much, but the silence of the teacher has often been misinterpreted by the over-enthusiastic, and imitated to the point where necessary help is withheld. It may also happen that particular learners are silent and apparently uninvolved for certain periods of the lesson. It may be that they are letting others conduct experiments with issues they have already sorted out for themselves, or it may be that they are working on the same issues, but internally, carefully watching and listening to see whether their hypotheses are confirmed by the members of the class who are overtly 'participating'. This explains how the Silent Way can work with large classes, providing everyone can see and hear what's going on.

Silent Way is unfashionable in the importance it gives to developing accuracy in grammar and pronunciation at the expense of emphasizing 'communication' and teaching lots of immediately usable language.

Suggestopedia attaches great importance to the physical and psychological comfort of the learners, to instilling confidence and enjoyment in using the language even before the stage at which accuracy begins to become automatic. It aims to stimulate learners' creative, artistic, musical, holistic faculties, associated with the right hemisphere of the brain, as well as the logical, analytical ones, associated with the left. The classical music used in the first 'concert reading' acts as a kind of 'carrier' which enables large amounts of new language to be taken in. The second reading helps this material to 'settle', and the learners then take this material away with them and begin to process it, not least during sleep. In subsequent lessons, a variety of game-like activities, as well as more traditional types of language practice and analysis, begin to activate this new language.

It's claimed that it doesn't matter whether or not the learners *like* the music, or whether or not they are familiar with western classical music; it will inevitably have the intended effect. The answer given to those who feel their attention uncomfortably divided between the music and the text is: It doesn't matter which you listen to. But if you really want a definite answer, listen to the music!

It seems that most, or even all, the trappings of physical comfort, music and so on, are expendable if the circumstances make it difficult to provide them and – crucially – if the teacher is appropriately trained. The one factor which is essential is the quality of benevolent authority of the teacher, which carries the bulk of the 'suggestion' that learners can achieve much more than they might believe.

It will be clear from the descriptions that both Suggestopedia and CLL rely, at least in their pure forms, on translation of the new language introduced. However, in work with non-beginners, there is no reason why they shouldn't be used with multi-language groups. In Suggestopedia, translation would be replaced by glossing, paraphrasing, forms of non-linguistic illustration and perhaps access to dictionaries.

Similarly, in CLL, in the case of a multi-language non-beginner class, the teacher can have the role of shaping and improving what the learners can already express in a rough-and-ready way. The question about unequal participation really has the same answers as in the Silent Way; participation is each individual's decision, and not talking isn't necessarily a sign of non-involvement and lack of learning.

The syllabus – such as it is – in CLL is determined entirely by the learners. This means, first of all, that they are getting what they need in order to fulfil their needs as they perceive them, and this is particularly important if they are in a target-language-speaking community. But, less obviously perhaps, it may happen that their interest in the language itself leads them to try out hypotheses about how the language works, and this can have the effect of shaping the progression into something like a structural syllabus. It's also possible for the teacher to shape the follow-up work on language from the conversations to highlight certain features in an ordered way.

5   Conclusions

Task 3

So what do these approaches have in common, and why are they called 'humanistic'?

Commentary ■ ■ ■

Here are two teachers' answers:

Giving space to the students, I suppose, minimal teacher imposition, a lot of use of quietness, of waiting, waiting for the students to take the initiative.
(KATE, UK)

They perceive the student as an individual, and not just a receptacle for language, someone with feeling and a capacity for creative thought. But I don't know how much I really believe that and how much is just that that's what I've been taught about them. I'd also like to think that that's something I believe about teaching generally, and something that I believed before I ever heard of any of these approaches.
(LIN, CZECH REPUBLIC)

There has sometimes been confusion over the word *humanistic* through association with others such as *humane, humanitarian* and the expectation that such teaching is soft-centred and insubstantial, or the contradictory observation that some Silent Way teachers, for example, seem to be extremely demanding and strict. It's probably more illuminating to consider 'humanistic' in the light of the general aims of humanistic psychology, helping people to fulfil the enormous human potential they possess, in this case as regards learning, and more specifically the learning of a foreign language. And the conviction that learning is entirely the learner's responsibility and the learner's achievement – and part of the learner's personal development – is what underlies the methods, techniques and materials, and what really defines the approaches.

It was the people, not the approaches – validating, not expecting, allowing things to happen, and waiting for the time to be right for any particular individual, not that everybody has to be there at a particular time – just allowing stuff to happen. So it's more to do with the person and their attitude than with an approach.
(ELLIE, UK) ■

6   What's in it for me?

What can these approaches offer a teacher who doesn't feel the need to pursue them in depth?

Well, plenty of tricks and techniques: Cuisenaire rods, playing music to influence atmosphere, playing ball games to practise language …

and:

Suggestopedia has given me a lot of important principles, like it's really important how comfortable students are, mentally and physically, and the importance of a non-stressful, non-threatening atmosphere, so although the actual technique is something I've never used, the general ideas behind it have become part of my teaching.

The thing that appeals to me about CLL is students being given the tools to say what they want to say and that's a principle I've taken into vocabulary teaching and grammar teaching and feedback from fluency activities, and I think is one of the most important, most successful parts of my teaching. Any fluency activity I do, after the feedback from the task, the first language feedback is always 'Was there anything that you wanted to say and couldn't, or that you said and are not satisfied with how *you said it, anything I can help you with?' And when you first do that with a group of students you get vocabulary questions, but if you persist that becomes a really significant part of any lesson.*

Silent Way: the basic principle of not wanting to be the decider of what's right and wrong, and trying to encourage students to do the deciding of what's good language and what isn't, and to take that responsibility. I think that unless they start to develop that awareness they're never going to be able to begin to continue learning language outside the classroom. That's important for any learner who's going to be successful. For example, a class of beginners bring back a homework exercise, look at it together, decide if the answers are the same or different, then letting them discuss and say which they think is right. That's their job, it's part of their learning.
(Lin, Czech Republic)

Task 4

What do you feel you might be able to gain from these approaches, which would be compatible with, and complementary to, your teaching style?

7   Recommended reading

Earl Stevick's *Memory, Meaning and Method* and *A Way and Ways* both contain very readable accounts of the author's own investigation of these approaches (Newbury House, 1976 and 1980).

For a mainstream view which describes these approaches and compares them with other, more traditional ones, see *Approaches and Methods in Language Teaching* by Jack Richards and Ted Rodgers (CUP 1986).

Chapter 12 Ten years' experience or one year experienced ten times?
Looking back and looking forward

You probably wouldn't have bothered to read this book unless you were motivated by beliefs or assumptions like these:

- English language teaching isn't a mechanical job where every lesson, every day, every week is the same as any other.

- Being a teacher of English – or of anything, for that matter – offers enormous scope for personal and professional development; and indeed, if we want to be as effective as we can, even *obliges* us to go on looking for ways of improving as long as we teach.

- Although we can benefit from being trained by people with more experience or expertise – and not only at the start of our careers but at any subsequent time, too – the development work we do as teachers is our own responsibility, in terms of motivation, planning, decision-making, research, focus, implementation and evaluation.

- By stepping outside our own perspective and looking into what other people have done, said and written, we can gather useful stimuli for our own development work.

We certainly hold these beliefs, and it is in this spirit that we have tried to draw your attention to certain practices, issues and beliefs in a way that may help you in investigating areas of interest in your own teaching. We also believe that teacher development is an open-ended process with no identifiable beginning and no predictable end, and that the next step of any developmental process is determined by where we are now. So rather than adopting a convergent perspective and only making recommendations, we have tried to open issues up and allow for divergent opinions, interpretations and conclusions. But at the same time, of course, we hold our own opinions about learning, teaching and language – even though we may sometimes have exasperated teachers we have worked with by being stubbornly non-committal! These opinions are sometimes acknowledged explicitly in what we have written; at other points they will be discernible just below the surface. We have also presented, we hope in a non-judgmental way, a small sample of the views of the extended community of teachers working in English language teaching today.

As we near the end of this book, we'd like to offer a few tasks which turn back from looking at specific topics within English language teaching to consider more general aspects of language learning, and the role of teaching. If at all possible, do them together with other teachers. We believe, and we hope this has become apparent by now, that learning about teaching, like all learning, is an individual responsibility and an individual achievement, but can be greatly facilitated by working together with others.

Task 1

Look back at the 'articles of faith' in Chapter 1 (p 7), and any additions you may have made to the list. Have your feelings about any of these changed, and would you like to add any more now?

Task 2

Do the same with the classroom metaphors in the section 'Beyond methods' (p 13). What does each chosen metaphor say about the roles of the teacher and the learners, and the interaction between them?

Task 3

What do you think are the absolute bare minimum requirements for language learning to take place? Certainly not coursebooks, dictionaries, cassettes and so on. Not even schools, classrooms and teachers – most of the language learning in the world happens without these. The answer will be more abstract than this.

Commentary ■ ■ ■

Our suggested answer is that there are four things:

- motivation;
- data (ie samples of the language, and information about the language);
- opportunities for experimentation;
- feedback

You may disagree with this, but whatever list you come up with, it might be a useful tool for thinking about what language learning and teaching consists of at a level beyond fashions, methods and approaches. Classroom-based language teaching involves an interaction between a triangle of forces: the language, the learner and the teacher. On historical and present global evidence, the teacher is not strictly *necessary* for language learning to take place – whereas the other two, the learner and the language, clearly are. How, then, does the teacher fit into the equation? What function can the teacher most usefully fulfil in relation to providing the minimum requirements of motivation, data, opportunities for experimentation, and feedback (or your own list)? And conversely, how can (do) teachers inhibit, interfere, get in the way of maximally effective language learning? ■

Task 4

Now here are some possible ways of looking at the process of language learning. Note which ones seem illuminating for you, and whether any others spring to mind.

Learning a language is like:

- building a wall;
- climbing a ladder;
- walking through a jungle;
- learning to ride a bike;
- developing a photograph;
- doing a jigsaw puzzle.

If you think of language learning in each of these ways, what are the implications for the role of the teacher? eg *Learning a language is like building a wall, and the role of the teacher is ...*

Commentary ■ ■ ■

We think that considering learning and teaching in these ways can help to reduce them to the fundamental issues which are sometimes obscured by theories and trends and methodologies, and can help teachers to interpret their own experience, and discover what their own theories are. ■

Task 5

What, if anything, do you think will change for you as a result of reading this book? In some cases, it's possible that the process of reading and reflection itself has brought about a shift in awareness which will have a noticeable effect on something you do in your teaching. In other cases, you may think *Hmm, that's interesting; I'd like to experiment with that,* or *I've never thought of doing that before; I wonder how my classes would react,* or *Yes, I think that's what I do, though I've never really thought about it before,* or *That sounds ridiculous, but if other teachers do it and say it works ...,* and so on.

Commentary ■ ■ ■

We suggest that if there are issues you'd like to follow up – whether mentioned explicitly in this book or not – it might be useful to turn your intention into a more rigorously-defined procedure, or action plan. There are various such possible procedures – here are a couple of imaginary examples, applied to two different teacher self-development issues.

Example 1

1 When I did my training to be an English language teacher, it was very strongly recommended – expected, even – that we should give models of new language, questions to learners, and class management instructions at least twice, maybe three times, to give adequate opportunity for learners to hear and understand. This felt a bit awkward initially but I soon got used to it and now it's pretty automatic.

2 I read in an ELT magazine a short article which said that teachers often waste their breath in repeating what they – and learners – have said. The writer claims that learners can often understand more than we give them credit for if we give them time to process what they've heard and formulate their response – which might take quite a bit of time and effort, especially at elementary levels. I instinctively react against this idea, but later, it returns to my thoughts and I remember a recent incident in a lesson: I asked a question, one of the class started to answer, but at the same moment I'd started to repeat the question. I remember my voice rising and quickening slightly so as to drown out the learner's voice, and his slightly annoyed expression and subsequent unwillingness to answer the question. I decide that perhaps there is something in what I read, after all.

3 I plan to try and gather some more substantial evidence on the issue.

4 Over a period of a couple of weeks, I tape-record my lessons whenever I remember to, just using any old cassette recorder placed at some convenient point in the classroom. I listen to the recordings whenever I get the chance, often when I'm doing something else about the house. Parts of the recordings aren't clear and I only half pay attention a lot of the time, but I listen more attentively to sections where I'm involved in dialogue with the class or with individuals. I notice that I do indeed tend to repeat myself, much more than I realized. And not only that; I also realize that I tend to repeat things the learners say, especially when they answer my questions – sometimes in order to make minor corrections, but sometimes even if what they said was perfectly OK.

5 I resolve to enlist the help of a couple of my classes – the ones I feel most comfortable and confident with. I play them some relevant bits of the classroom recordings and ask them if they remember the lessons and the incidents. In some cases the answer is no, but in some cases it's yes, and I ask how they felt about what happened, and what was going through their minds. Some of them haven't really got anything to say and don't seem to think it's very important; others, talking about the taped incidents and other similar ones they can recall, say that sometimes they do understand the first time and are distracted by my repetition when they're trying to formulate a response, or that they think they've understood me the first time, but then get confused because, as distinct from repeating verbatim what I've said, I paraphrase it or expand it, and they're not sure whether the question or the task is being changed. This introduces a new aspect of my investigation, and I recall instances from the recordings where this happened, but where I didn't notice it particularly. We have some discussion about whether or not I should repeat myself. Some say yes, it's helpful, others disagree and say they would welcome some silent time to prepare what they're going to say in reply. I also ask them how they feel when I repeat things they've said; some say it's good as a confirmation of what's right, some say they get confused because they don't know whether or not I'm correcting them, and others say they feel belittled or patronized, as if their saying it wasn't good enough and it has to be given my stamp of approval. I decide to leave this for further investigation and go back to the original issue of me repeating myself.

6 I continue to make recordings of lessons from time to time, but I notice a change in my awareness during lessons. Sometimes I notice repetitions after they occur, sometimes as they occur, and, increasingly, I'm aware beforehand of a moment when I can choose to repeat or not to repeat. At the same time, I become more able to notice and judge what's happening in the class, to detect signs of comprehension or incomprehension. (Sometimes I'm wrong, of course!) Often, silence is enough to enable learners to consider what I've said and respond. I find the silences unnatural at first, and long, though the evidence of the cassette recorder suggests it's usually a matter of five seconds at most, and I begin to get more accustomed to it, especially as I find myself able to put those few moments to good use in paying closer attention to the expressions in learners' faces, and to signals that say either *What?* or *Just a moment, I haven't quite got that*, or *Yes, OK, let me just think how to reply to that*, and so on.

7 Although there are setbacks, times when I overestimate learners and find I go too far in the opposite direction, I find generally that they benefit from my experiments in being able to do more for themselves without relying so much on me, and I benefit in having more space to observe them and tune into what they're doing. My recordings and discussions with classes have also suggested other possible fruitful lines of enquiry.

Example 2

A possible procedure for a group of teachers interested in working on their professional development.

1 Individually, brainstorm qualities of a good teacher (or of a good English language teacher specifically).

2 Compare lists in twos. This may suggest additions and alterations for clarification.

3 Gather everyone's suggestions together on a blackboard or flipchart. Edit the combined list to remove overlap, clarify, add anything new that arises.

4 Individually, select those qualities (a certain number could be specified) which are particularly important to you – at your stage of development as a teacher, or in the particular work you're doing at the moment.

5 From the resulting list, choose two or perhaps three qualities which you feel you succeed well in, and three where you would like to score better. (You could perhaps give yourself a score out of ten for each quality.)

6 For each high-scoring quality, write down how you can maintain and enhance your excellence. For each low-scoring quality write down how you can improve. It's most helpful if you write in concrete terms of behaviour which will be observable.

7 Work with a partner. Either show what you've written, or relate it verbally. Clarify as necessary, and, if you want, ask for comments and suggestions.

8 If your action plan is too long to be achievable, or even manageable, select a few points which can take priority and which can be implemented before the next meeting of the group.

9 Decide what kind of support, if any, you will want from your partner or other colleagues – some discussion after you've put some of your points into practice, someone to listen to you, someone to sit in and observe according to an agreed contract?

10 Ask yourself whether you really will do what you've intended. If you don't think you will, change it to make it less ambitious.

11 Decide how you will recognize when you have achieved what you intend.

12 Carry out your plan. Record the experience and the results in any way you think will be useful – keeping a journal, sharing it with a colleague ...

13 Bring the experience back to the group. If you're ready, move on to another, or revised set of issues.

You may find that you don't particularly need to adhere to procedures of this kind, and that you can work successfully on your teaching in a much more intuitive way. If so, fine. We find that many teachers are greatly helped, though, by giving themselves more structure – or, indeed, having structure imposed by someone else. We find that working in a group helps, even though the issues might be different for different members of the group, because the group can collectively impose a discipline that the individual may lack; because talking to others gives you a rich opportunity of finding out what you think, and because hearing other people's understanding of your own situation can give you new perspectives and help you shift your own awareness. Similarly, writing things down can be a valuable way of finding out what you think, thinking things through, being clear, being definite and imposing self-discipline.

You may think *I want to become as good a teacher as possible* – indeed, we hope you do aspire to this! – but we would emphasize a number of important ramifications of this apparently simple and uncontroversial aspiration. Firstly, the route which one teacher takes towards this destination will be different from the route taken by another teacher. But secondly, even the destination will be different for different teachers. There may be certain very fundamental qualities which are shared by a whole range of good teachers, but there are also differences, uniquenesses, idio-syncrasies. And thirdly, in order to reach the destination, in order to make the journey manageable, you need to identify and take the first step, then stop and have a look to see where you are, reconsider whether you are heading in what seems to be the right direction, then take the next step ... and so on. You will probably choose some steps by instinct, others by the kind of critical reflection, self-observation, experimentation, risk-taking and evaluation we have tried to make tangible in the pages of this book, so that each year's experience – and each week's, indeed – is not a repetition of the one that came before, but the next stage of a journey that takes you to somewhere recognizably new. ■

Recommended reading

Teacher Development, the newsletter of the IATEFL Teacher Development Special Interest Group, contains a wealth of articles by teachers around the world, reporting and reflecting on their attempt to take charge of their personal and professional development.

Julian Edge's *Cooperative Development* (Longman 1992) is a practical guide to activities teachers can use to work together on their development.

Index